Spirited Encounters

Spirited Encounters

American Indians Protest Museum Policies and Practices

Karen Coody Cooper

ALTAMIRA
PRESS

A Division of
ROWMAN & LITTLEFIELD PUBLISHERS, INC.
Lanham • New York • Toronto • Plymouth, UK

ALTAMIRA PRESS
A division of Rowman & Littlefield Publishers, Inc.
A wholly owned subsidiary of The Rowman & Littlefield Publishing Group, Inc.
4501 Forbes Boulevard, Suite 200
Lanham, MD 20706
www.altamirapress.com

Estover Road
Plymouth PL6 7PY
United Kingdom

British Library Cataloguing in Publication Information Available

Library of Congress Cataloguing-in-Publication Data

Cooper, Karen Coody.
  Spirited encounters : American Indians protest museum policies and
practices / Karen Coody Cooper.
    p. cm.
  Includes index.
  ISBN-13: 978-0-7591-1088-5 (cloth : alk. paper)
  ISBN-10: 0-7591-1088-3 (cloth : alk. paper)
  ISBN-13: 978-0-7591-1089-2 (pbk. : alk. paper)
  ISBN-10: 0-7591-1089-1 (pbk. : alk. paper)
  1. Indians of North America—Museums. 2. Indians of North America—
Material culture. 3. Indians of North America—Politics and government.
4. Museums—Management—Moral and ethical aspects. 5. Museum exhibits—
Moral and ethical aspects—United States. 6. Human remains (Archaeology)—
Repatriation—United States. 7. Cultural property—Repatriation—United
States. I. Title.
  E76.85.C66 2008
  323.1197—dc22   2007032074

Printed in the United States of America

Dedicated to all the participants of the battles worth fighting.

When someone else is telling your stories, in effect what they're doing is defining to the world who you are, what you are, and what they think you are and what they think you should be.

—Lenore Keeshig-Tobias, Ojibwa writer and Canada Parks
cultural interpreter (Ames 1991, 8)

Contents

Preface

The title of this book, *Spirited Encounters*, comes from combining key words associated with two museum exhibitions highly protested by Native people: *The Spirit Sings* and *First Encounters*, both of which are described in this book. The term "spirited encounters" captures the energetic battles waged by indigenous protestors who have been determined to force museums to recognize and redress long-held institutional biases regarding Native life and history. I spell *protestor* with an "o," staking a claim to whatever added authority and power the "o," as seen in *curator*, *senator*, or *administrator*, might provide.

I also capitalize Native when using the word to refer to indigenous people, following the editing preference of the National Museum of the American Indian's publications department. Without the capital letter, which regrettably can't be recognized when spoken (so I generally avoid it in speech), every president of the United States has been a native American, but not a Native American.

I have always intended this work to be a survey, a collection of happenings. I have not located every event, nor have I thoroughly mined, or researched, the events included within the manuscript. Instead, my desire has been to create a pile of concerns and issues that would rise high enough to capture interest and lead people to think about these events and the situations that caused them and the repercussions that follow them.

While most of the material presented within this book concerns events in the United States, important references are made to Canadian happenings, and I apologize to members of the First Nations if I cause offense through my ignorance of their sensibilities. I also regret that I know almost nothing about situations in Mexico, except that I am sure such knowledge could have enriched this volume immensely. As readers must know, the arbitrary borders between the three nations of North America sometimes cut through the hearts of Native territories, leaving treasured members of the family alienated from their kindred and speaking different foreign languages. Through the fortunes of war, I speak English and have experienced U.S. history.

Until the civil rights movement in the United States effectively illuminated the numerous grievances of minorities regarding mainstream institutions and helped change national attitudes toward minorities, museum curators had been in a position to generally assume they held the supreme knowledge, and therefore the authority, over the materials in their institutions, including undertaking the collection and study of human remains. With the institutional authority invested in them, curators determined what was to be said about cultural materials and how those materials were to be stored, handled, or disposed. Native Americans, alienated from museums, often felt not only a keen loss of ownership of materials emanating from their cultural heydays, which often contributed to a rift in their spiritual lives, but were further anguished at having lost the autonomy to protect the sanctity of ancestral remains and the integrity of collected sacred materials. Additionally, the lack of access to cultural and historical materials, in conjunction with the absence of knowing where materials had been taken, hamstrung Native efforts toward cultural continuity. Observing how wrongly museums related information about Native lives and materials, American Indians were continually frustrated at the usurpation of their right to define themselves to the world at large. For many American Indians, it seemed that museums— along with other institutions such as schools, publishing houses, and government agencies—were trying to execute the final dissolution of Native sovereignty and will.

Native communities, however, have possessed, and continue to possess, an uncompromising faith that they and their ancestors were and are valid and worthy, and that as strong people, their endurance and persistence shall be rewarded with continuation and a return of spiritual and political power. Although suffering from loss and dispossession, the survivors refuse to resign themselves, or their ancestors, to dissolution. We will continue in spite of the arsenal against us.

Spirited Encounters, then (if you will indulge me in an analogy), is about two powerful warriors—the Museum on the one hand, the American Indian on the other (or, as the cover art depicts, a gorilla I dub Museum in a face to face stance with an American Indian). In this story those entities clash like two titans that appear invincible; each has immense advantages.

Every blow in the course of the lengthy, sporadic battle serves to strengthen first one, then the other. They cannot help but gain respect for each other, like wrestlers who learn each other's scent and feel the other's heart beat against their own. Ultimately, at battle's end, they are transformed. Both are stronger, better informed, and have a shared experience to build upon. While, of course, museums and their workers are as varied as individual Native people are, I choose to offer the above story to describe the general way in which I intend to present the conflict between museums and Native peoples, as two entities, divided and struggling, learning and growing.

While this study focuses on actions by American Indians who challenged and, most importantly, changed museums, it must be noted that many people, non-Indian as well as Indian, played active roles in helping along the processes of change. But, because the purpose of this study is to identify and explore the role *American Indians* have played in changing museums through protests, the efforts of many others who supported change, who assisted, or who initiated good actions of their own volition may be overlooked, or the parts they played may seem diminished, in this study. That is because the purpose of this book is to exclaim that American Indians can be, and have been, active and forceful leaders of change within the museum world. In these pages, the stage is theirs. It is not my intention to make every non-Indian an enemy of American Indians (nor vice versa), or to proclaim museums to be hopelessly evil (nor to imply that every American Indian is faultlessly superior).

I have worked in museums for nearly thirty years and been a visitor of them for fifty years or more. I love museums. They have been my life's work. I am Cherokee and grew up in northeastern Oklahoma. My parents took me regularly to Tulsa's Gilcrease Museum, the Philbrook Art Center, and Woolaroc Museum. The State of Oklahoma, formerly Indian Territory, has preserved many sites related to my Cherokee heritage, including Fort Gibson which was the terminus of the Trail of Tears (a tragic event involving the relocation of my Cherokee ancestors) and Sequoyah's cabin, where the great Cherokee inventor of the Cherokee syllabary (and namesake of the giant trees of California), lived after migrating from his home in the Southeast. In 1963, while I was in high school, members of the Cherokee Nation of Oklahoma started a historical society, ultimately leading to the development of the Cherokee National Museum in Tahlequah.

There are thirty-nine resident tribes in Oklahoma, some being original inhabitants while others were forced, like the Cherokee, to resettle there. When I was a student, all children in the state were taught Oklahoma history in school, and much of that history involved information about American Indians. Additionally, the *Tulsa World* provided in-depth features on Native events and history. I was informed about many parts of

America's Native heritage, but soon discovered most other Americans from other states (especially from states with small Native populations) knew very little about our nation's indigenous peoples or their histories.

I moved to southern New England as a young bride in the late 1960s, leaving Oklahoma behind, and one of my early thoughts was, "Now I won't see any more American Indian people." That thought evoked a feeling of loneliness and loss. And, to me, the absence of Native people in Connecticut seemed to be a fact for many years, until a newspaper article informed me that there were still American Indians in the state (even though textbooks and dictionaries defined them as extinct despite their possession of reservations), and further, the news stories informed me that the people of the five state-recognized reservations had some issues to discuss with their non-Native neighbors.

An ensuing visit to the local historical society, not more than a half-hour drive from a reservation, failed to provide further information about the surviving Native people of Connecticut. On view in the small building was the skeleton of a "prehistoric" American Indian, a sight I would have preferred to prevent my accompanying children from viewing as it seemed grotesque and inappropriately displayed. The staff, probably volunteers, also showed me an issue of a nineteenth-century Cherokee newspaper. I was happy to learn that my newly adopted state had connections with my Native nation, which had the effect of making me feel closer to home.

Some Cherokee leaders, I learned, had been educated in a mission school in Connecticut in the early nineteenth century, and a couple of them had married Connecticut women (to the horror of the school's founders and most of the state's population). The children of one of the men were brought to Connecticut after the deaths of their parents to live with a maternal relative, and three of them are buried in a cemetery in the very town in which I lived when I discovered the old newspaper. This information, personal to me, delighted me. The sight of the exposed remains, however, saddened me, partly because the deceased person was presented and viewed as alien (while the non-Indians who had excavated and now possessed the bones were the true aliens, as intruders into the Native realm of sepulture), and because I believed it was inappropriate and irreverent to expose for public viewing the remains of someone who couldn't have given permission for exhumation, and probably would have found exhumation and display to tourists to be in opposition to the sensibilities they had once practiced.

Trekking to various other history museums in the state, I found virtually nothing about the history of Connecticut's Native people. Libraries provided little help, for very little had been published about Connecticut's Native people. What little I found consisted of colorful legends that were generally demeaning (tales of love-struck Native maidens jumping from cliffs), or prehistoric artifacts presented without context, and crafted items collected from American Indians outside of the state. During these visits, I found nothing to bridge the thousands of years of Native New England life that archaeology was in the process of discovering with the area's historic and contemporary Native life. Aboriginal people had been on the continent for millennia, colonists arrived, the Indians faded away, and a new story began; one people replaced the other, it seemed. But, I wanted to know the details of what had happened to the Algonquian-speaking people who met the colonists.

After reading that a children's museum in West Hartford had exhibits of American Indian materials, I took my son and daughter there to see what we could learn. Most of the exhibited material was from other areas of the country. But, on view we found another skeleton of a local American Indian displayed for the edification of children. I began to think that displaying the horror-evoking bones of ancient Indians was a favorite pastime of New England museums in the 1970s. It was, I deemed, a scary way to introduce children to an unfamiliar culture. Such displays reminded me of the roadside attractions so common in the 1950s, which sought audiences who were titillated by contrived horror and exotica. A decade after our visit to the children's museum, it de-accessioned its American Indian materials after having released the remains for reburial. Connecticut museums began offering to the Connecticut American Indian Affairs Council (comprised of representatives of the five state-recognized tribes) pertinent Native human remains for reburial within a state-protected cemetery. All attending the reburials were bound to secrecy of the site to prevent any non-Indians who harbored a desire to collect Native bones from digging up the remains again. When I attended my first reburial ceremony, I knew I was attending a historically important event. Museums, I realized, were waking up after a long slumber of relegating American Indians to a status that museums could control, or if they chose, ignore.

Literature, newspapers, stage presentations, television, and the cinema had etched pitiful images of American Indians onto the minds of citizens. American children grew up to be adults who knew almost nothing but false information regarding their nation's earliest resident people. Native Americans, if one relied on the paucity of information found in local museums and the bounty of negative information found in print and on the airwaves which were fed to our parents, were simply to be considered an unfortunate race who best belonged in a shrouded past. The general public was fed a steady diet of cultural pabulum during the twentieth century, in which it seemed nobody knew what had caused the apparent disappearance of American Indians from the many communities where they had once lived. According to the scanty information, and ensuing conjectures, many people assumed Native people had been less fit, or less worthy, than those who had invaded Native territories, and that is why, many believed, that Native people lost their land and suffered decline in numbers. It is the seeming long-term invisibility of American Indians that leads some people to believe that any contemporary Native American one might come into contact with is not actually real or authentic, but is a pretender, or an anachronism, pitifully out of place.

During my museum career, I once had a person reach out and poke one of my cheekbones to verify to herself that I might possibly be what I told her I was. Others have boldly told me I don't look like an American Indian. Another stranger, upon learning my cultural identity, chastised me for shaping my eyebrows. And, a child once prefaced a question to me with "when you were Indian." Indigenous identity is generally misunderstood and treated as suspect by those who are not Native people. Native identity is complex and layered. Those of us who are Native can connect to a vast network of other Native people, attending an array of Native-focused events and socializing with each other. It is hard for us to comprehend that people don't know we exist in their midst when we witness such a rich bounty of Native life wherever we live, even if far from our original homelands.

For most museum attendees, it has seemed as if all American Indians conveniently left after colonists learned the Native names of local mountains and rivers (for we know many of those words survive on today's maps). When I first arrived in Connecticut after living in Oklahoma, and heard the words Mattatuck, Quinnipiac, Shepaug, Quassapaug, Naugatuck, Weekeepeemee, Housatonic, I whispered them, savoring their sounds, and wondered what had become of the people who had once spoke them so purposefully in the past. Eventually, I found Connecticut's Native history in colonial archives, in ancient books, in descendants' memories. I learned about the early people's heroic efforts to survive smallpox, enslavement, deportation, military invasions, punitive restrictions, and arbitrary punishments. I learned the names of many of the historic Native leaders of southern New England: Wamsutta, Miantinomo, Sassacus, Weetamoo, Weramaug, Uncas, Ninigrit, and others. I learned about the Native people's recent histories as well. I witnessed the new generations' determination to survive. I met others with the same interest I had in Native history. Ultimately, I got the opportunity to absorb much of what I learned because of a museum.

A singular museum sprang up in Connecticut in the 1970s devoted to informing visitors and schools about the state's first people. The American Indian Archaeological Institute (now the Institute for American Indian Studies) became a powerhouse for informing Connecticut citizens about 10,000 years of Native life, and began introducing students to contemporary Native people. I cut my professional museum teeth there in the little town of Washington and am grateful to the two directors I worked for who had the faith to take this shy, but opinionated, Cherokee woman into their facility and let my wings spread as I grew from the information and experience they made possible for me to encounter. The rest, as they say, is history, both in regards to me and for Connecticut's Native population.

Presently, the Mashantucket Pequot successfully tell their own story thanks to their own mega-museum, the Mashantucket Pequot Museum and Research Center, which opened in 1998 after the Pequot's arduous and successful effort to gain federal recognition. Since the 1637 Pequot War, which was the colonists' effort to rid the area of all Pequots, the surviving members of the tribe had lived quietly (the safest way for Native people to survive when in a hostile environment) and in abject poverty. Melding into the populations of dark-skinned residents (people with African heritage, immigrant Portuguese fishermen, and various other segregated peoples), they survived. Achieving federal recognition, the Pequots gained the legal status to develop gaming enterprises, which in turn provided the funds for their government to establish public works, employment, housing (on reservations, it has been the practice of lenders to refuse mortgages). Additionally, they provide education and training for their citizens.

When I first arrived in Connecticut in the 1960s, dictionaries, along with textbooks, defined both the Pequot and the Mohegan tribes as extinct. Hardly anyone in the state knew they (along with the state's Paugussett and Schaghticoke tribes) existed, despite the fact that they each retained reserved lands and were recognized by state government. Interestingly, a Mohegan family had operated one of the nation's oldest Native museums, the Tantaquidgeon Indian Museum, founded in 1931, near Fort Shantok.

During my young adult life and through my museum career, I have followed with avid interest the many instances of Native activism, from California through the Midwest and to Washington, D.C. I especially took interest in protests that focused on museums. Gradually, I saw huge changes occur in the museum world. Paradigm shifts of enormous power quietly evolved, transforming museums and our lives. Often, these gradual changes go unnoticed by the majority of the population, and are unregistered in the minds of new professionals who have never known anything differently about their line of work. These groundswells deserve to be studied and considered. My findings published here are not by any means exhaustive. Much more remains to be explored. Published studies concerning Native people and museums now occur steadily in museum journals, professional history and education publications, anthropology writings, and in the Native press. Still, the effort to inform must increase as it takes an army of researchers and writers to transform information and experience into commonly shared knowledge.

Recently, I gained use of the term *indigenization* from the book *Voices of a Thousand People* by Patricia Pierce Erikson (2002). The publication is an ethnographic study of a Native museum—the Makah Cultural and Research Center in Neah Bay, Washington—in which the author presents the idea of indigenization of Native museums. Erikson describes how the Makah cultural center took the museum model and reformed it to suit their purposes. More about them occurs later in this volume.

What I have written here in *Spirited Encounters* suggests that Native efforts through protest has led to the indigenization of established museums across North American, not just of Native museums. Indeed, museums around the world are experiencing indigenization through realizations that they must talk to those whose materials they hold, that they must let cultural voices be heard in exhibitions and in public programs, that they must consider who really owns museum collections, that objects are living rather than inert (and must be treated accordingly), that inaccuracies hurt the teller's reputation, harm Native communities, and shortchange visitors, that power has shifted and institutional policies must adapt.

We face an exciting era of change in museums because of the work and sacrifices of hundreds of Native people who would not be still, who would not be quiet. It is their story I strive to reveal in the pages of *Spirited Encounters*.

Introduction

American Indians, Museums, and Protests

"When someone else is telling your stories," Ojibwa writer and storyteller Lenore Keeshig-Tobias has noted, "in effect what they're doing is defining to the world who you are, what you are, and what they think you are and what they think you should be" (Ames 1991, 8). Her words resonate strongly with American Indian communities across not only the continent, but throughout the hemisphere as well. Museums, along with other venerable institutions such as schools, publishing houses, the media, and government entities have long engaged in defining American Indians. Too often the information, presented to the public as scholarly fact, has instead been self-serving, biased, inaccurate, and/or incomplete.

"Until the museum community begins to accept the First Peoples' version of who the Indian, Inuit, and Metis are today and change the way they are 're-presented' through our eyes in museums and galleries, we will not be presenting an accurate view of the whole 'truth' of Canadian society to our publics," Nancy Hall, editor of *Muse*, the magazine of the Canadian Museums Association noted on the editor's page of the publication (1987).

She describes the outcry of an Inuit leader, Mark R. Gordon, during constitutional negotiations with Canadian officials in the early 1980s. Hall noted that Gordon pounded his fist on the table during a discussion where officials appeared to be ignoring contemporary realities and exclaimed, "We don't live in your bloody museums down here in the south," he said as he tried to hammer home the idea that the Inuit culture

1

was not frozen in time as museum exhibits had often made them seem (Hall 1987).

Not only have museums been telling the controlling culture's limiting version of the Native story, they have been hoarding the material culture of indigenous peoples, preventing us from experiencing an intimacy with our own pasts. Further, by taking part in the invasion of American Indian graves and by "owning" American Indian human remains and "grave goods" (the materials intended to accompany the deceased into the afterworld), the museum community proved to be patently unethical and insensitive to American Indian cultures. Museums made themselves into places that were not just uncomfortable and unwelcoming to indigenous people as visitors, but were viewed by many Native people who struggled to accomplish research as being downright antagonistic toward them. Museums preferred to show their treasures to credentialed researchers from universities and publishing houses. Inexperienced researchers, noted museum personnel, needed help, took too much time, and didn't know the proper way to handle materials. A tribe in the midst of building a community archives or working on a tribal history often found their representatives either turned away, or so frustrated by unfamiliar regulations and unfriendly staff, that they left, vowing never to return. Museums were, it seemed to Native people, part of a system intent on destroying Native people.

Museums (whether they intend to be) are nation builders (or state or community builders). The values museums instill through their careful selection of objects, images, and interpretations, unified in themes, serve to propel citizens toward a shared understanding. Nineteenth- and twentieth-century American museums joined publishers, filmmakers, journalists, illustrators, teachers, legislators, and other culture shapers in deciding what our nation should think of its Native residents.

The following chapters will outline individual protests and describe their causes, steps taken, museum reactions, and the culmination of resulting changes. But, first, in this introduction, I lay the foundation for what museums are like as institutions, how Americans have embraced protest as a change-agent, and how American Indians came to be so effective as protestors.

Initially, during the formative years of modern American museum development (from the 1920s through the 1950s), American Indian pleas and comments designed to correct museum lessons regarding Native life found few listeners and few who would engage in active and constructive response. Over the decades, frustration mounted, wounds festered, time marched on until a new era dawned during, and following, the civil rights movement in the middle of the twentieth century. With raised voices, American Indians took the opportunity to raise their voices to museums, and the museums which listened either did not like what they heard, or were surprised at the depth of feeling they encountered and realized they had been generally unknowing, and at times, calloused. When American Indians confronted museums and historic sites with demands regarding human remains and with requests that Native people be allowed to tell their own stories and control their own material culture, they were most often rebuffed and vilified by museum directors, curators, board members, museum support groups, governors and other political leaders, and various other powerful mainstream spokespeople who were, of course, raised on the misinformation and bias provided by textbooks, school lessons, and museum exhibitions. There was a closed loop of information serving to exclude American Indian knowledge and sensitivities. Unless the barrier was broken, American Indians would be forever excluded.

Ronald Wright noted in his book, *Stolen Continents: The New World through Indian Eyes since 1492*, "a foreign version of what had happened" is a "form of oppression in itself" (Wright 1992, 188). The telling of American Indian stories in museums had been, until recently, almost exclusively presented from the point of view of the non-Indian: either as a scientist talking about a study subject (generally in larger museums) or the "settler as hero" where the community-preferred story placed American Indians as foes (generally found in local history museums). Such museums never considered that American Indians might enter their rooms and feel rebuffed. Museum staff members had not yet attained the creed that their work should be relieved of a one-sided bias (that they might instead choose to avoid lockstep thinking) and that their charge instead should be to accurately inform people. It had not occurred to them that the public might hunger for the authentic voice. They didn't consider that citizens might want to hear "real" Indians rather than see the filtered thoughts of curators, who most often based their museum labels on information from non-Indian authorities.

During the 1970s, the American public learned through the publicity of American Indian protests that American Indians still existed and that they had grievances. What was the real story, many wondered. Soon, books by American Indian writers appeared. As some segments of the American population became more informed, it became clear that museum exhibits needed to catch up.

Prior to the 1970s, the three major types of museums known to impart information about American Indians were the natural history museum, the history museum, and the art museum. Generally, the greatest number of museum visitors received the most information about American Indians during visits to natural history museums. These museums typically focused on the flora and fauna of given continents. Following this guideline, such a museum would traditionally have described the natural (meaning pre-Colombian) lives of American Indians (as human animals living in an environment), along with the plants and animals of the "wild" American continents. Because of the lack of historical information in natural history museums, visitors typically learned little about American Indians as cultural beings or as contemporary people and virtually nothing about what happened to them as a result of contact with Europeans and other foreign groups.

It was not the mission of natural history museums to connect past ways of life to contemporary life, and their mission did not impel them to try to discuss how American Indian cultures contributed to, and helped shape, American life. There was a disconnect between what could be learned from a natural history exhibition about American Indian life, and understanding historical and contemporary American Indian life. Museum visitors, therefore, too often understood American Indians to be eternally of the past and irrelevant to America's continuing history and current times. Natural history museums contributed to people's understanding of Indians as something extinct (of the past) and aided the perception that Indians were "backward" (or mentally inferior) when compared with "advanced" (or modern European-based) humans. Most natural history museums in the Americas neglected to tell about prehistoric Europeans, which would have aided in understanding people comparatively. Instead, one could assume, after leaving most natural history museums in the United States, that Europeans apparently sprang forth fully adept at scientific inquiry and with an aptitude for learning far superior to the "primitive" people who were depicted in such museums. Indigenous people's knowledge of the sciences (botany, horticulture, medicine, astronomy, mathematics) was hardly explored in natural history museums, and consequently most visitors assumed indigenous people lived simple, untutored lives without bodies of knowledge.

Interestingly, history museums failed to amend the problem. History is not an unbiased social science. History museums, including community historical societies, had rarely sought to balance the story. Most historical societies were formed solely to relate the story of their "founding fathers." With that mission in mind, the founders were the "heroes" and if anything, or anyone, had impeded the advance of their dreams, those characters were antiheroic. And, so, American Indians were either absent from the local story or were the villains. The local museum usually would celebrate their community's victorious founders' "removal" of American Indians (with removal being a much sanitized connotation of the true actions) and then sending any remnants of surviving refugees ever westward or into marginal landscapes such as craggy terrain, barren lands, or marshes. That often was the end of the story regarding Native people in the museums of their former, or perhaps current, homelands. Nor did the emigrant Native arrivals become the beginning of a new story in a new homeland. Native accommodations to modern life, the treaties they signed, the sufferings of forced relocations, their achievements and participation in historical events were little noted in the history museums of the areas they came from, passed through, or settled in for a generation or more, nor were they much discussed in larger history museums. In many small towns across America, a few artifacts brought in by farmers from their fields are often the extent of the discussion of resident Native peoples. Consequently, some tribes' stories are hardly told in their entirety. For instance, the Delaware nation, enduring the first and most treaties and resettlements, have parts of their stories occurring in Pennsylvania, New Jersey, New York, Connecticut, Delaware, Maryland, Massachusetts, Ohio, Wisconsin, Indiana, Kansas, Texas, Oklahoma, parts of Canada, and other locations. While groups of the Delaware nation strive to maintain facilities and to tell their arduous history, rarely has the mainstream museum community tried to accurately portray such a complex tale.

If a history museum gave mention of resident Native people, those museums rarely allowed the Native history to be told by Native voices. And, again, most history museums failed to provide any clues that might inform their visitors that American Indians live on as contemporary people, often in the very communities that strive to ignore them today. This lack of information serves to contribute to the widespread public belief that surviving American Indians are an incredible rarity, or that American Indians who live modern lives in the midst of other Americans are not actually bona fide American Indians.

The type of museum where you will most likely see the least about American Indians is the art museum, except for the few institutions solely dedicated to Native art. Some North American art museums with older holdings have exhibited many memorable images of American Indians, most of them, of course, created by non-Indians. Many of the artworks of the past were politically motivated and served to perpetuate stereotypes about Indian "types" (as savages, as lusty seducers, as pitiful dregs of humanity, as exotically mystical, or as the disappearing last of a breed). Such artworks have been impressed upon our minds through repeated use in textbooks and literature. Many of the pieces evoke powerful emotions and often color the viewer's opinions of Native people.

One of the greatest injustices is that typically visitors to America's art museums would never know that there are successful contemporary American Indian artists (watercolorists, printmakers, sculptors, glass artists, photographers, painters, ceramicists, etc.). Art museums have generally categorized American Indian art as ethnographic material and, consequently, have rarely devoted exhibitions to modern-day American Indian artists. Instead, art museums may collect traditional pottery and weavings, but rarely purchase contemporary paintings, weaving, or sculptures by Native artists.

For American Indian artists navigating the gallery and museum world, there are complex issues of identity. When American Indian art has been lifted outside the bounds of ethnographic treatment and actually considered to be fine art, it has been treated as if it is "foreign" and is generally not considered as representative of "American art" (just as American Indian music is rarely included in any discussion of American music). American Indians have perennially been excluded from joining the American mélange in ways that appeal to them, and instead have often been forced into avenues that are restrictive and marginal. For instance, the movie industry used to insist on casting known studio stars to play characters like Geronimo or Osceola. The stars not only didn't look like Native people, but they didn't act or speak like us either. They relied on fake words, poor costuming, brown makeup, sign language, and exaggerated body language. Only recently have a number of American Indians found success in Hollywood as actors, directors and screenwriters. Today, Wes Studi, Graham Greene, Adam Beach, Chris Eyre, Irene Bedard, and others show up at various film festivals and awards programs joining Tantoo Cardinal, a seasoned veteran in the industry.

As little as a generation ago, there were few American Indians working in positions of authority in America's museums. As a result of the litany of insults America's museums heaped upon American Indians, museums became absolutely anathema in the minds and hearts of most American Indian peoples. Exhibited materials were often incorrectly labeled. Items of different time periods and from different cultures were often shown together in dioramas implying that such an arrangement was common to whatever tribe the exhibit title proclaimed. Ceremonial items were commonly mixed with household materials. Practices were often incorrectly described. Burial materials were often displayed as household goods. Denigrating language and illustrations were often employed. Visiting American Indians asking questions about items in collections were often turned away being told they didn't have the required credentials of researchers. American Indians who had, upon occasion, entered museums and did not like what they saw, shared their museum-related horror stories within Native communities. These communities became more certain that mainstream museums were places of intolerance and abuse.

Consequently, when American Indian communities became active in cultural preservation, they were eager to develop photo archives and to preserve oral histories, but many were loathe to create something called a museum. Many Native communities, while opting to develop exhibits in their homelands, instead decided to use terms like cultural center or heritage center (spelled "centre" in Canada) and sought to develop models for community institutions that differed from mainstream museums. The first part of this study looks at Native junctures with museums, and then proceeds to examine protests by American Indians regarding exhibition policies and practices; the second part looks at the growth and success of the movement to regain inappropriately-held materials from mainstream museums which culminated in the Native American Graves Protection and Repatriation Act (NAGPRA) of 1990; the third part is concerned with protests directed at mainstream museums supporting American heroes, icons, and events deemed oppositional to American Indians; and the fourth part looks at the battle for Native management of sites. The book is about protest, adversarial relationships, anger, and frustration; but it is just as importantly about partnerships, growth, dynamics, and evolution.

Protest, as a political action, has not been a uniquely American Indian occupation. The colonial-era protest concerning taxation, where the Sons of Liberty masqueraded as Mohawk Indians and dumped East India Company tea into Boston's harbor, served to launch the revolution that led to the creation of the United States of America. The British, of course, were not pleased with the "tea party" (the point of view regarding a protest varies by where one is standing). The new nation continued to be challenged by additional protests involving such topics as personal freedom, states' rights, workers' rights, women's suffrage, civil rights, ecological awareness, antiwar movements, and countless other citizens' concerns. The literary icon Henry David Thoreau encouraged thoughtful resistance in his 1849 essay "Civil Disobedience." And, while many protestors have been labeled un-American, they instead are true Americans, voicing their concerns in a land that cherishes freedom of speech.

Protest has shaped the policies of America. The achievements brought about by civil unrest in the middle of the twentieth century, as well as the relative success of battles fought on the legal front, probably did much to spur American Indians to action. It might have seemed that American Indians had been quietly compliant during the first half of the twentieth century. Instead, they had many life-sustaining issues to address within their own communities, and they had enormous legal activities to concern themselves with in various state houses and legislatures. Different tactics suited different times. The middle of the twentieth century was ripe for cultural protest.

In reality, there have been American Indian protests throughout time. Some of the protests went underground becoming quiet resistance, while other protests were instant and forceful. But Native concerns were rarely publicized and early protests generally brought terrible repercussions upon the protestors, including massacre, impoundment, starvation, removal, reduction of lands or rights, execution, curtailment of treaty agreements, and other punishments. However, those early protests were not in vain. Many modern American Indian protestors have attributed their spirit of dedication to the brave people who came before and suffered so much. Protests by American Indians during the twentieth century achieved more of the goals sought by the protesting groups, due in part to the leverage provided by increasingly complex laws concerned with historic preservation, freedom of religion, and with human rights that grew out of the civil rights movement (Price 1991, 19–41). As the United States matured, its citizens became more enlightened and tolerant. As Americans felt secure economically and politically, they began to foster more benevolent reactions to the protests staged by minorities. An opportunity to gain attention for Native causes did not escape the vigilance of American Indian activists who joined the civil rights fray in the 1970s with protest marches and occupations of various sites from San Francisco, through middle America, to Washington, D.C., fighting a variety of federal bureaucracies along the way.

An 1865 treaty agreement noted that military land should revert to its original owners (to American Indians in many cases) if the property were to be declared surplus by the government (HistoryLink.org 2005). In 1962 when the federal government decided to close the prison on Alcatraz Island, American Indians in San Francisco asked if they could have the property to use for an American Indian center and tourist outlet. Their request, however, was denied.

In 1969, the San Francisco Indian Center was lost to fire, and the local American Indians who dreamed of owning Alcatraz were themselves further ignited. A publicity float-by "occupation" was planned for November 9 by area American Indians. However, during the excursion several people jumped ship and swam through the frigid waters to the island and actually stayed overnight. On November 20, the full occupation of Alcatraz by Indians of All Nations began, and soon there were nearly eighty people on the island (Smith and Warrior 1996, 16–18). The press and television media found the occupation of keen interest.

At times, the atmosphere on Alcatraz was festive; at other times there was strife and disarray. The federal government was embarrassed, and perplexed, at how to handle the situation. The Nixon administration began a series of negotiations. The old prison facility was decrepit and unsanitary. The weather on the island could be raw. Whole families had come to the island, not sure how long they would be needed. Their situation was often perilous. Sometimes there was a feast of donated foods for the occupiers; other times there was little to comfort the hungry protestors and their resident children. Publicity was widespread, American Indians throughout the nation were inspired, and public sentiments seemed to favor the Native cause (or would if the federal government acted too severely). The Indians of All Nations hoped to gain cessions from the government to meet their demands of having a cultural center of their own (Reyhner and Eder 1989, 124).

By March 1970, following intense negotiations, the accidental death of a child due to a fall from heights, and the coming and going of supporters, government officials offered plans to build a museum and cultural center on the island. The offer, however, was made without giving title of the facilities or the island to the Native group, who in turn rejected the offer. As the occupation dragged on, public and participant interest slowly waned, and on June 11, 1971, federal forces removed the final fifteen occupiers (Smith and Warrior 1996, 78–109). Today, Alcatraz, a National Park Service site, chronicles the American Indian occupation in a section of the exhibits shown there.

As the protest at Alcatraz waned, some members of the same protesting group became involved in an effort to acquire a section of Fort Lawton, adjacent to the Magnolia District of Seattle, which was being declared as surplus by the federal government. On March 8, 1970 about one hundred members of the United Indian People's Council attempted to enter the 1,100-acre property. Among the activists were Leonard Peltier, Jane Fonda, Bernie Whitebear, and Bob Satiacum. About thirty members managed to gain entrance, but were quickly ousted. Scenes of resisters being carried through brambles and of children crying in jail gained sympathy for the group's cause (HistoryLink.org). Ultimately, the effort was successful. In 1977, the Daybreak Star Arts Center, Seattle, was opened and continues to flourish under Native control (Graves and de los Angeles 1980, 3).

Meanwhile, the American Indian Movement (AIM) began informally in 1968 by a mostly Chippewa group concerned mainly about being hassled by police. They attended American Indian conferences, handing out materials, and soon a powerful group coalesced, holding its first national meeting in St. Paul, Minnesota in 1970. As the membership expanded, the group's concerns became more nationally focused. AIM's primary leaders were Dennis Banks, Vernon Bellecourt, and Russell Means (Fikes 1996, 113–24; Smith and Warrior 1996, 128–33).

Widely publicized American Indian demonstrations followed the formalization of the organization and included an occupation at Mount Rushmore (Fikes 1996, 122), the Trail of Broken Treaties, which culminated in the takeover of the Bureau of Indian Affairs headquarters in Washington, D.C. in 1972, and the armed standoff at Wounded Knee, South Dakota, in 1973 (Burnette and Koster 1974, 124).

A couple of AIM's actions peripherally included a museum. In 1972, following a demonstration in Gordon, Nebraska, a caravan of demonstrators returning to Pine Ridge took a detour to the Wounded Knee Trading Post and Museum. Resentful of the practices of the owners, the demonstrators made threats and reportedly stole objects and broke pottery. The owners valued the losses at $50,000 (Smith and Warrior 1996, 118). A year later, during the occupation of Wounded Knee, the trading post and its museum were thoroughly destroyed, all objects were stolen or broken, and the owners became hostages for a time during the siege (Smith and Warrior 1996, 202). Two years later, two FBI agents lost their lives during a shoot-out at Pine Ridge and Leonard Peltier was sentenced to life in prison. Many believe he is innocent and his cause has become a focus of protests continuing through the ensuing years (Smith and Warrior 1996, 276–77).

Rampant American Indian poverty, federal and public disregard for treaty rights, and assaults on cultural practices had led to unbridled anger, despair, and frustration across American Indian reservations and urban communities, especially among younger American Indians. It seemed the only way to gain needed attention to important matters was to fight the system the American way: throw the tea overboard, engage in revolution.

Interestingly, several current American Indian museum professionals participated in some of these protests and became inspired to stay active in the cultural wars by gaining employment with museums, or by serving as consultants to museums and other related institutions. Other current American Indian museum professionals (myself included) were simply inspired by what they saw on television, or read in newspapers and news magazines, and chose to enter the fray by becoming part of the museum field, where we hoped we could re-educate the American public. Even as we work in museums, we are constantly protesting them, challenging their decisions, demanding changes.

George Horse Capture (Gros Ventre), former director of the Plains Indian Museum in Cody, Wyoming, noted in a memoir titled "From the reservation to the Smithsonian via Alcatraz," that the Alcatraz protest "changed my life and the Indian world." He goes on to say, "Like a nova, its force and brilliance had exploded and reshaped the psyche of the Indian world, and the force generated is still being felt today" (Horse Capture 1994, 139).

In 1973, another building linked to Native protest was destroyed. Pembroke State University's Old Main building had once been North Carolina's only school of higher education open to Native students. It often served as a rallying place for Robeson County's Tuscarora and Lumbee citizens. In 1972, the university's board of trustees voted to demolish the building. A group of Native people known as The Save Old Main committee struggled to raise money and gain support for restoration of the old building and suggested that it be established as a tribal museum. They gained support from the National Congress of American Indians and the Commissioner of Indian Affairs. At the same time, other area Native people believed that the building was too decrepit to save. When the building mysteriously burned one evening, tribal members joined together to request a new building. In 1975, the new building was dedicated as the Pembroke State University Native American Resource Center (Lumbee Petition for Recognition 1987, 111–13). Across the nation's campuses, Native students fought for centers in which to meet and exhibit information, and they struggled to change the attitude of institutions of higher learning as well. They argued that universities should promote increased knowledge of Native heritage among their student bodies.

The Woodland Cultural Centre, Brantford, Ontario, an Iroquois institution with its administration offices housed in a former boarding school building (causing some Native members painful memories upon visiting the center), opened an exhibition on stereotypes about American Indians in the fall of 1988. The idea for *Fluffs and Feathers. An Exhibit on the Symbols of Indianness* first occurred to the center's director, Tom Hill, in 1983 (Doxtator 1993, 21–23). A portion of the exhibition was devoted to the stereotyping conducted by museums and many of the ideas discussed here in this book appeared in the exhibition. The act of creating this exhibition can be considered as one of the many American Indian protests of museums documented in these pages.

Mainstream museums had already been the targets of localized protests, but were about to become targets of nationally publicized protests. Museums dislike protests, which are public relations nightmares that can cost museums essential support in terms of revenue through loss of grant awards, donations, memberships, object loans, entrance fees, sales, and volunteer hours. The American Indian protests directed at museums occurred just as many museums, becoming aware of their own shortcomings during the civil rights movement, tried to head off controversy by creating American Indian advisory committees, using American Indian consultants, and hiring American Indians as staff members. These were good things, of course, though these options rarely opened the doors wide enough to satisfy American Indians. Plus, many Native advisory committees, Native consultants, and American Indian staff members thought themselves ill-used and resented that their advisement was often ignored, while museums, on the other hand, often thought these Native advisors were asking for unqualified changes in museum practices, all creating further conflict and disgruntlement between Native people and museums. It was, strictly speaking, a conflict of cultures.

On the negative side of the outcomes of protests, it is possible that many museums avoided launching new exhibitions on American Indian topics and some divested themselves of American Indian collections, while others may have become reluctant to increase their Native collections. Materials left in the hands of private owners are free to flow to lucrative foreign markets (Jensen 1995). Other museums may have simply pushed their indigenous collections into deeper recesses within the museum, postponing research and the hiring of specialists to care for them. In protest, the physics axiom might be said to apply: for all action there is reaction.

The forceful demonstrations of the American Indian Movement and other protesting Native groups, however, were aptly understood by some museums along with other cultural institutions as a signal that a new relationship with American Indians, and with the American Indian materials held by museums, would soon follow.

The passage of the Native American Graves Protection and Repatriation Act (1990), the Indian Arts and Crafts Act (1990), and the formation of the new, Native-directed and Native-advised National Museum of the American Indian (mandated in 1989 and opened in 2004 in Washington, D.C.), along with the work of the Assembly of First Nations/Canadian Museums Association Task Force on Museums and First People (all of which will be discussed later in the book) point to major changes in public consciousness about American Indian issues that will dramatically change and propel museums to greater interactions with Native authorities and, as a result, to deeper understanding and increased knowledge (Berlo and Phillips 1993, 29). Much of the recent legislation in the United States has forced a positive exchange between museums and American Indians and has supported the birth and growth of Native-operated museums.

General American Indian protests continue. In 2005, the FBI reported that American Indians in the United States, representing 1 percent of the population, accounted for 2 percent of the victims of racially motivated hate crimes. Native protestors in Farmington, New Mexico, have taken to the streets protesting a series of murders of Navajo citizens (Buchanan 2006, 43). A lawsuit concerning the Bureau of Indian Affairs' mishandling of Native trust funds has been undertaken. Fishing and hunting rights, guaranteed by treaty, have long been issues of survival for several Native nations, and there has been active participation in protests over these issues. The phrase "save a fish, spear an Indian" demonstrates the hatred for American Indians that still exists within some quarters of the American public. The issue of sports mascots employing logos and names offensive to American Indians has drawn protestors. Poor health care fulfillment and unauthorized medical procedures, such as sterilization, have merited protests. Additionally, there are protests of offensive murals of past eras found in college and government buildings, along with boycotts of commercial products using stereotypical images or whose product names demean Native heroes and icons. American Indians are so beleaguered with issues of consequence including housing (traditional mortgages are unavailable on reservations), employment (businesses can't get traditional mortgages to construct enterprises), education, health, and finances that it is hard to imagine that American Indians have time or energy to battle cultural issues. But, for many American Indians, cultural issues are seen as the foundation upon which strengths can be built for battling wider problems. And, they believe, demeaned and abused people will not be respected, or have self-respect, until those who oppress them are re-educated and allow an arena of equality where self-respect can flourish.

While American Indian protests regarding museums was unfolding in North America, Native peoples throughout the world, including the Maori, Australian Aborigines, Native Hawaiians, South American Indians, African Blacks, Sami, Ainu, and others, undertook their own independent efforts to encourage changes in museums. As a result, the International Council of Museums is aware of, and regularly discusses, the issues brought forth by indigenous peoples.

The extent to which American Indian resistance to museum policies has contributed to changes in museums can never absolutely be discerned. However, this study chronicles the major protests enacted by a variety of American Indians concerning museums and the changes that have resulted, so it should become evident as the reader continues reading that American Indians have indeed had a profound effect upon museums in North America, and consequently, upon museums throughout the world.

I

PROTESTING EXHIBITIONS

Museums have had a long experience of exhibiting American Indian material. Charles Willson Peale is often considered the father of American museums having opened a facility in Philadelphia in 1786. As the father of museums in the United States, it is not surprising to learn that his son Rembrandt Peale opened a similar facility in Baltimore. Both had among their exhibited materials American Indian "curiosities." Yet, two hundred years later, it became evident that museums had hardly learned how to interpret, or properly display, the materials and culture of American Indians.

Only a few American Indians have had the opportunity to view most major exhibitions and collections due to the general geographic remoteness of Native homelands from major museum sites and lack of monetary resources to indulge in visiting museum-rich areas. Most Native people have not been asked to discuss their opinions concerning museum exhibitions about their cultures and, therefore, have not often even considered whether exhibitions affect their lives or not. Even most staff members of tribal museums rarely visit non-Indian museums or see the large exhibitions that crisscross the continent during itineraries taking them to major cities distant to most American Indian populations.

There are many reasons why exhibitions about American Indians could become candidates for protest by American Indians. There is much to know about American Indians since there are more than five hundred existing tribal groups in the United States alone. It is easy for the inexperienced to err in presenting information on such a vast topic. Without in-depth research, a curator might simply regurgitate existing erroneous information, or viewpoints, from mid-nineteenth century accounts. They might inadvertently relay sensitive ceremonial information to the public or trespass upon Native intellectual property when using reference materials from early anthropological studies or collector's notes. Some of the information that has been published, and exhibited, about American Indians was not intended by Native people to be shared with the public (there are religious sensitivities with some rites while other bits of information may lead treasure hunters to private locations). American Indian personal musical passages, totemic symbols, and philosophical statements become vulnerable to commercial abuses. There is also great concern about exhibitions instilling or perpetuating lies and stereotypes when viewers might see an object without reading revelatory labels or read a quote out of context. And there are valid worries about how young minds (both American Indian and non-Indian) can be negatively influenced by museum exhibitions.

"Did you kill the Indians?" or "Are they really stuffed?" asked some young visitors upon viewing a typical museum diorama depicting an American Indian prehistoric scene (Smith 1960, 21). While working in museum education, I was once asked a question by a student, who prefaced his query with, "When you were an Indian." Most children only know Native people from books and movies, which generally focus on the past. It is hard for them to comprehend that American Indians live today.

There are many ways to offend Native sensibilities in exhibitions. The use of words like "prehistory" or "New World," so often found in museums, is of questionable appropriateness to the Native point of view. They are words that clearly identify an opposing point of view to an American Indian's perspective of the Native world as one that is ancient and having a long rich history, retained through Native oral traditions or recorded through mnemonic devices such as pictures retained on bark tablets, leather hides, and on stone markers. Words like "primitive" or "simple" insult the ingenuity of early people living from the land. It isn't just that museums might lie or omit facts, but they too often have distorted viewers' perceptions of Native culture. Such distortions often appear, on the surface, to be benign and acceptable, and generally go unrecognized by most label readers as well as by the text writers who simply regurgitate the point of view they have learned from non-Native instructors. However, covert racism (which is all too often uncontested and generally unrecognized) is the most dangerous of all discriminations. It subtly shapes minds and is accepted as unquestionably appropriate, leaving no room for the consideration of different information or points of view.

For example, over-attention to warfare in exhibitions (and in movies and literature) has helped many Americans to believe that all American Indians were a savage and warring people, deserving of the losses they suffered (and causes nursery-school age children to consider Indians to be frightening). Many small museums showcase the stone materials brought in by farmers, and they label axe heads, chisels, adzes, and hoes as weapons because they cannot imagine that American Indians had an array of sophisticated tools used in carrying on their daily work as farmers, craftspeople, and builders.

At the time the initial research for this book began in the mid-1990s, the Smithsonian Institution's National Museum of Natural History depicted, at the eye-level of a third-grader, a drawn image of American Indians burning a white frontiersman at the stake (the image had appeared in the exhibit for as much as two decades, but since the opening of the National Museum of the American Indian, it has been removed along with the rest of the age-worn exhibits in the former American Indian hall). Most Americans believe (and the thousands of children who saw that dreadful image will believe) that battles with Indians were instigated solely by unprovoked bloodthirsty warriors, when in truth, most of the fighting with non-Indian settlers by American Indians occurred either in self-defense or was undertaken while serving as an ally to a European entity (with the French and Indian War, the American Revolution, and the War of 1812 serving as vivid examples). More truthful still is the fact that most American Indians were peaceful, even as wars raged about them. I often ask an audience to contemplate whether the United States should be described as peaceful, or as a warring nation. Considering how many modern Americans reenact wars or collect war memorabilia, how Americans go off to war nearly every generation, and how wars have been used to track and order our history, it is surprising that most Americans consider their country to be a peaceful one. In any case, American Indians, too, consider themselves peaceful, and if they fought, it was most often for homeland security or against threats to economic viability. Wherever the truth lies, the stories are complex and varied. The facts, along with points of view, deserve to be explored more fully in America's museums. Museum label writing, written in sentences, has always been in the business of interpretation. If the telling of a story must be told from one side or another, then one could not fault American Indians for believing that it is long overdue for American Indians to gain the opportunity to tell their side of the story.

Over the years, there arose a few museum voices recognizing the bias in museum exhibitions. Stephan F. de Borhegyi, noted museologist and the former director of the Milwaukee Public Museum, stated in a museum conference paper in 1969:

Museum exhibits in general . . . instead of stirring the imagination of visitors, tend to perpetuate the visitors' stereotypes of "savages" and "quaint primitive"

cultures. . . . Museum anthropologists continue to be primarily object and tribal
rather than subject or concept oriented in their exhibits. (de Borhegyi 1969,
45–46)

Hans Jorg Furst, an anthropologist from the University of Vienna, noted
twenty years later, "exhibition styles that feature the contemporary state
and recent history of indigenous people, and include economic aspects
and human rights, are not prominent at all" (Furst 1989, 101).

If the museum profession had invited a group of American Indians to
comment on the state of exhibitions about American Indians, inquirers
would have been told virtually the same information as the noted museum experts reported above. But, until protests made museum professionals anxious to hear from American Indians, they were rarely included
in museum conference presentations. Today, thankfully, it is not unusual
to hear an American Indian making a presentation at a museum conference and occasionally an American Indian author's thoughts are published in a museum journal.

In 1988, writing for the Canadian Museums Association magazine,
Deborah Doxtator, one of the outspoken Native voices who had finished
graduate museum studies, wrote about points of view regarding American Indian exhibits. She noted, "The public and the museum do not want
to acknowledge that what is being presented is a story, just a perception
of another culture." She continues, "Perhaps it is time that the museum
explained to the public that the stories they want and expect to hear in the
museum about other peoples are based upon a particular point of view,
not upon absolute truth and indisputable fact" (Doxtator 1988). When Native voices began to tell their stories in the opening exhibitions of the new
National Museum of the American Indian, experienced exhibition critics
distrusted the factualness and decried the lack of academic authority.
American Indians, of course, have long distrusted the factualness of academic presentations.

There is need for more Native voices in museums and for greater
scrutiny of museum policies and practices by American Indian advisors.
It is the responsibility of the museum world to foster such interactions because many minority people will be reticent about offering their opinions
to those they deem as remote and uncaring.

American Indian protests concerning museum exhibitions, interestingly, have rarely focused on text or tone. Perhaps that is because American Indians have repeatedly been disenfranchised, treated as if they have
not understood history, and described as if their historic roles were minimal at best, detrimental at worst. Scholars stood arrayed against their
voices. So, perhaps it is not surprising that it has been mainly policies and
practices, rather than exhibition labels and content, attracting the greatest

number of protests. The areas of contention include: (1) exhibition sponsorship from corporations known to be in political opposition to American Indian concerns; (2) the inappropriate display of items used in religious practice; (3) the display of human remains or items from burials; and (4) the attempts to define and limit categories or styles of exhibited American Indian art. While American Indians rarely gained attention for saying an exhibit did not describe their culture adequately or appropriately, the exhibit content that has most raised Native ire has been exhibits focused on the hero dimensions of people like Christopher Columbus while ignoring, or diminishing, his genocidal actions of enslaving, murdering, and kidnapping Native people.

The exhibition protests described in this book have ranged from quietly mild to near-violent and have included picketing, writing a letter of protest, filing a court injunction, gaining and using media support, invading exhibition areas (including defacing exhibitions), and enduring arrest.

Locations where the most publicized protests regarding exhibitions occurred were Dickson Mounds Museum (Lewistown, Illinois), the Glenbow Museum (Calgary, Alberta, Canada), the Science Museum of Minnesota (St. Paul), the Florida Museum of Natural History (Gainesville), and the Little Bighorn Battlefield National Monument in Montana.

Protests regarding exhibition practices have been undertaken by various groups, including the Lubicon Lake Band of the Cree in Canada, a group called United Indian Nations, some Native American artists, members of the American Indian Movement (AIM), the Pueblo of Zuni, and the Grand Council of Chiefs of the Haudenosaunee. The following pages chronicle these protests and their achievements.

Figure 1.1. The cross-country run transporting the 1988 Olympic torch to Calgary was called Share the Flame. First Nations citizens who protested the exhibit The Spirit Sings, including Alvin Wanderingspirit, pictured above, used placards to parody the run's slogan. The protest gained international attention and led to museum reformation.

1

Politics and Sponsorship of
The Spirit Sings

In 1983, the Glenbow Museum, in Calgary, Alberta, began planning an exhibition to be held in conjunction with the 1988 Winter Olympics. *The Spirit Sings: Artistic Traditions of Canada's First Peoples*, was to showcase 650 artifacts of the indigenous peoples of Canada with most of those objects borrowed from 110 institutions (Harrison 1988a, 12). Julia Harrison of the Glenbow Museum served as chief curator for the exhibition. Her curatorial team consisted of Ruth Whitehead, of the Nova Scotia Museum; Ruth Phillips, of Carleton University in Ottawa, Ontario; Ted Brasser, from the Canadian Museum of Civilization in Ottawa; Bernadette Driscoll, of Johns Hopkins University in Baltimore; Judith Thompson, from the Canadian Museum of Civilization; Martine Reid, an independent scholar; and Bill Reid (1920–1998), a Haida artist, "who attended some of the committee meetings" (Harrison 1988c, 6) and who is not always included in listings of the team (Harrison 1988b, 33; Stott 1988, 78). Reid would have been the only First Nations representative on the curatorial team (First Nations and Aboriginal are the terms of referral preferred by Canadian Native people).

Curator Harrison stated that committee members were selected not only for their academic backgrounds, which included art history, anthropology, philosophy, and Canadian studies, but that they also "brought to the project a knowledge of foreign collections which, when pooled with the knowledge of a European advisor to the project, would identify the majority of the collections, public and private, relevant to the exhibition" (Harrison 1988c, 6). A laudable attribute of the exhibition was its goal of locating and exhibiting artifacts that had been removed from Canada during the early years of exploration and colonization. The objects selected for *The Spirit Sings* would represent a treasure trove that had been largely unknown to present-day North Americans. As such, the exhibit was an extremely important one. However, the exhibition became even more significant due to protests launched by a group of First Nations people.

In 1986, the Lubicon Lake Band of Cree of Peace River in northern Alberta called for a boycott of the Olympics to draw attention to a fifty-year effort to settle a land claim with the Canadian government. According to Lubicon chief Bernard Ominayak, the boycott was directed at "that small group of wealthy and powerful interests in Alberta who are trying to wipe us out." Ominayak stated that the Lubicon Lake Band did not have a problem "with the athletic competition or with cultural displays" (Ames 1991, 9).

However, when the Glenbow Museum refused to honor the boycott of the Olympics, the band and its boycott supporters turned their attention to the exhibition. Shell Oil Canada Limited, providing nearly half the support for the exhibition, was viewed by the Lubicon Lake Band as an adversary because the company was drilling for oil on land claimed by the band. Protesting the involvement of Shell Oil, the Lubicon Lake Band, unsuccessful at negotiating with the Glenbow Museum regarding their issues, put out a plea to the museums scheduled to make loans to the exhibition to refuse to lend their artifacts to the Glenbow Museum (Ames 1991, 9).

The Lubicon chief and his advisors made several trips to Europe to attract European support for the new boycott (Harrison 1988c, 6). Reacting to the Lubicon request, twelve institutions, for a variety of reasons, decided not to follow through on loans to the Glenbow Museum (Harrison 1988a, 12). Approximately 160 objects were withheld from the exhibition by foreign museums (McManus 1991, 204). Some of the withdrawals pertained to support of the Lubicon Lake Band, while others were enacted to avoid placing materials in harm's way should the boycott escalate into violent protests.

The following points concerning the Glenbow exhibition were noted by protestors:

- The museum borrowed First Nations artifacts without informing or involving First Nations people.
- The museum used money from sources involved in disputes with First Nations.
- The exhibition ignored contemporary issues.
- Non-First Nations people were employed to curate the exhibition.
- The museum pleaded political neutrality failing to see the role it had played in supporting one side while repressing another (Ames 1991, 9).

Polarization began to occur as people, groups, and institutions were forced to decide where they stood on the issue. Tom Hill, director of the Woodland Cultural Centre, Brantford, Ontario, recalled a debate on the boycott occurring at the Canadian Museums Association conference in 1986. According to Hill, a trustee of a major museum stated that he preferred to see Indians in display cases rather than in boardrooms making policy. "I was witnessing . . . a gentleman in a position of power feeling threatened by the increasing influence of First Nations," Hill noted (Hill 1988).

Such comments led the editor of the *Edmonton Journal* to write an editorial titled "The Spirit Weeps" about his fellow citizens, noting, "(W)e actually prefer our native culture in museums. We certainly do not prefer it running the Department of Indian Affairs. Nor do we prefer it announcing the news on national television or determining its own political destiny" (Hume 1988).

In November 1987, the Canadian Ethnology Society passed a resolution to register their support of the Native opposition to *The Spirit Sings*. Their statement includes, "Museums which are engaged in activities relating to living ethnic groups should, whenever possible, consult with appropriate members of those groups, and such museums should avoid using ethnic materials in any way which might be detrimental and/or offensive to such groups." Additionally, the International Council of Museums (ICOM) passed a resolution outlining appropriate relationships between museums and Native people at their November 1987 meeting. However, they claimed this action was not related to the boycott (Harrison 1988c, 7).

Conflicting viewpoints served to create havoc inside many of the involved museums. Writer Evan Roth reported in a 1992 issue of *Museum News*, the official journal of the American Association of Museums, that the Smithsonian Institution was persuaded not to loan objects to the exhibition (Roth 1992, 30). In actuality, while Smithsonian curators sympathized with the boycott, the institution did loan most of the requested objects. However, those loans did not go through without some internal struggles. The curators of North American ethnology at the Smithsonian's National Museum of Natural History, Dr. William C. Sturtevant and Dr. William Merrill, opposed sending Smithsonian materials to the exhibition and prevented several items from being loaned by applying the most stringent of conservation criteria regarding soundness of objects. They were able to find some objects unsuitable for travel (Sturtevant personal communication 1995; Merrill personal communication 1995).

Bruce G. Trigger resigned his honorary curatorship from McGill University's McCord Museum when its board of governors refused to withdraw its loan to the Glenbow Museum (Trigger 1988, 9). Discord and discussion shook the foundations of museum thinking and reached out to create fomentation within various associated cultural institutions.

According to anthropologist M. L. Vanessa Vogel, who described the protest in *Museum Anthropology*, "The question arose in the mind of many Native peoples if, once again, their highly valued cultural heritage was being used to decorate and make beautiful the white man's festivities, while at the same time ignoring the disintegration and even in some cases sabotaging the survival and maintenance of nearby Native American communities . . . one might further conclude that the Glenbow show best served the interest of the regional oil company" (Vogel 1990, 8).

Ojibwe artist Rebecca Belmore used herself in a protest art piece during the running of the Olympic torch as it was carried through Thunder Bay, Ontario. She sat inside a large art frame bearing the label "Artifact #671B 1988." The number refers to the Ontario Liquor Control Board's product number for an inexpensive wine. Belmore was illuminating the irony of Native heritage being celebrated while contemporary Native issues were ignored (Butler 1999, 87–88).

The exhibition opened as scheduled, if not as planned, on January 14, 1988. Approximately 150 protestors marched in front of the museum on opening day while 3,500 viewed the exhibitions inside. Picketers protested throughout the festival. The protest received extensive media attention including meetings with camera crews and journalists from throughout the world. Organizations supporting the boycott included the World Council of Churches, the European Parliament, and members of the academic community (Harrison 1988c, 6).

In response to critics' concerns, Curator Harrison noted that the Glenbow Museum provided a festival of First Peoples' arts and crafts to complement the exhibition. She wrote, "The Celebration allowed Native peoples to present a variety of contemporary cultural expressions to the public. It included contemporary dance performances, traditional craft demonstrations . . . story telling, contemporary and traditional fashion shows, and readings by contemporary Native authors. A variety of Native peoples from western Canada participated" (Harrison 1988c, 6).

Harrison's writings defending the exhibition suggest that she felt the festival allowed adequate representation of contemporary Native life and that the festival provided as much of a Native voice in museum affairs as was deemed necessary by herself and the museum culture she represented. To Native thought, however, the most urgent issues were political and economic, being issues of survival, and these matters were ignored in the exhibition and its accompanying programs. In her article, *"The Spirit Sings* and the Future of Anthropology," published in *Anthropology Today*, Harrison defends the museums' choice of sponsorship by suggesting museums are forced to accept money wherever it might be forthcoming. She says, "This does not mean that corporate sponsors play editorial roles in the theme and focus of the projects that they fund. Nor is there any evidence that the public confuses corporate support for a museum as a museum's support for corporate policy" (Harrison 1988c, 8). Again, her answers did not square with Native opinion. A corporate sponsor is afforded the opportunity of appearing as benevolent and good through its association with the museum, while any less than ideal interactions it has concerning Native communities go unexplored in the museum project, and therefore seem nonexistent or nonproblematical. Increasingly, museum professionals were beginning to feel the sand shifting beneath them as they witnessed the discourse and began to hear answers (or even to provide answers) that were not adequate any more.

Before the exhibition traveled to Ottawa for an opening date there of July 1, 1988 (Assembly of First Nations and Canadian Museums Association 1992, 1), Georges Erasmus, then National Chief of the Assembly of First Nations (AFN), invited George MacDonald, director of the Canadian Museum of Civilization, to cosponsor a symposium on the issues raised by the Lubicon boycott (Roth 1992, 30). That meeting, held in November 1988, led to the formation of a task force jointly sponsored by the Assembly of First Nations (AFN) and the Canadian Museums Association (CMA) (Wilson 1992, 6).

Erasmus said during his introductory comments at the symposium, "We want to leave behind situations where . . . the last people they consider are the very people whose way of life is going to be presented" (Erasmus 1992, 8).

The task force first met as a group at the Woodland Cultural Centre, a museum on the Iroquois reserve in Brantford, Ontario, and at the Royal Ontario Museum in Toronto in February 1990. From those meetings three major actions were requested of museums:

1. Increased involvement of Aboriginal peoples in the interpretation of their culture and history by cultural institutions.
2. Improved access to museum collections by Aboriginal peoples.
3. Repatriation of artifacts and human remains. (AFN and CMA 1992, 1)

Task force leaders Tom Hill, representing the Woodland Cultural Centre, and Trudy Nicks, from the Royal Ontario Museum, chose to divide members into regional working committees. Over 4,000 requests for statements were distributed to American Indian leaders and museum officials. After two years of meetings, reading contributed statements, and drafting a report, the task force released *Turning the Page: Forging New Partnerships Between Museums and First Peoples* (Penney 1992, 10). During the process of creating the twenty-one-page report, invaluable dialogues and insights occurred. In November 1991, the Canadian Museums Association Council accepted the report unanimously (Penny 1992).

A section of the report states seven principles for establishing partnerships between First Peoples and Canadian Museums. They are:

1. Museums and First Peoples will work together to correct inequities that have characterized their relationships in the past. In particular the desire and authority of First Peoples to speak for themselves should be recognized and affirmed by museums.
2. An equal partnership involves mutual appreciation of the conceptual knowledge and approaches characteristic of First Peoples, and the empirical knowledge and approaches of academically-trained workers.
3. First Peoples and museums recognize mutual interests in the cultural materials and knowledge of the past, along with the contemporary existence of First Peoples.
4. First Peoples and museums must accept the philosophy of comanagement and coresponsibility as the ethical basis for principles and procedures pertaining to collections related to Aboriginal cultures contained in museums.
5. Appropriate representatives of First Peoples will be involved as equal partners in any museum exhibition, program, or project dealing with Aboriginal heritage, history, or culture.
6. First Peoples and museums must recognize a commonality of interest in the research, documentation, presentation, promotion, and education of various publics, including museum professionals and academics, in the richness, variety, and validity of Aboriginal heritage, history, and culture.
7. First Peoples must be fully involved in the development of policies and funding programs related to Aboriginal heritage, history, and culture. (AFN and CMA 1992, 7)

Recommendations put forth by the task force report are included under the five stated categories of interpretation, access, repatriation, training, and implementation. Recommendations listed under the heading "Interpretation" are:

a. Museums should ensure that First Peoples are involved in the processes of planning, research, implementation, presentation, and maintenance of all exhibitions, programs, and/or projects that include Aboriginal cultures.
b. Interpretation or representation of information relating to First Peoples should conform to an ethic of responsibility to the com-

munity represented, as well as to the scholarly or professional ethics of the academic and museum communities.

c. In partnership with First Peoples, museums should refine the nature of information relating to their collections, activities, and practices. Identification of items in their collections and in exhibitions using Aboriginal languages is recommended. (AFN and CMA 1992, 8)

A section of recommendations termed "Access" addresses issues of inclusion as members of governing boards, programs designed for Native audiences, legitimate opportunities for employment, access to sacred objects and relevant documents, recognition of concerns by Native people about treatment of aboriginal materials, and wider sharing of information about sizes and contents of collections, plus inclusion of Native artists' works in collections (AFN and CMA 1992, 8).

The AFN and CMA discussed plans to lobby the Canadian and provincial governments for financial support and to seek national adherence to the principles stated in the task force report. Annual reports on the progress of implementation were scheduled as well as planned reviews following the report's release (AFN and CMA 1992, 8–10). While not all follow-up actions have occurred on schedule, the increased dialogues have served to improve the way Canadian museums work with Native communities.

According to David W. Penney, "Key to the task force recommendations is the notion that museum and first peoples relations are to be governed by 'moral and ethical criteria'" (Penney 1992, 10).

Even so, Mohawk museologist Deborah Doxtator noted that the report perpetuated an imbalance of power between museums and First Nations. "American Indians are given a somewhat passive role in these recommendations," she wrote in an essay titled "The Implications of Canadian Nationalism on Aboriginal Cultural Autonomy" (Doxtator 1994). While changes may seem sweeping at times, it is usually in stages that things progress. It is not easy for a whole group of people to suddenly have the veil fall from their eyes.

The task force report states, "'The Spirit Sings' exhibition was a watershed in Canadian museology" (AFN and CMA 1992, 7). It can be suggested that the exhibition was a watershed for North American Indian/museum relationships as well. Had it not been for the Lubicon boycott which drew worldwide attention and created a call for action to which Canada responded in an enlightening fashion while the world watched, positive changes in policy and practice regarding First Nations (and, quite likely, indigenous people throughout the world) would have been, I believe, slower to come, and not as extensive as the progress that has been made since the exhibition's protest.

No other protest led to the creation of a task force which produced such an all-encompassing report; caused active debate within museums between curators and directors and museum boards, some of which resulted in resignations and dismissals; attracted support from so many diverse quarters (churches, anthropologists, the international museum community) and caused museums to address questions on a variety of fronts including financial sponsorship, equally-shared ethnic participation, and acknowledgment of contemporary issues.

Vogel noted in a 1989 presentation that "many a curator will cautiously weigh a proposal of sponsorship against the museum's need to protect itself from an embarrassing conflict of public interest that mars the integrity of the exhibition" (Vogel 1990, 7). And exhibition reviewer Margaret A. Stott said, "There is no doubt that *The Spirit Sings*, through generating debate, has performed a service to museum professionals, forcing us to re-examine the role of museums" (Stott 1988, 78).

Reverberations continued. The 1996 Report of the Royal Commission on Aboriginal Peoples makes extensive references to *Turning the Page* and much of the sensitiveness of the commission's report appears to be in response to the outcomes of the changing attitudes caused by the protest and its aftermath of analysis.

Scholars and students still study the exhibit and the protests and publish their thoughts. Moira McLoughlin noted in a paper she prepared for the *Canadian Journal of Communication* that in calling back, through use of exhibit loans, items that had been out of Canada for up to three hundred years, there had been an opportunity in 1988 to let the history of those items and their journeys "speak of the disruption and extinction, the change or the loss, that was evident on their return" (McLoughlin 1993). That premise would have produced a very exciting exhibit.

Recently, the Glenbow Museum has employed a Native advisor to serve as a liaison for projects involving Native communities. One of the museum's permanent exhibitions is called Niitsitapiisini *Our Way of Life* and is presented online as a virtual museum not only in English and French, but in the language of the Blackfoot as well. The exhibition is noted as a collaboration between the Blackfoot Nation and the museum, and several Native advisors are noted on the Web site. The Glenbow Museum appears to have learned much from its experience, and seemingly is the better for it in improved capacity for future exhibitions and programs on Native life.

2

⁜

Display of Sacred Objects

The traditional practices of the Zuni Pueblo people are quite different from the traditional practices of the Six Nations of the Iroquois or from those of the Lakota people. Most museum curators are scarcely familiar with the beliefs, practices, sanctions, and uses of sacred objects of the entire diversity of American Indian nations represented in their collections. Most specialize in only a handful of Native cultures while their museums may have collections and exhibitions representing a large number of Native groups. Lack of needed knowledge can only lead to missteps.

Almost every religion has sacred materials, materials that were hallowed for or by ceremonial practice. A curator experienced in any religious practice would know there are sensitivities involved in many rites. To the practitioners of a religion, these are serious matters.

While art museums often display art that politically satirizes people or practices of the mainstream world, they usually do so with full knowledge of the territory they are invading. Mainstream museums might display art containing a representation of something sacred to a majority religion (which has sufficient numbers and widespread acceptance, making its future secure). Art museums have displayed art that profanes things highly regarded by majority religions. Such practices, and the ensuing outcry by a portion of society, can be seen as an internal dialogue between components of that mainstream society, which is using the tools of dialogue that the society itself has created and cultivated.

Minority beliefs and practices, however, are vulnerable, and a mainstream museum would seem a bully to threaten them. Many Native practices and many communities' entire religious rites have been lost, and remaining ones

29

Figure 2.1. To respect Native practices, museums must learn and practice protocols regarding how to exhibit and manage Native materials, especially those of ceremonial significance. The Buffalo Bill Historical Center in Cody, Wyoming, appropriately exhibits unconnected pipe bowls and stems as shown in this photograph of an exhibit case at the center.

Courtesy of the Buffalo Bill Historical Center, Cody, Wyoming.

are extremely endangered. Art museums don't generally know much about American Indians and their beliefs and practices, and they have unwittingly, at times, abased American Indian consecrated items held in their collections and shown in their exhibitions.

When Kevin Smith was cultural coordinator at Tulsa's American Indian Heritage Center, he remembers seeing a Pawnee medicine bundle on display at the Museum of Modern Art in New York. Although not Pawnee, but Cherokee, Smith felt "extremely offended. I remember thinking, 'This should offend anyone with feelings for the sanctity of another person's religion.'" (Bilger 1993). The term *medicine* can be a spiritual energy comprised of forces that can keep a person or the world in balance, or can lead to chaos if disturbed or not respected.

According to university educator and museum professional Richard Hill (Tuscarora):

> Non-Indian museum professionals must acknowledge several points: 1. The Indian concepts of religion are culturally very different from their own. 2. The Indian concepts of sacredness and religious duty are still very much alive. 3. The method by which many objects were acquired has resulted in cultural genocide. 4. The American Indian Religious Freedom Act will have a direct impact on museums. (Hill 1980, 181)

The American Indian Religious Freedom Act was signed by President Jimmy Carter in 1979. The law states, "it shall be the policy of the United States to protect and preserve for American Indians their inherent right of freedom to believe, express, and exercise the traditional religions of the American Indian, Eskimo, Aleut, and Native Hawaiians, including but not limited to access to sites, use and possession of sacred objects, and the freedom to worship through ceremonials and traditional rites" (Hill 1980, 182). The necessity for such a law informs us that rights were being impinged. The law would hopefully address and right previous errors. American Indians had hoped the law would give them access to long-separated ceremonial materials residing in museum collections, but it actually provided very little teeth in accessing and using ceremonial materials held by museums. Some of the problems concerning access involved different understandings (or misunderstandings) of what is sacred. Non-Native curators too often believed that the religious practices of Native people were long abandoned (or they might believe those practices should be abandoned). Uninformed curators could easily believe nothing in their museums should be needed for living ceremonial practices. But, the truth is, Native traditional people still remain. American Indian spiritual practitioners were often parted from their ceremonial materials under duress. Not knowing the reality of the situation of how collections made their way into museums, many curators may have mistrusted any American Indian requesting access to ceremonial materials, and turned them away. After the passage of the American Indian Religious Freedom Act, Native people kept knocking on the door, often to no avail, despite the hoped-for protection of law.

The definition of a sacred object has been defined by the Zuni tribe of New Mexico with the following words:

> For American Indians, Eskimos, Aleuts and Native Hawaiians, Native sacred objects are those objects which were created for a specific ritual or spiritual purpose, that are currently a vital part of an ongoing religion and have continuing religious significance or are of important significance in the practice of a Native religious rite. Such objects would be communally owned, made for the spiritual use and benefit of a community or tribe as a whole. (Davies 1979, 136)

It is a common misconception that Native Americans freely gave or sold ceremonial objects no longer valued by them to museums. Under this misconception people rationalize that museums should be able to utilize items in collections as they see fit. However, a different scenario is realized when the accession history of many items in collections are examined. During the past five hundred years, American Indians have suffered persecution for their religious practices and, in many an instance, ceremonial objects were taken from them by government agents (Hill 1980, 184). At times, ceremonies fell into disuse through inability to practice them due to sanctions imposed by outside entities. Persecution and extensive government efforts to see that Native children were raised without involvement in traditions termed "heathenish" produced the result of many traditional practitioners being succeeded by nonpracticing descendants. Thus, many inherited objects were discarded or destroyed, when, in some instances of Native practice, such objects should have been shifted to fellow adherents of the faith or should have been buried with the last practitioner (Finster 1975, 41). Many of the items buried with owners were later retrieved as booty by archaeologists and pot hunters (people who search for old objects for their own personal gain ignoring cultural context). In other cases, dependent Native elderly were pressured by nontraditional family members to part with objects in order to obtain badly needed cash (Breen 1991, 289). Many such objects were the property of the cultural group, not of individuals, and were improperly placed with institutions outside of the culture (Davies 1979, 136; Gulliford 1992, 27). Some objects now in museum collections were actually stolen objects (Isaac 1995, 29; Lurie 1976, 235; Echo-Hawk 1985, 7).

In fact, many tribes and individuals tried to reclaim objects more than a century ago but were not afforded protection of the law. In 1899, the Onondaga Nation filed a New York suit seeking to invalidate the sale of materials they viewed as tribally held materials. The case was dismissed because the court found (erroneously) that the governing Indian group, the Confederacy of the Six Nations, had ceased to exist (in the federal view) and the material, therefore, could not be seen as communally held (Echo-Hawk 1985, 4). Today, the finding would be different, but for the decades when museums were doing their heaviest collecting, Indian rights were ignored.

Although many sacred objects continue to be in the possession of museums, the people of the Zuni Pueblo, the Iroquois of the Longhouse tradition, and other religiously focused Native Americans have actively resisted the display and ownership by museums of items of importance to their traditional religions. "Indians believe the first step is to remove sacred or questionable items from exhibit," states Richard Hill, Iroquois museologist (Hill 1980, 184). In 1974 the Buffalo and Erie County Historical Society established an Iroquois Advisory Committee and on March 25, 1975, the museum agreed to remove all medicine masks from exhibition (Gonyea and Hill 1981, 2).

In 1979, Oren Lyons, speaking for the Onondaga Chiefs Council at the American Indian Museums Association meeting in Denver, said, "I saw on exhibit a false face mask, and on the side was the name of a person who said, these masks had been prepared for exhibition. I can tell you, there is no ceremony that prepares a mask for exhibition and a person does not have the authority to exhibit or to prepare for exhibit material that regards this society. The society itself would have to gather, and it would have to agree, which will never happen. They will never agree that these masks be prepared for exhibition" (American Indian Museums Association 1979).

In 1980, the Grand Council of the Haudenosaunee (sometimes spelled Hodenosaunee) of the Six Nations Iroquois Confederacy, adopted a policy statement regarding medicine masks. The following excerpt contains the portion of the statement concerning exhibition of sacred masks.

The public exhibition of all medicine masks is forbidden. Medicine masks are not intended for everyone to see and such exhibition does not recognize the sacred duties and special functions of the masks.

The exhibition of masks by museums does not serve to enlighten the public regarding the culture of the Hodenosaunee, as such an exhibition violates the intended purpose of the mask and contributes to the desecration of the sacred image.

In addition, information regarding medicine societies is not meant for general distribution. The non-Indian public does not have a right to examine, interpret nor present the beliefs, functions and duties of the secret medicine societies of the Hodenosaunee. The sovereign responsibility of the Hodenosaunee over their spiritual duties must be respected by the removal of all medicine masks for exhibition and from access to non-Indians.

Reproductions, castings, photographs or illustrations of medicine masks should not be used in exhibitions, as the image of the medicine masks is sacred and is not to be used in these fashions. To subject the image of the medicine masks to ridicule or misrepresentation is a violation of the sacred functions of the masks.

The Council of Chiefs find that there is no proper way to explain, interpret, or present the significance of the medicine masks and therefore, ask that no attempt be made by museums to do other than explain the wishes of the Hodenosaunee in this matter (Grand Council of Chiefs 1980).

The Grand Council of the Haudenosaunee represents the traditional Iroquois. These leaders acknowledged that some masks had been carved by Iroquois for commercial purposes, but they maintain that there cannot be a nonsacred Iroquois mask. The Council requested that all masks be removed from exhibition, be removed from sale, and that all masks be returned to the Iroquois. Their policy statement was distributed to museums in 1980. While many museums ignored the request, the Rochester Museum, the New York State Museum, the Denver Museum of Natural History, and many others responded with removal of Iroquois masks from display (Gonyea and Hill 1981, 2). The three named museums, however, did not return the masks (personal communication with respective curators Dan Barber, Lisa Anderson, and Robert Pickering 1996). Further, the Rochester Museum only removed masks from Iroquois exhibits and did not remove Iroquois masks from an exhibition concerning masks of the world (Barber 1996).

During the Lubicon Cree protest of the 1988 exhibition *The Spirit Sings*, a group of Mohawk chiefs went to Calgary and succeeded in obtaining a court injunction during their effort to remove from the exhibition a False Face mask lent by the Royal Ontario Museum of Toronto. The injunction removed the mask from gallery walls for two weeks. "The claim concerning the mask was that it should not have been on view to the public since it was only to be seen by members of the respective medicine societies," wrote exhibition curator Julia Harrison (1993, 339). The court, finding that the mask had been exhibited before and had been reproduced in publications, declined to permanently remove the mask from the Calgary exhibition and it was returned to its place in the show. However, the mask was removed before the exhibition was set up in Ottawa due to a letter from "appropriate leaders of the reserve" which was received and honored by the museum (Harrison 1993, 340). "Appropriate leaders" often means those elected according to the methods ordained by non-Indian authorities, which may not be in keeping with the Native nation's traditional selection of leaders. Since many Native people refuse to participate in elections not based on traditional selection of leaders, such "official" leaders may or may not speak for the majority of the group, and may or may not be sensitive to those members of the group who practice traditional religion. Native tradition bearers are often ignored by museum and government authorities unless the "appropriate" spokespeople (meaning elected or government appointed office holders who oftentimes are non-traditional members of a nation) actively sanction the spiritual leaders.

Since 1978, following passage in the United States of the American Indian Religious Freedom Act, the Zuni Pueblo sought to have their War Gods (*Ahayu:da*) removed from public display and returned to their altars (Zuni efforts to achieve repatriation are described in the second section of this book). Altars for War Gods are in remote rocky overhangs and have been vulnerable to thieves. Without express protection of law, Zuni War Gods were regarded in the non-Indian world as abandoned property. Immediately following passage of the religious freedom act, the Zuni Pueblo initiated three formal legal actions concerning the War Gods (Clifford 1988, 209).

"It hurts us that, throughout the whole world, religious items/artifacts, belonging to the Zuni people, are displayed in museums. . . . These display places are far removed from Zuni land for whose benefit those items/artifacts were created," explained T. J. Ferguson, Zuni tribal archaeologist (American Indian Museums Association 1979).

Zuni councilman Barton Martza noted, regarding War Gods in museums, that in the 1970s "we did view the War God on display. And after contacting the Denver Art Museum it was taken off display. I guess from there, that from that time on, that I started working with individuals and also museums that have these artifacts. There were a lot of legal problems, but right now it's getting to the point where a lot of museum boards are getting probably more educated in this" (Ferguson 1990, 9–10).

The Museum of Modern Art had planned to include a Zuni War God belonging to a Berlin collection in an exhibition, but changed plans when informed that exhibition of the carving was not allowed by Zuni belief (Clifford 1988, 209). The Zuni Pueblo, as did the Iroquois, found that many museums responded to formal requests for removal from exhibition, while others required more pressure (calls from lawyers, adverse publicity, and/or court action).

In 1991, the Brooklyn Museum opened an exhibition, *Objects of Myth and Memory*. No War Gods were exhibited (in fact they were returned to Zuni leaders in the spring of 1991). Additionally, Zuni masks were also not exhibited in deference to Zuni beliefs. Zuni consultants to the project requested that the masks not be displayed, "since they find it offensive for part of a sacred costume ensemble to be exhibited alone, especially for view by the uninitiated" (Berlo and Phillips 1993, 39). For the Zuni Pueblo, their coordinated actions were accumulating success stories.

In 1981, a Hopi altar in the Field Museum, Chicago, was removed from exhibition following multiple requests. "If such objects are displayed or even handled indiscriminately by scholars, they are profaned," explains Emory Sekaquaptewa, Hopi lawyer and anthropologist (Page 1983, 60–61). Robert Breunig, curator of the Heard Museum, Phoenix, explains further, "some kinds of knowledge are power, and that power can be dissipated or dangerous if it falls into the wrong hands . . . like having that altar on display" (Page 1983, 63).

In 1992, two members of the Minneapolis American Indian community, Dale Kakkak and Sammy Watso, reviewed the Minneapolis Institute of Arts exhibition *Visions of the People*. They likened the public display of pipes in the exhibition to pornography. The museum responded by agreeing to replace the fifteen pipes with fifteen stones collected from the Missouri and Mississippi rivers (Garfield 1993, 12). The fifteen stones became proxies for the pipes, and the altered display served to inform visitors about Native American sensitivities.

The above situation points to a shortcoming of the majority of museum exhibits, in that once installed, museums are not proficient at making wholesale changes in exhibitions (which, oddly enough, allows plenty of time for protests to organize). It has always alarmed me that museums often respond to a request from the public regarding a mistake in an exhibit by replying that once the exhibit is open, it can't be changed, and therefore any requests for change must simply wait for the exhibit to close. Often, misspelled words have been left as is throughout the course of an exhibit. A common excuse is that exhibit staff people are working on the next exhibit, so no one is available to undertake the corrections. Costs for corrections are not included in an exhibit's budget.

One exhibit I greatly appreciated, *Darkened Waters*, by the Pratt Museum of Homer, Alaska, did allow for changes, as they fluidly provided updates on the oil spill in Prince William Sound and the ensuing court settlements. As fastidious as museums generally are, it seems odd that most of them, the big ones especially, resist correcting erroneous or misleading exhibited information. At least, such an attitude is changing in forward-thinking museums, which are increasingly focused on providing better responses to community concerns. Removing the pipes and replacing them with river stones represented an elegant response to public concerns.

In other cases regarding pipes, protests centered on the exhibitors improperly connecting bowls to pipe stems during exhibition, or placing pipes in an inferior position to other objects, both of which cause concern amongst people who are knowledgeable in proper care and use of pipes (Lynch 1993, 54; Gulliford 1992, 31). Pipe bowls and stems are only connected during ceremonies because the act of connecting the pieces brings the pipe to its full power. Additionally, pipes are always highly respected and treated reverently and should not be placed in inferior positions.

Walter Echo-Hawk, representing the Native American Rights Fund, told attendees at the American Indian Museums Association conference in 1979, "if, for example, a museum has a collection of sacred objects, they should have to have substantial input from Native religious leaders in the form of a permanent, formalized Advisory Board; so that this Advisory Board could advise the museum as to proper ways of handling and displaying the sacred objects which are in its possession" (American Indian Museums Association 1979, 50).

It will be interesting to see if all of the above mentioned religious articles (ceremonial pipes, masks, bundles, altars) are to be repatriated in the future, making exhibiting them a moot question. However, even if all items were to be repatriated, there undoubtedly will be dissension in the future over exhibition of replicas and photographs of sacred objects. Native American advisory committees will still be needed to examine exhibition texts for accuracy, sensitivity, and with regard to ownership of knowledge. Conflicts over exhibition of sacred objects, even if sacred objects become absent from museum collections, are far from over.

Meanwhile, the museum world is evolving. In 1990, the Zuni opened their own museum, A:shiwi A:wan Museum and Heritage Center, and are managing a rapidly expanding archives plus a large photograph collection. Ganondagan State Park, New York, is the site of a historic Seneca village, managed by Peter Jemison (also a Seneca artist), recently on the board of the American Association of Museums. Increasingly, Native museums and mainstream museums are creating and supporting Native museum professionals, who then are able to re-inform mainstream museum professionals about proper treatment of Native materials.

Figure 3.1.   For almost sixty years, tourists and school children viewed the exposed remains of Native people in a popular roadside exhibit in Saline County, Kansas, which
first opened in the 1930s. Following Native protests and lobbying, the Kansas legislature
closed the exhibit in 1989 and reburied the remains the following year.
Courtesy of the Kansas State Historical Society.

3

Display of Human Remains

In 1978, the American Association of Museums (AAM) stated:

> Although it is occasionally necessary to use skeletal and other sensitive material in interpretive exhibitions, this must be done with tact and with respect for the feelings for human dignity held by all peoples. Such an exhibit exists to convey to the visitor an understanding of the lives of those who lived or live under very different circumstances (AAM 1978, 15).

Native protests brought before the public eye the concern of American Indians regarding the public display of human remains, and AAM and museums across the continent struggled for policy adjustments to handle the issue. By 1994 the AAM code of ethics backed away from mentioning exhibits, and simply stated that the "special nature of human remains and funerary and sacred objects is recognized" (AAM 1994).

Having Native sensibilities, I am often jarred by television programs on archaeology in Peru, the former Egypt, China, and other distant lands when an enthusiastic archaeologist invites the camera to view a recently uncovered crypt. Excitedly, the scientist points to a cracked skull, discusses the teeth, notes a broken femur, and dismantles the remains of a formerly living human before our eyes. Would this same scientist, with cameras in tow, be welcomed into any small town's funeral home or into a close-knit family cemetery to analyze the bodies there? For some of us, time is irrelevant. Don't we bury our dead with ceremony to recognize the sacredness of their lives? Don't we seal and cover the burials to keep them from being seen above ground? Who gave permission to our contemporaries to expose these apparently beloved people of the past? How is it that modern investigators presume so many rights in opposition to the rights and desires of others? While it is appropriate for science to be analytical and dispassionate, we must be assured that scientists are not allowed to presume ownership of all human realms without consideration of citizens who harbor sensitivities regarding souls and spirits, rights of the dead, honor of ancestors, and the sanctity of bodies.

Gordon Pullar, a former president of the Keepers of the Treasures, an organization concerned with protecting Native heritage sites and materials, observed in the chapter he wrote in *Reckoning with the Dead*, that "respect" has different meanings to Native peoples than it does to non-Natives. After being assured by Smithsonian staff that no skeletal material from Pullar's Alaska region was on display, he discovered an exhibition with the statement, "Back defects among Eskimos have increased through inbreeding." Some of the displayed material was from Kodiak Island, Pullar's home. Pullar wrote, "I did not consider the display respectful at all" (Pullar 1994, 19).

The display of American Indian remains was considered de rigueur by most public museums up to, and including, the middle of the twentieth century. Many of today's adults remember skeletal displays in local or state historical society exhibitions or have seen photographs of such exhibitions in newspapers, books, or magazines. Generally, American Indians have disputed the rights of archaeologists to excavate and claim Native bones, but non-Indians have generally failed to understand indigenous respect of ancestral remains, and no legal protection existed until recently for what non-Indians considered to be abandoned graves (Tivy 1985, 12). To American Indians, there's no such thing as abandoned graves.

During the 1970s, protests against displaying human remains increased and began to gain momentum. The Museum of New Mexico was one of the first museums to remove skeletons from public display (Guillory 1990, 23). Their decision, made in 1965, was not due to protests, according to institutional memory (Freshour 1999), but one wonders why they once exhibited remains and then came to the conclusion that exhibiting remains was not appropriate. The museum, whether the change was solely under their own initiative or prompted by Native concerns, is to be lauded for its positive and early action. Other museums were not so forward thinking. After formal Iroquois protests occurred in 1971, the Albany State Museum agreed to remove all displays involving American Indian skeletons and to replace them with drafted renditions or plastic reproductions (Case 1972). The agreement was a compromise, at best, because the exhibition of skeletal material, real or reproduced, is considered unacceptable by many because issues of respect could still be viewed as inadequately addressed. In 1972, protests resulted in the Iowa State Historical Museum removing bones from exhibition by order of the governor (Tivy 1985, 12). That same year, the Milwaukee Public Museum took Native remains out of their exhibitions (Guillory 1990, 23). A few years later, the Saskatchewan Museum of Natural History removed skeletal materials from exhibition in response to Native protests (Conaty 1989, 410).

In 1978, the American Indian Religious Freedom Act provided leverage for stopping displays of human remains (Guillory 1990, 24). As state authorities studied the law, they began writing their own restrictions concerning display of American Indian remains; as many as fourteen states now provide restrictions regarding display of human remains (United States Department of Agriculture 1993; Price 1991) and many possibly think such a restriction is no longer necessary because display facilities in their states have stopped showing human remains.

During the 1980s protests continued and more museums responded by removing remains from public display. In 1983, the display of two skulls and a tibia at Fort Worth Museum of Science and History caught the attention of four members of American Indians Against Desecration, a protest group founded to oppose the display of Native remains. The group contacted newspapers and before the museum could react to requests to remove the materials from exhibition, the story was in the news. Materials were removed from one exhibition immediately and replacements were found at a later date for the other exhibition, which had previously been approved by a local Native group (Floyd 1985, 11).

The Cleveland Museum of Natural History established a policy in 1987 to no longer display human remains (Price 1992, 96). Chicago's Field Museum removed its last display of American Indian human remains in 1989 (Hass 1990, 16), as did the American Museum of Natural History in New York (Guillory 1990, 23). One by one, museums removed human remains from galleries. The museums that found it hardest to change were the museums whose main subject matter focused on Indian skeletons—such as burial mound museums.

The most contentious battle—or perhaps the most widely publicized, and certainly the incident involving the most remains (237) in a single display—involved the Dickson Mounds Museum in Lewistown, Illinois (Illinois State Museum 1992, 6). "Indians have had their eyes on Dickson Mounds for 50 years. They see it as a cynical and tragic desecration," noted David Hilligoss, a professor at nearby Sangamon State University (Guillory 1990, 24). According to the 1990/1991 biennial report of the Illinois State Museum, which oversees the Lewistown facility, "The Dickson Mounds Museum has been the site of numerous demonstrations by American Indians and their supporters" (Illinois State Museum 1992, 6). With those few words, the museum authorities provided one of the briefest summations of a long-standing battle that had been waged for half a century between the museum and hundreds of American Indian protestors.

In 1927, amateur archaeologist, Dr. Don Dickson, a chiropractor by trade, began excavating mounds that existed on property held by his family since the Civil War era. The mounds were from the Mississippian and Woodland cultures and dated from 900 to 1250. Dickson established a private museum, which became a state park in 1945. In 1965, Dickson Mounds became part of the state museum system (Guillory 1990, 21) and in 1972 a $2.5 million museum was constructed over the exposed graves (Pridmore 1992, 18).

Prior to the new facility's dedication, Native Americans threatened to disrupt the opening ceremony. Native American groups and sympathetic scholars periodically spoke out against the display. In 1989, the World Archaeological Congress, convening in Vermillion, South Dakota, officially noted the exhibition as unacceptable (Pridmore 1992, 18).

The Native American Rights Fund and Indian Treaty Rights Committee went on record as opposing the Dickson Mounds exhibition. Additionally, the Sierra Club, the American Association of Museums, the Society for American Archaeology, and the U.S. Forest Service supplied letters supporting closure of the exhibition (Guillory 1990, 24).

Meanwhile, the director of Dickson Mounds Museum, Dr. Judith Franke, recommended to Illinois governor Jim Thompson that the burial exhibition portion of the museum close, but Thompson vacillated. When a local newspaper announced the closing of the exhibition, local residents arose in protest, maintaining that the exhibition was an established part of local history. With the 1990 election approaching, Thompson retreated from taking a stance (Pridmore 1992, 19).

Native protests accelerated. In one incident Native Americans jumped over the railing and into the burial area to cover remains with blankets. Next, a group of over fifty protestors, some from Oklahoma, marched in with shovels to attempt to rebury remains. Although police were required to remove protestors, no arrests were made (Pridmore 1992, 19).

Finally, on April 3, 1992, the burial exhibition was closed to the public (Franke 1995a, 3). At the closing ceremony, Michael Haney, a spokesperson for United Indian Nations in Oklahoma said, "I am rejoicing that our ancestors will be treated with respect" (Lawton Constitution 1992).

In September 1994, a newly renovated Dickson Mounds Museum, minus the burial display, opened after being closed for one year. In addition to upgrading the mechanical systems and providing handicap access, new exhibitions, museum shops, and a discovery center were added. The new exhibitions not only discuss Native life, but the environmental life of the region as well (Franke 1995a, 3). The area over the graves is an open, dark space with hanging scrims upon which are projected images of nature, artifacts, petroglyphs, and of people's hands planting and harvesting. There is a soundtrack with wind and other natural sounds and some spoken text (Hill 2000, 107–8).

Museologist Richard Hill (Tuscarora) visited the new facility and declared its exhibitions "satisfying." He noted, "The exhibition is an extension of Indian beliefs that allows the visitor to experience Native world views with the kind of emotions necessary to transcend science" (Hill 2000, 108).

However, not everyone is pleased with the compromise employed to close the display. Besides grumbles from physical anthropologists and local history buffs, many Native Americans are also unsatisfied. The original remains are covered with a concrete slab over protective cedar planking (Franke 1995b). A magazine report suggests that the slab hints at the possibility of future reopening of the site (Pridmore 1992, 18). Further, the concrete entombment using protective cedar planking is designed to preserve the site, rather than serve as a method encouraging the natural return of the remains to the earth.

Not everything original to the site is in situ. Early in the display's history of being open to the public, and before accurate mapping was completed, some objects were moved to other locations within the excavation to provide a clear pathway for lecturers. Additionally, break-ins had resulted in some objects being stolen (Harn 1980, 3). However, the museum does not know of the existence of any materials at other locations and has not taken any materials out of the site for its own collections or exhibitions (Franke 1995b). At least for the present, the entire burial site is now discreetly removed from the prying eyes of the ever-curious public.

In Salina, Kansas, another popular exposed Indian burial had been a much-visited tourist attraction since the 1930s. Local elementary students were regularly brought to the site on field trips. But in 1986, Pawnee leaders sought closure of the site, determining that the 169 exposed remains could be their ancestral people, together with the related tribes of the Arikara and Wichita. Gaining assistance from the Kansas legislature, the site was shut down in 1989 (Echo-Hawk and Echo-Hawk 1994, 66–69). Other burial excavation displays, including one in Moundville, Alabama, also closed (Pridmore 1992, 18; Guillory 1990, 24).

On September 12, 1989, the Smithsonian Institution announced its decision to return human remains (Guillory 1990, 23) to tribal authorities opening the way for the landmark Native American Graves Protection and Repatriation Act, which followed in 1990 (Price 1990, 32) affecting all the museums in the United States that receive federal support. Federal support generally refers to the receipt of grants, but federal financial support also occurs in the benefit of tax exemption (Mahoney 1999; McKeown 2007). Following the resulting extensive repatriation of Native human remains, and a steady increase in state laws protecting burial sites and prohibiting the sale and display of remains, it would have seemed that the exhibition of American Indian remains in the United States would have soon become a faint memory of an ugly, eerie past.

However, several conflicts over displays of the dead still occurred. When the Florida International Museum in St. Petersburg, Florida, announced it would open the exhibition *Mysteries of Peru* in October 1998, members of the Florida Indian Alliance were aghast to realize the exhibition would display Peruvian Native mummies and funerary objects. Making matters worse was the disrespectful promotion of the exhibition, using Halloween themes to encourage visitors to view "human skulls," "a sorceress," and "human sacrifice." The St. Petersburg *Times* ran an irreverent piece titled, "Despite their rap, mummies are really very chummy" on October 23. The article carried two photographs of mummified remains, one bearing the phrase, "a face only a mummy could love" (Sanders 1998). For American Indians, who generally are taught by their families to feel a responsibility to ancestors, these disrespectful comments about the remains of ancient Native people deliver pain and insult.

While the exhibit had the approval of the Peruvian government, it did not have the blessing of the Indigenous peoples of Peru. The Florida branch of the American Indian Movement joined the protest effort along with the International Indian Treaty Council, which asked Yachay Wasi, an indigenous nonprofit corporation in New York City and in Cuzco, Peru to also join the protest. These organizations ultimately prepared a statement for presentation at the World Archaeological Congress in Cape Town, South Africa, in January 1999, decrying the exhibit and the disrespect to Native remains. They also undertook a campaign seeking repatriation of the remains, which they referred to as "Indigenous Prisoners of War." The exhibition closed as scheduled in March 1999 (Yachay Wasi, 1999).

That same year the Nevada State Museum was at work on an exhibition about mummified remains they called Spirit Cave Man. Found in 1940, it wasn't until 1995 that the museum learned the remains were more than 10,000 years old. Further, the Bureau of Land Management ultimately decreed that the mummified remains were not related to any people, living or dead, denying the remains any connection to today's Native people, and seemingly bypassing any possibility of repatriation. The Fallon Paiute-Shoshone tribe, however, took exception (Mullen 2002).

"We have always lived in this valley," Donna Cossette, Fallon Paiute-Shoshone tribe chairperson noted, explaining that her tribe's knowledge and beliefs place their beginning in the area (Mullen 2002).

The museum, planning an exhibit about the remains and the museum's findings about early Native life, contracted forensic sculptor Sharon Long to create a facial reconstruction of Spirit Cave Man. The Fallon Paiute-

Shoshone asked that the depiction of the remains not be publicly shown. Yet, in 1998, the reconstruction of the ancient man's face appeared on the cover of *Newsweek* magazine, raising the ire and apprehension of Nevada Native residents (Chandler 2001).

The museum's plan to mount an exhibition about Spirit Cave Man became of great concern to Nevada Native people. What would the exhibit show, what would it say, and how fairly would the message be presented? When newly elected state governor Kenny Guinn met with Nevada tribal leaders, the leaders registered their objection to the exhibition as well as to further studies of the remains. Once the governor had his new appointee in place at the Department of Cultural Affairs, the exhibition was promptly canceled and further analysis of the remains was halted. In place of an exhibition focused on Spirit Cave Man, the museum instead began work on a collaborative exhibition honoring Nevada's Native people (Nevada Division of Museums and History 2006).

Initial planning meetings between museum staff and Nevada Native representatives were begun with trepidation, but soon the process proved enriching and successful. *Under One Sky* opened in June 2002 at the Nevada State Museum in Carson City and set new records of attendance by Native visitors to the museum. Programs presented by Native presenters proved successful and the museum plans to continue such programming following the close of the exhibition (Nevada Division of Museums and History 2006).

"Certainly, it's one of the Museum's most important projects in recent history. The collaboration among cultural organizations and agencies and the involvement of Native Americans has been extraordinary," reported museum director, Jim Barmore. *Under One Sky* proved so successful that, following its closing, parts of the exhibit were installed in the museum's main exhibition area (Anderson 2002).

Meanwhile, the Fallon Paiute-Shoshone tribe is engaged in a claim of the remains, which is now pending court deliberations. The tribe seeks to protect the remains from further scientific probing, to prevent further exploitation of his remains, and to return the remains to the natural world. Regrettably, the replicated image, as well as photographs of the remains, have been published, filmed, and dispersed throughout the Internet, giving anguish to traditional members of the 1,000-member tribe. The museum, at least, has said it will not display the replication in accordance with the tribe's preferences (Mullen 2002).

While some U.S. museums are willing to repatriate human remains to nations outside of the United States, they are not yet required to do so. Some museums, however, are willing to consider the return of remains to requesting authorities regardless of country of origin. While museums in North America have generally become more thoughtful about the display of Native remains and about the discussion of human remains in exhibitions, not all are as sensitive as American Indians would like them to be.

What about American Indian remains in other parts of the world? A survey in England of twenty-four museums determined that while nineteen of the participating museums displayed human remains, none continued to display Native American, Australian Aboriginal, or Maori remains. Seventeen museums indicated that they had removed all human remains from display. Four stated that they had done so as the direct result of external pressures (Simpson 1994, 28). The Pitt-Rivers Museum in Oxford, England, responded to a request from Pacific Northwest Coast tribes to remove remains from an exhibition focused on the practice of artificial deformation of crania. After a series of discussions, the museum complied (Jones 1994, 29).

While cultures around the world have divergent attitudes about managing human remains, it is important for institutions to respect the sensitivities of all people. American Indian protests have made it apparent that museum exhibitions are not appropriate places for the remains of American Indians.

In the summer of 2006, members of the Inter Tribal Council of Arizona along with a group of Native American community leaders met with the Arizona Science Center to discuss Native concerns about the center's intention to bring in the controversial *Body Worlds*, an exhibition of preserved human bodies designed to instruct about human anatomy. Actual bodies, none American Indian, and all apparently donated for educational purposes, had been "plastinated" and arranged to show how organs and muscles are arranged. The popular exhibition began traveling in 1995 and was shown in twenty-seven cities worldwide before its scheduled trip to Arizona (Nilsen 2006). Although, Arizona American Indian concerns might not prevent the opening of such exhibits, the controversy gave Native people a chance to explain their views regarding display of human remains. Bringing the discussion of the ethics of displays of human remains to community forums is important, and American Indians are serving an active role in such discussions.

Meanwhile, the display of Egyptian mummies and of exhibitions like *Body Worlds* continues to thrill the public and to fill museum galleries. Such displays prevent many American Indians from entering museums. Some tribes believe that unhappy spirits of the dead can maintain negative energy and that entering buildings where such spirits reside can be dangerous. For others, it is not a spiritual taboo that prevents them from enjoying exhibits of human remains, but instead they believe that cultural institutions should not own the remains of other cultures. Many museums possess and hold mummies and human remains from throughout the world, and from throughout the millennia of human existence. Thus, the current practices of some museums prevent some American Indians from benefiting from the wisdom and knowledge within those museum's walls and within the brilliant minds of their informed staff members.

One way to overcome this barrier is to house research facilities and human remains separate from exhibition facilities and to stop the exhibition of all human remains, using replicated pieces for medical exhibits. Some time in the future, museums may bear a symbol to inform visitors that no human remains are housed within the building, just as facilities today are required to inform about hazardous materials within its premises.

While American Indians and European-Americans may never agree on how to proceed to address the study, preservation, and exhibition of human remains versus Native reverence for deceased humans, museums have at least begun to understand that American Indian concerns exist, and that effective laws now aid in protection of future and current American Indian burial sites, and of past excavated, or found, Native remains. And, there is a growing body of laws prohibiting the display of American Indian remains in the United States.

Figure 4.1. Lakota artist Oscar Howe (1915–1983), who produced modern paintings such as Victory Dance above, found that most museums and art markets limited opportunities for innovative American Indian artists. Today's Native artists still struggle against preconceived expectations regarding Native art.

Oscar Howe, *Victory Dance*, 1954. Museum purchase, 1954.6. © 2007 The Philbrook Museum of Art, Inc., Tulsa, Oklahoma

4

Art Confined
to a Reservation of Its Own

Museums of art differ from other museums in that their collections are considered fine art, which means a museum provides little, or no, interpretation of their exhibitions, or they provide a different context regarding symbolism, technique, psychoanalysis of the artist, and a review of art developments. One would expect art to be solely a matter of aesthetics (which is hard to define and often culture-bound although universal aspects are often obvious). But more than appropriate aesthetics determines which pieces of art are purchased by museums, or which are shown on their gallery walls.

Art museums, more than other kinds of museums, see a market response to their efforts. Whoever is lucky enough to have an entire show devoted to his or her work realizes a rise in the value of that work. The determination of what is collected by art museums affects the pocketbooks of artists, collectors, and art brokers. The selections are often influenced by fame and value, which are controlled by personalities and power. These factors provide plenty of room for controversy.

Art museums have been able to avoid conflicts about human remains and biased translations of Native history, yet conflict has occurred at the single juncture where the two worlds (art museums and American Indians) meet, which is in a museum's policy affecting the ability of American Indian artists and their creations to gain entrance, or be barred.

American Indian artists face a struggle to gain acceptance in the art world. They are caught in a double bind. Once one's identity is known as American Indian, there will be expectations concerning one's work. Native artists can be criticized if their work does not reflect Native life and themes, and they can be criticized if their work does reflect Native life and themes.

When one's work does reflect Native themes, the artist's career can seem pigeonholed into a category of ethnic art and the artist may not receive prestigious mainstream showings. The critics and the public don't usually know how to respond to works from a strictly Native aesthetic. Those untutored in American Indian history won't appreciate the work in the same way they appreciate the kinds of works they have been schooled to see and understand. In other words, whether the public has been exposed in depth to European-based art, or have only viewed a few classics in textbooks and classroom materials, they have been prepared to regard European-based art as true art.

In this way, American Indians have become exotics in their own homeland. A Native artist can paint about the life she or he experiences in America, but most Americans won't recognize the themes as American. Mainstream art magazines rarely discuss, or spotlight, American Indian artists. People are generally only exposed to kitsch Native-style art as seen in Sunday magazine sections selling commemorative plates or in fundraising mailings from missionary schools.

It is difficult for the general citizen to learn about contemporary American Indian art. To demonstrate how basic are the problems facing those interested in researching contemporary American Indian art, visit any library and search the shelves, card files, or directory for "American Indian art." After realizing you may have to look under American Indian, Native American, Indian, and various other designations, you move on to "art" within those files. What you will find are mostly references to pre-Columbian or historic ethnographic materials being referred to as art. Ferreting out any contemporary art information takes diligence and some beforehand knowledge of the subject. This "lost in the crowd" scenario for contemporary Native issues such as art reflects the general trend by Americans to consider Indians as a thing of the past. People rarely think of American Indians in contemporary terms. For an artist hoping to create a following, being relegated to the past is deadly. It is particularly deadly to the spirit of one's innovative growth, so important to creativity, and it is deadly to the Native business of generating income, or a career, in the art world.

Indeed, American Indian art has a long history. Before Europeans arrived, many aesthetics had developed on this continent. Northwest Coast Native art was dominated by bold lines and solid color blocks, often with multiple faces and many eyes found in totem pole carving, elaborate wooden masks, and weavings. Parfleche trunks of the Great Plains were painted with stark, dramatic geometric designs. Buffalo robes often had radiating fine lines leading to breath-taking intricacy providing a powerful dynamic of energy. Tipi covers and winter counts portrayed pictorial silhouettes, pure in style and duplicated with sure sophistication to reflect herds, battles, villages, mountain ranges, or forests.

Curvilinear designs became common in the art of Woodland groups, looking like vines, curling bark, and sweeping petals. In the Southwest, intricate mazes and repeating patterns provide an art style that is complicated and practiced. They also used graceful silhouettes of wildlife. These descriptions only touch the surface of the varieties of Native art found through time and space in the Americas. For those knowledgeable of Native art, particular styles and preferred palettes of color are easily discernable, tribe from tribe, place from place, period to period.

Currently, Native ceramicists, basket makers, jewelers, and weavers, as well as sculptors and painters, using both contemporary and traditional mediums and tools, create American Indian art. But there are also American Indian glass artists, large-scale metalworkers, printmakers, and other nontraditional forms of art being created by American Indians. One of the central issues facing these artists is the question of who controls and/or defines American Indian art. Is it instructors, curators, gallery owners, agents, juries, critics, the media, or artists? Since, until recently, most of the people bearing the titles just listed were non-Indian, American Indian artists have been frustrated by non-Indian entities and individuals who have demanded, or confiscated, the power to shape, control, and describe American Indian work.

Among the earliest Native artworks employing European-style depictions, or "realist" art, were watercolors produced by the Tuscarora brothers, David and Dennis Cusick, in the beginning of the nineteenth century. Following the War of 1812, they began depicting their tribe's cultural practices. After an initial period when their art was admired, their productions became forgotten and are now known mostly among historians (Anthropolog 2006).

In 1875, Cheyenne, Kiowa, Arapaho, and Comanche men, imprisoned at what was then called Fort Marion in St. Augustine, Florida, were encouraged to draw on ledger pages to fill their time. Having previously drawn on hides with oil and mineral paints, the idea of recording activities through drawing was a familiar one. The work of the men was found to be marketable to visitors and fort employees and provided a small sum of spending money for the Native artists. Completed ledger books were sold for $2 and included subjects remembered from the artists' formerly free lives as well as special events occurring at the fort along with everyday prison scenes including the Christian preacher, classroom teachers, and soldiers practicing their drills (Hoebel and Petersen 1964, 9–10). Although none of the men received formal Western training in art, their work is now found in several museum and library collections (Hoebel and Petersen 1964, 91–93). And their bold line work inspires their descendants today.

From 1917 to 1926, Susan Peters, an Indian Service field matron, provided art instruction to young Kiowa students near Anadarko, Oklahoma. These students—Spencer Asah, James Auchiah, Jack Hokeah, Stephen Mopope, Louise (Lois) Smokey, and Monroe Tsatoke—soon enrolled in special courses at the University of Oklahoma, Norman under the tutelage of Edith Mahier and Oscar Jacobson (Warner 1986, 190; Rushing 1992, 8). This group's art attracted a wide audience and they were among some of the earliest Native artists to be regarded as "artists" by mainstream authority.

Between 1931 and 1937, Dorothy Dunn created a studio at the Santa Fe Indian School (Warner 1986, 194). Allan Houser, who became one of the most widely celebrated American Indian artists, later observed, "My only objection to Dorothy Dunn was this: she trained us all the same way" and "it was the old Traditional style . . . wanted from you or none at all." Fellow Santa Fe students comprise a host of successful artists including Oscar Howe, Fred Kabotie, Pablita Velarde, Joe Herrera, and Harrison Begay (Hill 1995, 48).

In 1935, an art program was established at Bacone Junior College in Muskogee, Oklahoma, with Native artists as instructors. Acee Blue Eagle, Woody Crumbo, and Dick West Sr., all renowned artists, had the privilege of teaching such students as Fred Beaver, Blackbear Bosin, Ruth Blalock Jones, Sharron Ahtone Harjo, and Jerome Tiger. These and many others also became successful artists (Hill 1995, 90). While the art style taught at Santa Fe was referred to by that city's name and also as the Studio style, the style emerging from Bacone College and the University of Oklahoma was referred to as the Oklahoma style. These styles emerging from Oklahoma and New Mexico were similar and were generally termed "traditional" (Warner 1986, 194).

A definition in *The Arts of the North American Indian* defines the "traditional" style as emphasizing "flat colors, clear outlines, and sinuous curves, with a stress laid on line, which was used to separate discrete color areas. The subject matter of the painting, in the main, was nostalgic and traditional-minded in that it depicted scenes of dancing, warfare, buffalo hunting, horses, and so on" (Warner 1986, 190). Houser noted that when one student came upon a way of depicting something, members of the group began copying it. He referred to the manner in which Harrison Begay portrayed trees that led to others creating the same form of trees (Highwater 1976, 149). The traditional style was very much a conformist art. The acceptance of this style as traditional Indian art was based as much on non-Indian perspectives (what patrons expected) as it was on a continuation of Southwestern Indian flat art types (and, of course, we must remember that not all Indians were from the Southwest or Oklahoma). Additionally, it is important to understand that an overly aggressive emphasis on tradition ignores the fact that cultures continually evolve and that they can proactively change without being destroyed or lost (Jonaitis 1992, 47). The choice to make change should not be denied to a culture.

A selection of one style of Native art to serve to define all American Indian art excluded, or diminished, the opportunity of those of other American Indian cultures to participate in, or reap any benefits, from any "craze for," or popular pursuit of, American Indian art. Such a selection served to seemingly make disreputable other forms of American Indian art. For instance, Northwest Coast artists, staying true to cultural styles, could have found their art being rejected by shows and markets because it wasn't thought to be "native." Such artists would then have the choice of maintaining their skills by producing images that were not appropriate to their heritage, or continuing their style without a market, or not creating art at all (and not passing their skills to the next generation). Such restrictions were serious setbacks for many groups of Native artists, and to their cultures, as well.

In 1946, the Philbrook Art Center in Tulsa, Oklahoma, began its Annual National Exhibition of American Indian Painting. *Time* magazine noted that in 1947 the art world for American Indians was centered in Tulsa's Philbrook (Strickland 1980, 9). The Indian Annual, as the competition and exhibition was called, served as an important venue for American Indian artists. However, as a measure of control, Philbrook distributed to artists a description of the kind of art it would support and told jurors to exclude nontraditional styles. The Art Center called for "flat design and solid color areas" as well as traditional themes (Strickland 1980, 12). The so-called "national exhibition" was not truly national in its scope of Native style.

As one would expect, "traditional" was becoming ever increasingly difficult to define, as well as to defend. Even art authorities at Philbrook were divided. The work of Patrick Desjarlait titled *Maple Sugar Time*, was rejected from the first Indian Annual because it was rendered in a style similar to Mexican muralists, yet it was deemed important enough to be purchased by the museum for its permanent collection (Strickland 1980, 12–13). While jurors of the art competition were of one mind, curators were apparently of another mind.

During this time period, Pueblo artists were encouraged by their purchasers to continue the complicated and repetitive lines and patterns of earlier Pueblo potters (Warner 1986, 194) and Joe H. Herrera (Cochiti Pueblo) held a successful one-man show full of abstract art based on pottery designs at the Museum of New Mexico in 1952 (Highwater 1976, 90).

Herrera noted that his Modernist paintings were a direct challenge to the Studio style and suggested that the Studio style should not be called traditional (Archuleta and Strickland 1991, 13). Meanwhile in Oklahoma, Fred Beaver (Creek/Seminole), considering himself to be a traditional Indian artist, was criticized by Susan Peters for including nontraditional wooden structures in a painting accepted by the Indian Annual (Strickland 1980, 13). Ultimately, a letter from Oscar Howe (see below), a Sioux artist, whose cubist-looking art was rejected from the 1958 Indian Annual, assailed the Philbrook barriers.

Howe's work was asymmetrical, had "chromatic energy," and carried a "dynamic, fluid movement based upon edge and contour" (Quintal and Day 1982, 8). In the *South Dakota Review*, an arts journal, Howe explained that his work was solidly based on Dakota traditions (Howe 1969, 69–79) and he took "violent issue" with writers who insisted that his style developed while he was in the Army in Europe viewing modern art (Dockstader 1982, 13, 15). He said, "The basic design is *Tahokmu* (meaning spider web). From an all-Indian background I developed my own style" (Harjo 1996).

When Howe's submission to the Philbrook Art Center was rejected on the basis of being nontraditional, Howe exploded with a powerful response:

> Who ever said, that my paintings are not in the traditional Indian style, has poor knowledge of Indian Art indeed. There is much more to Indian Art, than pretty, stylized pictures. There was also power and strength and individualism (emotional and intellectual insight) in the old Indian paintings. Every bit in my paintings is a true studied fact of Indian paintings. Are we to be held back forever with one phase of Indian painting, that is the most common way? We are to be herded like a bunch of sheep, with no right for individualism, dictated as the Indian has always been, put on reservations and treated like a child, and only the White Man knows what is best for him. Now, even in Art, "You little child do what we think is best for you, nothing different." Well, I am not going to stand for it. Indian Art can compete with any Art in the world, but not as a suppressed Art. I see so much of the mismanagement and treatment of my people. It makes me cry inside to look at these poor people. My father died there about three years ago in a little shack, my two brothers still living there in shacks, never enough to eat, never enough clothing, treated as second-class citizens. This is one of the reasons I have tried to keep the fine ways and culture of my forefathers alive. But one could easily turn to become a social protest painter. I only hope, the Art World will not be one more contributor to holding us in chains. (Stickland 1980, 13)

While Howe's letter presented a powerful protest of Philbrook policies, his wasn't the first, of course. Others had protested against the arbitrary influence the Philbrook was wielding, as an earlier letter to Philbrook director Denys Myers from Fred Beaver in 1955 demonstrates.

[S]ome of the original Indian painters quit exhibiting and some others have dropped out or submit fewer paintings . . . due to the fact that some of the exhibitors were submitting abstract art . . . and some of the judges . . . would select some of this type as prize winners. . . . At one time, [Philbrook] told us that they would create a separate division for this type of art aside from the original Indian art. (Strickland 1980, 14)

Although, Howe's and Beaver's protests were not supporting the same views regarding artistic styles, they both represented a plea from American Indian artists for the Tulsa art center to cease wielding potentially damaging practices in the American Indian art world.

Jeanne Snodgrass (later Jeanne Snodgrass King, Cherokee), curator of the Indian Annual, appealed to Philbrook's board following receipt of Howe's letter, "If Indian art is to survive it must not be dictated to and controlled; it must be allowed freedom to develop" (Strickland 1980, 14). In response to Howe's protest, along with the knowledge of the concerns of his fellow artists, the center increased the categories of art styles acceptable in the Indian Annual to encompass modern forms as well as traditional forms of art. Howe's work garnered prizes at Philbrook in 1960 and 1961 (Harjo 1996).

The University of Arizona hosted a conference to explore the future of American Indian art, and as a result, the Indian Art Project was held in the summers of 1960 through 1962, funded by the Rockefeller Foundation (Highwater 1976). Students of the project were encouraged to experiment and explore new directions in art. From this project the Institute of American Indian Arts, Santa Fe, was born in 1962 as a federally supported school, and was privatized in 1988 (Harjo 1996). Lloyd Kiva New (Cherokee) and other American Indian artists had begun the push to have an arena suitable to their needs, rather than having their art shaped by non-Indian instructors. The school, attracting many of the most successful American Indian artists to serve as instructors, has produced an impressive new generation of successful Native artists, one of the first being T. C. Cannon (Kiowa and Caddo), and including Roxanne Swentzell (Santa Clara Pueblo).

In 1992, the IAIA Museum opened under the direction of Richard Hill (Tuscarora) in the old post office building in the center of Santa Fe, providing a showcase for Native produced artwork (Harjo 1996).

IAIA began as a two-year degree institution using a portion of the aged facilities of an existing college, has grown to offer four years of study, and opened a new campus on the outskirts of Santa Fe in 2001. It currently offers a museum studies degree along with its programs focusing on fine arts with the goal of helping Native artists continue the dynamics of Native creativity.

Although the situation at Philbrook Art Center encouraged participants in the world of Indian art to look more holistically at Indian art, the entrenchment of and the enchantment with, the idea of traditional Indian art has been slow to die. In 1973, the Heard Museum selected four American Indian artists to serve as their panel of judges for their Annual All-Indian Arts and Crafts Exhibition. The judges, divided in their opinions, wound up awarding Best in Show to a decidedly nontraditional sculpture called "Horse of a Different Color," produced by Dommick LaDucer. The museum's categories for entries consisted of the simple divisions according to medium. Artists and patrons expressed dismay with the winning entry, and one of the judges who preferred traditional Indian art noted that he was "disgusted and discouraged" by the winning selection (Wade 1981, 15–17). While it is heartening that there is increased placement of Indian artists on judging panels, there still continues to be conflict about style, tradition, and, increasingly, even about identity. Questions are posed regarding how much Indian blood quantum a particular person possesses or whether one has had adequate extent of experience in one's tribal life and cultural practice. These questions are raised as much by American Indians as by others. Legislation regarding the Indian Arts and Crafts Board's work with Native artists has addressed the issue of which artists can call themselves "American Indian," relying on tribal enrollments and federal designations, which in some cases, gave the appearance that non-Indians still exerted extensive control of Native identity.

Two American Indian artists received a boost in 1972 when the Smithsonian opened *Two American Painters*, an exhibition of works by T. C. Cannon and Fritz Scholder, which then toured European capitals the following year. The show was described as witty and biting with their works using metaphors for modern Native experiences. The exposure launched both artists into a realm of success previously unknown by many artists. Soon, their works appeared as widely distributed prints, posters, and note card images (Harjo 1996).

In 1974, a project was initiated to provide collaboration among existing Indian Cultural Coordinators in western states. That project led to a meeting December 7–8, 1977 in Phoenix at the Heard Museum culminating in the development of Atlatl National Service Organization for Native American Arts (Atlatl 1977). The organization continues to serve American Indian artists today with a biennial conference, an active Web site to promote artists and offers of advice, technical assistance, and networking.

Urban Native groups in North America began founding organizations to facilitate services to needy American Indian people who were either relocated to cities by government programs or who migrated to urban areas on their own in search of employment. The continuation and support of American Indian art and artists was often also supported by these organizations. In 1977, the Daybreak Star Arts Center was founded in Seattle. In 1978, the American Indian Community House founded the American Indian Gallery in New York City. In 1983, the American Indian Contemporary Arts gallery was founded in San Francisco. Similar galleries may be found in Wichita, Minneapolis, Chicago, Philadelphia, Baltimore, and other cities throughout the nation. Galleries and organizations were increasingly developing to support American Indian artists, and increasingly, American Indians were founding, directing, and managing these new organizations.

In 1976, a group of Native artists joined by the American Indian Movement and Artists for Democracy, protested the opening in Britain of the American exhibition *Sacred Circles: Two Thousand Years of North American Art*. They criticized the show because it failed to discuss how the objects were obtained and it ignored the existence of contemporary American Indians (Fisher 1992, 44). Later versions of the exhibition corrected some of the failings of the first version. For example, three photo mannequins of contemporary Native people were produced to stand at the exit of the last gallery.

Ray Gonyea (Onondaga) curated a 1977 exhibition of contemporary art sponsored by the American Indian Society of Washington, D.C. Gonyea noted, "By selecting Indian artists who exemplify the mainstream of modern Indian art . . . rather than feature the more traditional forms of Indian art, the exhibition can help dispel stereotypes of Native Americans held by the general public" (Gonyea 1977, 5).

A continuing challenge facing American Indian artists is the exclusion of a significant representation of American Indian artists in the galleries and collections of most art museums (Ames 1991, 8). Also, at issue is whether museum curators treat the few American Indian artworks they show as the equals of other fine arts materials in their collections. Do their collected Native materials and exhibitions focus on the ethnographic side of the works rather than portraying the works as belonging fully in the spectrum of art? Do they consider (and subsequently treat) their Native works as art of lesser credibility? Do they fully understand and appreciate the work they are showing?

Canada also progressed through stages in coming to terms with its Native artists. In the 1950s, the Canadian government instituted a production and marketing program for Inuit sculptures. Baffin Island administrator, James A. Houston, a trained artist, introduced stone-block printmaking to Native artisans who adeptly adopted the art form and found successful markets. Native cooperatives began to spring up in other Canadian locations.

During this time, Ojibwe artist Norval Morriseau began creating works using mythological and shamanistic images in what became known as the Legend Painting School or Woodland Art Style, and other young artists followed his success with their own adaptations (McDonald 2005, 42). In October 1978, the first Native artists symposium held in Canada occurred (Houle and Podedworny 1993, 14).

In 1977, the Canadian Museum of Civilization hired its first curator of contemporary Indian art, Robert Houle (Saulteaux-Ojibwa). However, in 1980, Houle, frustrated with the museum's attitudes, resigned, saying, "I began to realize that the people who worked there, from the director down, did not see these works as standing on their own merit at all. They were seen as extensions of the ethnological collections without any appreciation of their esthetic values" (Houle and Hargittay 1988, 58). Houle's resignation protested the then-prevalent attitudes of museums regarding Native art.

In 1990, Houle was asked to participate as a consultant for a study about issues in the exhibiting of contemporary Native art. The Thunder Bay Art Gallery in Ontario called for the study with a questionnaire distributed to 306 individuals and organizations having been identified as working with American Indian art, or were themselves American Indian artists. The project culminated in the 1993 publication of essays by American Indian artists and Native curators along with the results of the survey. One of the key questions was, "Do you perceive there to be a problem with the museological treatment of contemporary Native art in Canadian art galleries?" Eighty-two responded "yes" while twenty-three said "no" (Houle and Podedworny 1993, 80).

In 1998, Irvine J. Scalplock (Blackfoot), curator of the Siksika Nation Museum, provided a review to the Canadian museum magazine *Muse* on the Syncrude Gallery of Aboriginal Culture's exhibit on Alberta's Native people, which had opened at the Provincial Museum of Alberta. While the review finds good things to say of the exhibit, Scalplock discusses one area of contention. During advance publicity of the exhibit while it was being developed, readers became aware that Asian artists had been hired to provide the exhibition murals. First Nations people objected, demanding that the remaining mural be provided by one of their artists. Resulting consultations made it clear that Native people no longer would tolerate being left out of planning for exhibitions that would tell their lives, and that their artists should be considered for museum work contracts (Scalplock 1998, 13). This incident demonstrates that museums can be slow to learn, or have short memories, for the province of Alberta is the province where the 1988 protest of *The Spirit Sings* at the Glenbow Museum occurred. Too often, breakthroughs don't self-maintain. Protests, it seems, must be periodic in order to keep moving forward.

One of the most effective ways for artists to create work and to protest simultaneously is through performance art. James Luna (Luiseno), burst onto the national scene in 1987 with *The Artifact Piece* at the San Diego Museum of Man. Lying on a bed of sand, Luna was the exhibit. His display led viewers to understand that Native people are contemporary and that they are tired of being viewed as specimens. Since then Luna has performed in Japan, Canada, Italy, and major cities in the United States (Lowe 2005, 16). Most recently Luna performed *Emendatio* in the 2005 Venice Bienniale, sponsored by the National Museum of the American Indian.

Richard Hill, Tuscarora artist and museum professional, writing for the 1995 premier issue of *Indian Artist* magazine, noted, "Many Native artists have come to the conclusion that there are no conclusions. People change how they live their lives. Beliefs change. Perspectives change. The art of any individual will therefore change over the years. In the past, archaeologists have tried to define the arts by their similarity over the years (however) . . . change is actually traditional" (Hill 1995, 90).

Native people feel very strongly that their art should be viewed as one of the pillars of American art—as art that is distinctly of this continent. America's seeming rejection, or overlooking, of American Indian art is viewed as untenable by Native people who vow to do battle with the staid art world. There will, no doubt, be protests concerning this issue in the future. Meanwhile, Native artists struggle to find their audience of collectors and supportive gallery owners and look to museums to provide more wall space, to increase purchases of Native-produced fine arts, and to help develop related marketable products. Recent successes of American Indian film makers, musicians, clothing designers, jewelers, and other Native artists points to a promising future for Native arts, but it won't be without struggles and vigilance.

One singular sign that the art museum world is becoming more broadly aware of Native issues is the 2006 published report of the Association of Art Museum Directors Subcommitte on the Acquisition and Stewardship of Sacred Objects. The report encourages museums to "adopt special stewardship or interpretive responsibilities for sacred objects" and to work with not only federally recognized Native entities, but to also consider nonfederally recognized tribes, First Nation cultures in Canada, indigenous Mexican cultures, and other worldwide groups (Association of Art Museum Directors 2006).

II

⚜

THE LONG ROAD TO REPATRIATION

Public museums as we know them today, with formalized policies and practices, are relatively new institutions. The earliest manifestations of what would become museums first appeared as private "cabinets of curiosities." These cabinets, or collections, belonged to wealthy individuals who traveled and collected mementos from exotic places and enjoyed collecting strange and rare materials. The first public museums in the United States developed well after the nation was established and were generally full of exotic and eclectic materials displayed with little descriptive information (Alexander 1983, 3). The objects themselves, it was deemed, were fascinating enough to draw viewers.

In the nineteenth century, the belief that American Indian cultures were disappearing caused a great clamor by museums, private collectors, and universities for American Indian objects. Time for putting together comprehensive collections of indigenous cultures was running out, collectors believed, because they thought American Indians were disappearing. Wealthy benefactors helped underwrite the costs of collecting expeditions. The powerful American museums of the day (Chicago's Field Museum, New York City's Heye Foundation/Museum of the American Indian and the American Museum of Natural History, plus the Peabody Museum in Cambridge, Massachusetts) commanded great purchasing power. Competing with them were European collectors who were interested in adding to the collections already amassed during the colonizing of the Americas.

The very actions of collecting contributed to both the erosion of cultural practices and the transference of knowledge to institutions. Loss of access to items that had been touchstones of memory and practice served to weaken the links of cultural heritage for Native cultures. At a time when many American Indians were most vulnerable (reeling as they were from introduced diseases, poverty, displacement, and curtailment of rights), powerful museums sent collectors after American Indian objects. Janet Catherine Berlo says in the introduction to *The Early Years of Native American Art History*, "The Smithsonian's taking of 6,500 pots out of Zuni and Acoma within six years (1880–1885) destabilized pottery making traditions, as design sources were removed from the pueblos" (Berlo 1992, 3). While some objects were obtained legitimately within the law, many were not. Some of the so-called legitimately obtained objects were not procured with the best ethical practices. During the late nineteenth and early twentieth centuries, however, protests by Native voices opposed to removal of objects were generally ignored, and in the eyes of the law, Native communities were powerless to protect themselves.

The 1985 book *Captured Heritage. The Scramble for Northwest Coast Artifacts*, by Douglas Cole, details the merciless searches undertaken by museums for artifacts, which served to pillage the holdings of the tribes of the Northwest Coast. Similar ravaging occurred in Native communities across the Americas. Many of the early "heroes" of anthropology were actually ruthless collectors with ethnocentric views who ingratiated themselves to people they actually disdained and whose cultures they cannibalized. When Franz Boas, noted ethnologist, returned to the Northwest Coast after an absence of almost a quarter-century, he lamented, upon hearing the same potlatch speeches he had heard early in his career, that the objects of those ceremonies were absent. He noted that it was "remarkable how the people cling to the form though the content is almost gone . . . the bowls are no longer here. They are in the museums in New York and Berlin!" (Cole 1985, 279). They were in the museums due to the work of Boas and others like him. While the research notes of many collectors openly reveal thievery and subterfuge, it is not difficult to imagine that many collectors never made references to the underhanded methods they might have used in obtaining collections. The extent of stealing and trickery may be more extensive than records reveal.

Of greatest interest to American Indians were the hundreds of thousands of bones of ancestors lying on museum shelves or dumped into boxes sitting on storage room floors. Those of us who grew up seeing our relatives' remains exhibited were most anxious to get those remains back on their journey to the afterworld.

Although some museums repatriated an occasional object (generally when confronted with information that questioned the museum's title to an object), most museums turned a deaf ear to American Indian queries and complaints. The two cultures (museum and American Indian) viewed ownership and use of collected materials in very different ways. With so many claims arising from Native groups, it seemed that legislation was the only way to get the issue of repatriating to the proper owners resolved.

In 1986, Congress was prodded into considering a Native American Museum Claims Commission. A hearing was held on the proposal, but nothing occurred. Late in 1988, the American Indian Religious Freedom Coalition was formed, backed by nearly one hundred organizations and tribes, including the National Congress of American Indians, Association on American Indian Affairs, and the Native American Rights Fund (Association on American Indian Affairs, 1993–1994). When legislation occurred to establish the National Museum of the American Indian as part of the Smithsonian Institution in 1989, the coalition saw to it that amendments were attached requiring the Smithsonian to repatriate human remains and funerary objects.

The following year (1990), the Native American Graves Protection and Repatriation Act (NAGPRA) became law, providing a process for American Indians to regain materials that should never have been alienated from them. Powerful forces had been arrayed against the passage of the act. The president of the American Association of Museums suggested that instead of requiring museums to provide proof of ownership, Native groups should be required to provide proof that the objects in question had been taken without consent (Hill 1996, 83). Those opposing repatriation included archaeologists and physical anthropologists, governors and other political leaders, university presidents, museum directors and curators, and professional museum and anthropological associations with large memberships. For many American Indians, the passage of the law was the culmination of a long, arduous process of protests, legal battles, public relations work, and, ultimately, political lobbying.

NAGPRA affects institutions receiving federal funds (most museums rely on a portion of their funding coming from federally-funded grants and most enjoy tax-exempt status—which some museum analysts consider a form of federal funding). Museums and agencies receiving federal funding were required by the new law to inventory their collections and to send reports of the inventories to federally recognized tribal groups affiliated to the materials (with a copy also going to the national NAGPRA office at the National Park Service). Following examination of the inventories, tribes can request negotiations concerning the return of certain classes of objects including American Indian human remains, associated burial goods, ceremonial objects, and items of cultural patrimony (Tabah 1993, 55).

If a tribe requests return of certain qualifying items, if there are no other tribal entities laying claim to the objects, and if the claim is substantiated, the objects are to be repatriated to the requesting group without demands being made on the group concerning storage, curatorial care, or future use. In addition to museums, the act affects most of the following (depending on their reliance on government funding): historical societies, park services, libraries and archives, universities, government entities, and other repositories possessing ethnographic collections and human remains. The National Park

Service (themselves undergoing repatriation of the 20,000 human specimens which had accumulated in their collections) was charged with developing the processes under which the law was to be enacted (Preston 1989, 67).

C. Timothy McKeown, manager of the national NAGPRA office located within the Archeology and Ethnography Division of NPS, has noted, "This is not a piece of legislation intended to loot museums, but to return certain objects that museums don't have a right to possess" (Selby 1993, 13A).

Although the law does not pertain to private owners of materials (other than to prohibit the sale of materials described by the NAGPRA guidelines), it is more broadly sweeping than many had thought possible, given the forces that had to be overcome to create the law.

The following two chapters chronicle some of the early protests American Indian individuals and groups undertook to regain wrongfully lost properties. These early efforts helped lay the groundwork for the passage of NAGPRA by setting precedents, by creating momentum, and by bringing information forward. The first chapter in this section looks at Native American efforts to regain objects other than human remains; the other is concerned solely with the quest to get American Indian human remains off museum shelves and back to their communities (however some Native communities are averse to receiving human remains).

It is important to consider that the seeking of the return of museum-held materials has meaning beyond the objects. According to Dr. James D. Nason (Comanche), "Museum specimens are not only the physical representations of this heritage and identity, but also the symbols of the loss of American Indian autonomy and culture by military, legal and demographic processes" (Nason 1973, 21). Empowerment can begin to be realized through the recovery of the lost materials and the accompanying reassertion of possession.

The act has assured that the two estranged cultures—American Indian and museums—will have to communicate and will have to agree on some basic interactions involving such things as the setting of meetings, exchanging documentation, and determining how items will be delivered and received.

NAGPRA has successfully determined that my grandchildren will not view the old museum classic—an American Indian skeleton—during their formative years. By the middle of 2006, as required by NAGPRA, the eligibility for repatriation of the remains of 31,344 individuals and more than 770,000 artifacts had been registered through public notices published in the Federal Register (National Native American Graves Protection and Repatriation Program 2006). There had been 1,263 published notices by U.S. institutions. The process is ongoing as the records of collections continue to undergo research regarding identity of materials, and tribes confer regarding disposition of claimed materials.

5

⊹

Demands for Return of
Material Objects

Museum charters have long focused on objects, a term patently offensive to many Native Americans because it refutes the idea of animism, or life within the materials. And it seems to separate Native things from their roles in Native cultures, objectifying them as standalone pieces. Still, for most of us, no comfortable term has arisen to replace object, material, thing, artifact, or item, so I will use "objects" when talking about a large class of materials. I ask the reader to keep in mind that these objects are alive (science finds that everything has atoms active with moving protons and electrons) and that these objects have valued status in Native communities. Also, while the word artifact might serve well for those things manufactured by people, the word doesn't necessarily extend to natural things incorporated into daily Native life.

The phrase "the collection, preservation, and exhibition of objects" was central to most museum mission statements through the middle of the twentieth century and still remains a critical part of many such statements. Museums came to understand that their unique educational ability was that of object-based learning. The possession of objects made museums different from schools, libraries, and historic sites, and the use of objects in exhibitions made museums the unique institutions they are. Today, there are museums without collections and there are institutions other than museums that have collections and provide exhibits.

During the early years of museum development, curators of collections began to learn about extending the life of the materials under their care through staving off hungry insects, combating the deterioration caused by

Figure 5.1. The leather cover of an illustrated two-volume Bible of 1745 reads, "The gift of the Rev. D. Francis Ayscough to the Indian Congregation at Housatonnic in New England. MDCCXLV." Following a succession of moves and resettling by New England Natives, the set disappeared. Later discovered in a New England museum, the Stockbridge-Munsee of Wisconsin regained possession of the set in 1991.

heat and light, understanding the damaging effects of constantly changing, or extremes of, humidity and temperature, and the need for nonabrasive and inert, or nonchemical-releasing, storage materials. The more curators learned, the more they protected the objects, and the more centrally important the preservation of objects became to curators. Their behavior soon bordered on obsessive and they began to develop a code of ethics regarding care of objects, ignoring that ethics had often been overlooked during the collecting of many of the ethnographic and physiological objects in their care. Some of the objects that curators sought to preserve were actually created by their makers with the intent that the objects would disintegrate naturally (as in the case of the Zuni War Gods). Therefore, extreme efforts to preserve some items might be considered unethical.

Further, while some in the museum field obsessed about the ethics of proper care of objects, others in the museum field were unethically selling and trading objects from the collections they were charged with protecting. For example, in 1975, the attorney general of New York charged the Museum of the American Indian's trustees and director with failure to care for the museum's collections. An examination discovered that records were inadequate and materials were improperly stored (Weil 1982, 50–51). Ultimately, the director was said to be de-accessioning materials without the knowledge of the trustees (Blair 1979, 129). The director was removed, six trustees resigned and a computerized inventory was ordered as a result of the investigation (Weil 1982, 51). In 1990, it was discovered that a longtime employee of the museum had stolen twenty-five objects over a period of time. One of the items was a Northwest Coast mask said to be worth $200,000 (*Oklahoma City Times*, March 28, 1991). Similar scandals have occurred in museums across the nation, many of them involving museums focused on Native American collections. "Safeguarded" items were protected well enough to make it hard for American Indians to view them, but not well enough to protect them from unscrupulous museum directors and employees.

Access to stored materials was often reserved for academic researchers, or at the very least, only academic researchers understood how to gain access. In 1985, Michael Bush, the executive director of the American Indian Community House, New York City, called upon the Museum of the American Indian to provide access to Indians or to give the collections back to the Indians (Hill 1996, 88).

It is little wonder that American Indians have generally been distrustful of the habits of museums. In the following pages, the pursuits taken by American Indians seeking return of wrongfully held materials are explored. The following studies concern a Hidatsa ceremonial bundle, Iroquois wampum belts, Kwakiutl potlatch materials, the Omaha Sacred Pole, Zuni War Gods, archaeological treasures, and a tribal Bible. The latter appears unusual in the list of Native materials, but the Bible had been communally held tribal property since 1745, making it older than the Declaration of Independence and many other American icons.

Through recent decades, the numbers of American Indians requesting return of objects grew, not because they had lacked desire to have them before, but because events made modern times more appropriate for long-ignored voices to be heard. The cases here represent only a sampling of the struggles.

HIDATSA BUNDLE

One of the first repatriations occurred in 1938 from the Museum of the American Indian to the Waterbuster Clan of the Hidatsa of North Dakota. In 1888, Small Ankle, a Hidatsa Indian and keeper of the sacred bundle of the Waterbuster Clan died. In 1907, his son Wolf Chief, a convert to Christianity and not a member of the same clan, sold the bundle for $100 to Gilbert Wilson, who made the purchase at the request of George Heye, whose collections founded the Museum of the American Indian in New York City. Although Wolf Chief had tried, following his father's death, to turn the bundle over to clan members, none had accepted the responsibility. Wolf Chief was undecided about accepting the offer from Wilson, but then quickly made the decision to relieve himself of the burden of responsibility for the bundle he found mystical and intimidating. Since receiving the property upon his father's death, Wolf Chief's immediate family had endured several tragedies. He was anxious to rid himself of something he considered powerful and beyond his abilities to manage (Gilman and Schneider 1987, 296–300).

However, according to tribal convention, Wolf Chief had no authority to sell the bundle. Clan members were outraged when they heard of the sale and lodged a protest with authorities. Wilson's permit to enter the reservation was suspended during the investigation. But the sale was ultimately allowed. Not until 1938, after suffering the successive droughts of the Dust Bowl era, could the Waterbuster Clan members gain allies in the Bureau of Indian Affairs and, with their help, were able to persuade the Museum of the American Indian to repatriate the bundle. That summer abundant rain returned to the reservation (Gilman and Schneider 1987, 315). In 1977, during a forced inventory, the museum discovered it had not given up the entire bundle contents, and returned what remained of the original materials (Jacknis 2006: 533).

The bundle is presently under the care of clan members. The Hidatsa are affiliated with two other tribes: the Mandan and the Arikara. Together, they support their own museum, the Three Affiliated Tribes Museum, in New Town, North Dakota.

IROQUOIS WAMPUM

Another early effort to regain lost property was initiated by two groups of Iroquois traditionalists in the waning years of the nineteenth century, but was not resolved until recent times. The Iroquois Confederacy (currently comprised of six nations: the Onondaga, the Mohawk, the Seneca, the Oneida, the Cayuga, and the Tuscarora) was organized before there was a United States.

Wampum, comprised of purple beads from quahog clamshells and white beads from whelk shells, is a sacred medium for the Iroquois nations. Wampum belts are woven mnemonic devices (meaning they are intended to prompt the memory about past events). Pictures and symbols created by the weaving process can be "read" by traditional leaders and serve to document and communicate the history and covenants of the group. The Onondaga Nation is the fire keeper of the Confederacy and is charged with keeping the Confederacy's wampum. With the advent of the hostilities that eventually separated the American colonies from England, the Iroquois Confederacy became divided, often due to their varied connections (political and economic) to foreign powers (Abrams 1994, 352–58).

The Six Nations of the Confederacy met during the troubled time, and its leaders agreed to split the Confederacy's wampum in line with the fact that they were physically divided by the border between Canada and the United States. The Loyalists located themselves in 1784 on the Grand River and became known as the Six Nations. Meanwhile, the New York reservations were successively diminished in land holdings. In 1847 members of the Onondaga returned to the site of their ancient council fire in New York. The Confederacy was constantly under siege due to pressures within and forces without compounded by the cumulative processes of relocation, political separations, impoverishment, and diminishment of rights of self-governance. Some segments of the population believed the old system of hereditary chiefs could no longer work. Reforms were suggested. Modern difficulties intervened. While people were distracted, events occurred to separate long-valued wampum from its owners (Fenton 1989, 401–2).

In 1893, Chief John Buck, called Skanawati, the keeper of wampum for the Six Nations Iroquois at Grand River, Ontario, died and not long afterward the belts he had kept were dispersed by his son, Joshua Buck, who held no authentic claim to the communally-owned objects (Green 1988, 25).

Acting on behalf of Joshua Buck, was his sister Clara's husband, Chief James Jamieson. Thomas R. Roddy, a Chicago trader, purchased eleven belts from the Jamiesons in 1899. Buck was reported to have held twenty-two belts. It is thought that Harriet Maxwell Converse, a folklorist, also purchased one of the belts (Fenton 1989, 404).

Meanwhile, in the same year of the death of Skanawati, the Council of Chiefs sent a delegation to retrieve the belts, but they were unsuccessful. The next year they recovered some of the belts that had been sold to David Boyle, a collector. The council discussed the issue at length, but failed to make a formal report of the situation to Canadian authorities (Fenton 1989, 404).

In 1900, Converse, on behalf of the Iroquois, wrote to the Indian superintendent at the Six Nations Reserve telling him that trader Roddy had offered a belt to the Buffalo Historical Society and she believed the belt was not rightfully his to sell (during this time, records indicate she also was in possession of one of the belts). The superintendent was told by his superiors to warn Roddy that the belts were not alienated from the nation. Meanwhile, Roddy was showing them to several possible buyers despite museums being warned away from the sale by Arthur C. Parker, New York state archaeologist and a descendant of a Seneca grandfather (Fenton 1989, 404).

The Council of Chiefs wrote to the governor general of Canada in 1909 requesting help in recovering the belts. Photos of the missing belts were circulated (Fenton 1989, 405).

Nevertheless, George G. Heye, founder of the Museum of the American Indian (MAI) in New York City acquired the belts in 1910 through an enterprise known as the Indian Trading Company. He paid $2,000 (Fenton 1989, 405-6).

Heye insisted, throughout the coming years of inquiry, that he had legally purchased the belts and he eventually donated them to the museum he founded. In 1915, the Council of the Six Nations passed a resolution declaring the wampum belts property of the Six Nations Indians of the Grand River and provided the names of six chiefs who could provide positive identification. However, the Canadian government was in the process of altering Native governments from traditional forms to elective systems formulated by the government. During this time, traditional people were often ignored and dismissed (Green 1988, 29). It is also possible that Canadian authorities believed they had offered the Iroquois a practical path of regaining the wampum by filing suit against the Buck family. However, the route of a lawsuit was not attractive to the Iroquois leaders who preferred to avoid public infighting, and were, no doubt, reluctant to submit to the decisions of a foreign legal system (Abrams 1994, 369).

In March 1977, the lawyer for the Union of Ontario Indians, Paul Williams, contacted the Museum of the American Indian and requested the museum provide information about how it had acquired the belts. An exchange of correspondence followed and both sides continued research into the matter. In May 1985, Williams again contacted the museum, this time as attorney for the Six Nations Confederacy chiefs. The Museum of the American Indian eventually agreed to turn over the eleven belts. The return was completed May 8, 1988 (Fenton 1989, 393–401). Probably, the MAI decision was prompted by concern about adverse publicity (which affects financial support) and a sense that judicial and legal authorities were increasingly responding to a modern public opinion differing from the patterns of earlier days.

Meanwhile, Iroquois traditionalists in the United States also fought to regain wampum lost to them in 1891 when Onondaga Chief Thomas Webster sold four belts to a U.S. Indian agent. In 1893, John B. Thatcher, mayor of Albany, bought the belts. In 1897, Chief Webster was removed from office and a suit was filed against Thatcher seeking return of wampum belts in his possession (Hill 1996, 84–85). It is reported that Harriet Converse, mentioned in the other Iroquois wampum case, persuaded the Onondaga chiefs to appoint her as their attorney and subsequently to agree that the board of regents of the New York State Museum (or New York State Cabinet of Antiquities as it was then known) would serve as caretakers of the wampum (Blair 1979a, 18). Twenty-six belts ultimately became the property of the museum. Again, the Iroquois failed to regain their wampum in the midst of governmental policies seeking to restructure Native governments. The courts ultimately determined Iroquois nations to be extinct with no standing (a decision that stood at the time, but no longer stands). In 1909, the New York legislature appointed itself as wampum keeper. The Thatcher belts were donated to the State Museum in 1927 (Hill 1996, 85).

In 1970, a group of Onondaga, supported by other Iroquois and non-Iroquois Indian activists, called for the return of the wampum to the Onondaga. Their argument gained support from some anthropologists and other supportive non-Indians (Lurie 1976, 244).

However, alarmed curators and historians from the Smithsonian Institution, the Field Museum of Natural History (Chicago), the University of Southern Illinois, the State University of New York, and the Peabody Museum of Salem, Massachusetts, representing the Committee on Anthropological Research in Museums, wrote to the governor of New York, Nelson Rockefeller, protesting the possibility that wampum in the state's possession was being considered for repatriation to the Iroquois.

They said in a letter dated Feb. 23, 1970, "The allegation of the Indians that they need the wampum now for their religion is only partly

true. . . . [S]tate property should not be legislated away lightly in the il-
lusion of religiosity or as capital in the civil rights movement." (Henry
1970; Council on Museum Anthropology 1970).

Still, in 1971, the New York State Legislature, after much continued
pressure from Iroquois leaders, passed a bill promising return of
wampum belts held by the New York State Museum on the condition that
the Onondaga build a satisfactory storage facility to protect and display
the belts. Since many reputable museums were storing their own Native
collections in poor facilities under substandard conditions, the require-
ment had the appearance of a stalling factor with paternalistic overtones.
The stipulations imposed on the Onondaga delayed transferal of the contested wampum for almost eighteen years (Hill 1977, 45). In the minds of
many Native people, it is inappropriate for museums and governments to
impose standards of care on objects owned by Native entities (and we
have found it especially galling to visit non-Native museum facilities that
do not meet, or have not met, basic standards of protective care, and are
not, nor have been, required to meet such standards themselves).

Meanwhile, the Iroquois were seeking returns from other wampum-
holding museums. In 1974, the Iroquois Advisory Committee of the Buffalo and Erie County Historical Society requested that wampum beads be
returned to the Council of Chiefs, along with Iroquois human remains.
The committee also made inquiries about the return of ceremonial masks.
The museum responded by requiring that assurances be given to guarantee that no returned objects find their way to the open market (Gonyea
and Hill 1981). Although such a response is typical of a museum point of
view, it is alienating to Native ears and seems paternalistic as well as ac-
cusatory, as it seems there is suspicion that Native communities won't attempt to protect the materials they regain. If the property is wrongly held
by museums, and rightfully belongs to American Indians, then it is not
appropriate for a museum to impose a stipulation, whether it is to develop appropriate storage facilities or to provide guarantees that items
won't be sold.

In 1975, the historical society returned human remains from their collections, offered the masks they held for ceremonial use, and returned
several thousand wampum beads on an annual loan basis (Gonyea and
Hill 1981).

In 1981, the Grand Council of the Haudenosaunee issued a formal policy statement regarding medicine masks (ceremonial masks vital to cur-
ing and other ceremonies). Included with the statement was a request for
the return of masks.

"There is no legal, moral or ethical way in which a medicine mask can
be obtained or possessed by a non-Indian individual or an institution . . .
in order for medicine masks to be removed from the society it would re-

quire the sanction of the Grand Council of Chiefs. This sanction has never been given" (Gonyea and Hill 1981).

In 1986, the Grand Council of Chiefs presented a statement read by Oren Lyons, Onondaga chief, as part of a panel discussion at Columbia University. The statement laid claim to "all sacred objects, human remains, and traditional territory as our cultural patrimony and our national cultural treasures." Lyons said, "The national cultural treasures of the Haudenosaunee are the property of today's generation of people and the governing body of chiefs who represent them" (Center for American Culture Studies 1986).

In summary, eleven wampum belts were retrieved in 1988 from the Museum of the American Indian, New York City, by the Grand River Iroquois in Ontario, Canada, with Ray Gonyea (an Onondaga working at the New York State Museum at the time) serving as mediator. Then, in October 1989, twelve wampum belts were returned by the New York State Museum to the Onondaga Nation, again with Gonyea interceding (Gonyea 1993, 4). That same year, the Haudenosaunee Standing Committee, comprised of members representing each of the six nations of the Iroquois Confederacy, was formed to protect Iroquois burial sites. It soon became involved in repatriation pursuits (American Indian Ritual Object Repatriation Foundation 1996). With the advent of NAGPRA, the Iroquois will be reunited with more items from a variety of museums, and will not be obligated to adhere to any imposed restrictions or requirements regarding those returned objects as had occurred in pre-NAGPRA times.

KWAKWAKA'WAKW POTLACK MATERIALS

In December 1921, a large gathering of Kwakwaka'wakw First Nations or kwak'wala speaking people (then referred to as the Kwakiutl) in British Columbia attended a very large potlatch. But ceremony soon turned into lamentations when the potlatch was interrupted by Canadian government officials who confiscated more than 750 masks, coppers, regalia items, serving dishes, and other ceremonial and gift items (Carpenter 1981). The potlatch ceremony was hosted by Chief Dan Cranmer, a 'Namgis member of the Kwakwaka'wakw from Alert Bay, Cormorant Island in conjunction with his wife, Emma, and her family, the Mamalilikala of Village Island. The hosts were assisted by Chief Billy Assu (Lekwiltok) of Cape Mudge Village. During six days of ceremony, objects were displayed and gifts were distributed (Clifford 1991, 227).

A potlatch is a traditional and significant ceremony involving gift giving and is often held when people marry, receive names, mourn, engage in other rites of passage, or gain honors. Guests witnessing the honoring ceremony are provided with gifts as a means of payment for their services as witnesses to the business transacted during the ceremony. Guests accepting the gifts then also accepted the responsibility to verify and pass on the information about the business transacted for future reference. This is because the First Nations people did not have a written language so history was passed on orally. Ceremonial objects owned by the hosting family are displayed. Missionaries and government agents frowned on the rites contending that such ceremonies prevented proper civilizing of the Native peoples involved. Additionally, the "authorities" needed to be able to provide a labor force for the burgeoning European-style economy. Naively, they believed the potlatch served to impoverish people through extravagant displays, expensive gifting, and seemingly wanton destruction of property.

In 1884, the first prohibition of potlatch passed was found to be ineffectual, and later strengthened. Although the Native people appealed for the persecution to stop, they were ignored. As time passed, the prohibition caused many owners of Native religious materials to sell objects since they feared they would face fines if found in possession of the materials. As new generations received less exposure to traditional ceremonies, their appreciation for the materials declined and more objects found their way to the marketplace. Such losses were hardly self-imposed. Even in the face of persecution, however, many remained faithful and practiced ceremonials in secret (Cole 1985, 249).

The 1921 raid occurred at Village Island, British Columbia, Canada, and forty-five people were initially arrested (U'mista brochure). The Cranmer potlatch was noted as the biggest ever recorded on the central coast. Among the gifts were gas boats, pool tables, sewing machines, and gramophones (Cole 1985, 250).

Ultimately, those arrested were offered suspensions if they would give up their potlatch materials, which also included traditional materials such as coppers (a shield-shaped plate of beaten copper) that represented a symbol of wealth, power, and prestige; masks; rattles; and whistles. The New York collector George Heye arrived on the scene and promptly bought thirty-five items from the arresting officials (Cole 1985, 251–52).

The remaining materials were sent to Ottawa and divided between the Victoria Memorial Museum, now the National Museum of Man in Ottawa, and the Royal Ontario Museum in Toronto (U'mista Cultural Centre brochure 1994). Eleven items went to the Indian Affairs office. The collection remained mostly intact, but occasional museum exchanges occurred resulting in the dispersal of some items (Cole 1985, 254).

Twenty people spent two to three months in prison. And the people of the various involved villages never forgot their losses. Eventually, tribal members were issued checks to pay for their lost valuables, but many refused to take the money. The total compensation amounted to $1,495, while the value of the items *at the time* was estimated to have been worth over $35,000. Although the tribe had sought to recover the items soon after confiscation, until repeal of the 1884 law, there was no effective recourse. The Native Indian Brotherhood fought for repeal of the anti-potlatch law and finally succeeded in 1951 when revision of the Indian Act deleted Section 149, the offending portion that had outlawed the potlatch (U'Mista Cultural Centre brochure 1994).

In 1963, James Sewid, a Kwakwaka'wakw leader, reported to the media that he had tried to buy back the confiscated materials held by Canada's national museum and his offer had been refused. By 1975, the Canadian government relented and arrangements were made which allowed two bands to separately hold and display the 313 items still in the possession of the government (Carpenter 1981). The agreement stipulated that the bands must construct museums to house the materials. Two tribal museums were formed and the collection was split between them. In 1979, the Kwagiulth Museum and Cultural Centre opened in Cape Mudge and in 1980, the U'mista Cultural Centre opened in Alert Bay (U'Mista Cultural Centre brochure 1994). In 1988, 75 more objects were returned from the Royal Ontario Museum (Kwagiulth Museum brochure 1994).

THE SACRED POLE OF THE OMAHA

The Sacred Pole of the Omaha was created in the mists of time as a burning tree that was not consumed. During its earliest times with the Omaha, it was known as the Venerable Man and was viewed as an elder. The pole represented the joining of halves: male and female, the Sky people with the Earth people. It renewed life, and kept the people safe and united (Ridington 1997, 68–70).

In 1888, Yellow Smoke, the keeper of the Sacred Pole of the Omaha, reportedly gave up the Pole in exchange for $45 from Francis La Flesche, a fellow tribesman who also happened to be an ethnologist employed by the Peabody Museum of Harvard University (Ridington 1997, 90). La Flesche had suggested to the elderly man, who was worried about the fate of the pole, that he should send it to the "great brick house" (Ridington 1997, xix), implying that the pole would be safest in the Peabody Museum.

In 1875, the last feast of renewal had been held and the last new wrappings were applied to the Pole. For several years the Omaha had been prevented from holding buffalo hunts, which had provided the necessary feast for the renewal ceremonies. Purchasing cattle for the feast was unaffordable. Without the feast and the renewal ceremony, the Sacred Pole

was not regularly seen by most of the Omaha population. The ceremonies, and those who practiced them, declined.

Yellow Smoke, approaching the end of his life without a keeper to follow him, had little choice but to seek whatever means of preservation he
could find for the Sacred Pole. The tribe had suffered through the effects
of allotment of their lands during the Omaha Severalty Act of 1882, which
scattered the people across the landscape and served to diminish their
ceremonial, political, and social lives. Robin Ridington, author of *Blessing
for a Long Time. The Sacred Pole of the Omaha Tribe*, suggests that Yellow
Smoke viewed the placement of the pole in the Peabody as one of "safekeeping" (23). Indeed, La Flesche and his mentor, Alice Fletcher, used the
word "safekeeping" in their 1911 Bureau of Ethnology report, *The Omaha
Tribe* (Ridington 1997, 53). Many Omaha people, however, believed that
the Pole had actually been stolen by La Flesche.

Efforts to retrieve the Sacred Pole began during a visit to the Peabody
in the 1970s when former tribal chairman Edward Cline saw the pole on
display in the Peabody. Believing the display disrespectful, he asked the
director to remove the Pole from exhibition and the museum agreed. In
1988, a century after the pole had arrived at the Peabody, tribal representatives arranged to see the pole outside in the courtyard of the Peabody
where they would touch it for the first time in their lifetimes (Ridington
1997, 28). The pole was possibly two centuries old when it was taken to
the Peabody in 1888 (Ridington 1997, 53). Omaha leaders believed that the
key to unity and cultural preservation was the return of the pole to its
people.

Upon returning home from their last trip to the Peabody in Massachusetts, tribal officials sent a formal request to the museum for the return of
the Sacred Pole. They received a letter that appeared to turn down the request. Further negotiations achieved a response that the Peabody would
engage in a three-year loan followed by beginning the process of legal
transfer of not only the pole, but of the entire Fletcher collection with the
provision that the tribe document where and how the collection would be
stored. The Joslyn Museum, Omaha, was proposed as repository and
would bear the shipping expenses (Ridington 1997, 201–3).

Planning for a 1989 arrival of the pole at the tribal powwow, negotiations became harried when the Joslyn changed its charter to become an art
museum making it no longer appropriate for, or interested in, housing the
collection. Luckily, the director of the Center for Great Plains Studies at
the University of Nebraska quickly agreed to house the Sacred Pole (Ridington 1997, 204–6). The following year, 280 objects were returned to the
Omaha tribe from the Peabody Museum (Ridington 1997, 193). Those objects, along with the White Buffalo Hide and the Sacred Pole, currently reside in the University of Nebraska State Museum (Ridington 1997, 235)

until the Omaha Tribe has its own collections facility. Current U.S. repatriation law does not require a tribe to satisfy concerns about future care of returned materials. Repatriated items, by U.S. law, are regarded as having returned to the ownership of the tribe, and a tribally owned item is the business of no one but the tribe.

A 28-minute news story produced by KUON-TV with support from Native American Public Telecommunications has been released as a film, *The Return of the Sacred Pole*, which documents the Omaha community's celebration of the pole's journey back home.

Another sacred Omaha item, the White Buffalo Hide, was stolen in 1898 by an unidentified thief. It was delivered to individuals who initially offered to sell it to the Peabody, but who instead sold it to another party, after which, unbeknownst to the tribe, the hide found its way in 1928 to George Gustav Heye, the founder of the Museum of the American Indian (Ridington 1997, 219–26). In 1982, Dennis Hastings, Omaha tribal historian, requested a list of Omaha holdings from the Museum of the American Indian and discovered the missing hide was listed among the many items. Filing the information away for a future time, probably because the tribe was busy with negotiations to retrieve the Sacred Pole, the tribe did not request the hide until the National Museum of the American Indian was formed in 1989. Subsequently, the hide was repatriated by NMAI in 1991 (Ridington 1997, 227).

Just days before the theft of the White Buffalo Hide occurred in 1898, La Flesche successfully persuaded the keeper of the hide to give it up to the Peabody so that future Omaha children would understand the ways of their ancestors (Ridington 1997, 219). Indeed, it was just such "children," the grown offspring of children not yet born when the pole and the hide were lost, who sought the return of the sacred materials from the Peabody and the National Museum of the American Indian generations later. It is apparent they understand the ways of their ancestors and take those ways very seriously.

ZUNI WAR GODS

In 1978, the Zuni Tribe began concerted efforts to gain return of Zuni War Gods, known as *Ahayu:da*. By 1991, the tribe had repatriated sixty-five War Gods from thirty-four museums and private collectors (Pueblo of Zuni press release 1991). By 2000, a total of eighty had been recovered (Ferguson, Anyon, and Ladd 2000, 243). Head Councilman Joseph Dishta noted, "Many people at Zuni Pueblo have worked together to achieve this success, including the Deer and Bear Clan leaders, the Bow Priests, and every Governor and Tribal Council during the last fourteen years.

We also gratefully acknowledge the technical and scholarly support provided by the Institute of the North American West and the Zuni Archaeology Program, and the legal guidance of attorneys in the Office of the Field Solicitor, Department of the Interior, and the Department of Justice" (Pueblo of Zuni press release 1991).

Ahayu:da are believed to be embodiments of sacred beings which protect the Zuni and the world around them. Every year their images are constructed and placed in outdoor shrines, which are located in remote locations. Because of the remoteness of locations, and because non-Indians regard such carved images as collectible art, many War Gods have been stolen and many have become the possessions of museums.

Museum collections workers have suggested that museums are proper repositories for War Gods saying that should the Zuni ever lose the practice and understanding of their War Gods, they could learn about them from museum collections. The Zuni responded to that suggestion by noting that such knowledge would be superficial. They say that it is the prayers and thoughts that are important and they cannot be learned from museum collections (Ferguson and Eriacho 1990, 11).

Barton Martza, who would serve later as head councilman of the Zuni tribe from 1987 to 1990, recalled in a Zuni publication how the search for War Gods residing in museums was launched. Sometime in the late 1970s, tribal members, who had just placed a War God in a shrine, discovered nearby a tin can with old papers inside. Martza was given the papers, which were dated in the 1800s. The information provided by the papers led to evidence of War Gods residing in the Denver Art Museum. Upon hearing this report, the Zuni religious leaders began discussing the idea of seeking the return of the War Gods. Martza was part of the first delegation to approach the museum. In 1978, the Zuni leaders declared they would seek the return of all War Gods from museums and collectors (Martza 1991, 12).

In response to the Zuni tribe's request for repatriation, representatives of the Denver Art Museum developed an argument resisting return citing five points: (1) the museum's first responsibility was to its general public; (2) the museum had a responsibility for the preservation of materials: (3) the museum should not simply give up objects; (4) the museum was not assured the objects would be cared for by the requesting recipients; (5) and the museum feared the objects might be resold.

The Zuni representatives countered that the War Gods had greater significance to the tribe than to the museum. The Zuni tribe developed criteria for qualifying sacred objects emphasizing the continuing religious significance of the objects. They argued that if an object were stolen, it should be returned to its rightful owners. They argued points of the law that cite that the burden of proof rests on the non-Indian to show legal acquisition

of the property once the Native representative has shown prior possession (Davies 1979, 136–37).

The Zuni also included a statement advising that the museum would be
freed from liability concerning illegal acquisition and of continued reten-
tion of stolen property if the museum released the War Gods to the tribe.
The attorney general of Colorado, backing the Zuni line of argument,
stated that he did not support a public institution's right to use of stolen
property (Davies 1979, 138).

In 1980, the Denver Art Museum returned the three War Gods to the
Zuni. That same year the Wheelwright Museum returned two War Gods
and the Museum of New Mexico returned four. In 1981, the Millicent
Rogers Museum and the University of Iowa Museum of Art returned one
each. The Tulsa Zoo returned one in 1985 (Ferguson 1990, 7). Some of
these War Gods found their way to public institutions after being donated
by collectors who had bought the items from dealers. Other War Gods
were bought directly by the institutions from dealers who had obtained
them from collectors. In most cases, the public institutions had not considered the items stolen. Most would have considered them originally
"abandoned" and subsequently legally transferred from owner to owner.
The Zuni enlightened many curators and directors as they continued their
pursuit of the War Gods.

In 1987, two Zuni War Gods were repatriated from the Smithsonian Institution (Owsley and Compton 1990, 11–12) as a result of negotiations,
which had begun in 1978 (Ferguson, Anyon, and Ladd 2000, 243). In 1988,
the Logan Museum of Anthropology returned three and the Milwaukee
Public Museum returned two. The Southwest Museum returned two War
Gods in 1989 (Ferguson 1990, 7).

The governor of the Pueblo of Zuni wrote to all U.S. museums known
to have *Ahayu:da* in their collections in February 1990. He requested the
return of the War Gods known to be in each museum's collection. Many
responded to the request (including one which was not on the original
list, but who, upon hearing about the request, initiated repatriation of the
War God in its collection) (Ferguson and Eriacho 1990, 8). In 1990, the following museums repatriated War Gods: Redrock State Park, American
Museum of Natural History, Museum of the American Indian, Hudson
Museum, Lowie Museum of Anthropology, Taylor Museum, and Arizona
State Museum (Ferguson 1990, 7).

During the sustained drive to repossess their War Gods, the Zuni also
repatriated War Gods from private individuals and art galleries as well
as an art brokerage firm and a corporation's private collection (Ferguson 1990, 7). Most of the response from private owners was due to the
mounting publicity and consequent awareness of the meaning of War
Gods.

At this time, all U.S. museum-possessed War Gods are believed to have been repatriated, and have been placed in protected shrines according to the wishes of the Zuni people.

Other notable returns in the Southwest include a return of kiva masks to requesting Hopi elders made by the Heard Museum, Phoenix. However, that return was repudiated in a 1977 magazine interview with the ensuing Heard director, Patrick Houlihan, who noted that he would have opted for a long-term loan to the tribe instead (Newsom and Silver 1977, 94). Houlihan went on to become director of the Southwest Museum, Los Angeles, from 1981 to 1987. In 1988 he became director of the Millicent Rogers Museum in Taos (Gibson 1993, 62). Then, in a 1989 inventory at the Southwest Museum, the discovery was made that 127 items including Navajo textiles, Hopi kachinas, baskets, and paintings were missing. Twenty-eight items were recovered and traced back to Houlihan, who had sold them. Houlihan was fined, sentenced to 120 days in the county jail, placed on five years probation, ordered to pay $70,000 to the museum in restitution, and ordered to serve 1,000 hours of community service without association with art, anthropology, or Southwestern culture (Gallo 1993, 22). Such have been the unstable ethics of a number of museum directors involved with American Indian collections.

The Wheelwright Museum, Santa Fe, returned sacred bundles to Navajo medicine men in 1977 (Blair 1979a, 18). In 1982, the Smithsonian responded to a request from a Pueblo community and returned a ceremonial vessel discovered to have been inappropriately obtained (Owsley and Compton 1990, 11–12).

In the eighteenth century, a Spanish artist painted a hide depicting Our Lady of Guadalupe and sculpted two saints for a Catholic church in the center of Zuni Pueblo. In the nineteenth century the mission properties reverted to Zuni ownership. In 1879, a Smithsonian collector removed the artifacts without permission from Zuni officials. In 1991, the Smithsonian's National Museum of American History agreed to repatriate the materials. Since one of the sculptures had been destroyed in a fire, the museum agreed to create a facsimile as a replacement (Ferguson, Anyon, and Ladd 2000, 256). These incidents represent a few of the many items repatriated back to Southwestern tribes.

TUNICA TREASURE

In 1968, Leonard Charrier began excavating a burial mound in Louisiana and eventually unearthed more than 100 graves. But it was not bones that interested the digger. In fact, he discarded most of the remains. He was after treasure. And he had found an extraordinary trove. He unearthed approximately 200,000 eighteenth-century artifacts representing the Tunica and their trading partners, including the French and English, as well as trade items from other geographic areas of the American continent (Hennessy 1995, 10).

When Charrier contacted the Peabody Museum of Harvard University in Massachusetts, a representative was dispatched to look at the materials. In 1970, the collection was shipped to the Peabody Museum after Charrier assured their representative he could prove title. In 1972, the excavator finally told the Peabody where the collection had been located and it became clear that title was uncertain. The museum had little concern, it seems, about the possibility of Native claims; the concern was whether the property owner had relinquished rights to the digger. When the property owner failed to provide clear title to Charrier, the excavator initiated suit against the property owner for the rights of ownership. Louisiana initiated its own suit against Charrier and bought the mound site (along with possible rights to the collection) from the property owner for $175,000. The case continued. However, in July 1981 the Tunica-Biloxi became a federally recognized tribe and joined the suit seeking rights to the collection. The state decided to back the tribe's claim of ownership (Hennessy 1995, 13–17).

"This will be a landmark case, " noted Jeffrey P. Brain, Peabody curator and author of *Tunica Treasure*, a book describing the excavation and the materials found, but, having been written before the trial was concluded, it did not report on the final disposition of the collection (Floyd 1985, 6–7).

In March 1985, the Appeals Court in Saint Francisville, Louisiana, declared that, as a burial site, the site could not be judged as abandoned. Thus, according to the court's finding, the materials belonged to the tribe. The case was appealed to the Louisiana Supreme Court, which upheld the decision in 1986 (Hill 1996, 89).

Although the materials were declared to belong to the Tunica-Biloxi tribe, as in so many other similar instances involving American Indian issues regarding collections, the tribe was required to have a proper facility to care for the materials before they could receive the items, which had been physically transferred from the Peabody Museum to the Cabildo Museum in New Orleans. According to Tunica representatives, the items were not receiving the kind of care they needed at the Cabildo. It was galling to the Tunica to realize, when they finally received the materials, that they believed the objects would have been better served if they had been placed in Tunica care earlier, however unprepared Tunica collections facilities may have been at the time. The materials had been placed in containers and stacked while at the Cabildo, but the containers were not appropriate for stacking and materials consequently had been damaged (Hennessy 1995, 17–18).

In 1989, the Tunica Treasure came home and much of it is currently exhibited in the Tunica-Biloxi Museum, Marksville, Louisiana, in proper climate-control, in darkness the majority of the time, and resting on chemically inert materials. The tribe developed its own conservation laboratory and is still in the painstaking process of conserving copper, iron, ceramics, and other degradable materials. The finding in the court ruling regarding the Tunica Treasure helped establish tribal rights to burial materials (Hennessy 1995, 17–18).

STOCKBRIDGE-MUNSEE BIBLE

In 1745, the Christian Indian congregation known as the Stockbridge Indians were presented with a two-volume Bible from Dr. Francis Ayscough, an emissary of the Prince of Wales (Stockbridge-Munsee Historical Committee 1990, 2). The Stockbridge Indians represented a band of the Mahicans, a large Algonquian group whose homeland had included portions of New England and New York. They were a subgroup of the large Delaware Nation, also known as the Lenape tribe.

During the Revolutionary War, Stockbridge Indian men fought as enrolled soldiers, but their absence from their property while fighting led to final losses of land. Disappointed by their poor treatment, they moved from Massachusetts in 1785 to live near the Oneida in western New York. They made an oak chest to protect the Bible and the tribe made its way west (Guthrie 1991).

In 1820, Stockbridge families again were forced to move; some stopped in Indiana while others continued to Wisconsin. The Wisconsin group linked up with the Munsee, a related group originally from Pennsylvania. After several moves within Wisconsin, the Stockbridge-Munsee settled in their present location in Shawano County in 1856. Their Bible was still with them (Guthrie 1991).

It was last known to be in the home of Sote Quinney in the 1920s. But, it seems, at Quinney's death, the pastor of the Presbyterian Church took the Bible from the home to the church basement. In the 1930s Mabel Choate of Massachusetts offered $1,000 to the Wisconsin church to purchase the Bible. She was intent on creating a Mission House museum at the home of the missionary who had led the conversion of the original Stockbridge congregation (Guthrie 1991).

The bill of sale was signed by two elders and by two trustees of the church (two of the signatories were tribal members). However, other tribal members objected to the sale when it became public knowledge, but by then the Bible was gone. Through the mists of time, as people mentioned the Bible, the knowledge of where it resided became uncertain.

And then in 1951, Jim and Grace Davids were making a pilgrimage east to the land of their forebears when they visited the Mission House Museum and saw their Bible on display. Their discovery led to several subsequent visits by tribal members throughout the ensuing years. In 1975, fifteen members, including nine students, made the trip to see the Bible. The students urged their elders to seek repossession of the two large books (Guthrie 1991).

Upon receiving the initial request from the Wisconsin Indians, the trustees of the Mission House Museum had to seek legal opinion regarding ownership of the Bible since Mabel Choate had turned her possessions over to the museum to be held "in perpetuity." The tribe's lawyer commented that he considered it ironic that the first Christianized Indians might have to sue to regain the representation of their conversion. Over the next fifteen years, letters and visits would bring the transfer closer to reality. Ultimately, the inscription in the Bible itself became the deciding factor, for it entrusted the Bible to the Stockbridge and their successors (Guthrie 1991).

Once the museum decided to relinquish the books, it imposed one familiar condition: it required that the tribe obtain a safe place for keeping the Bible. After some delays, a security system was installed in the tribe's library and cultural center. The Probate Court of Massachusetts made the approval for transfer in December 1990 (Guthrie 1991).

On March 11, 1991, ten members of the Stockbridge-Munsee tribe participated in a ceremony at the Mission House Museum where they received the Bible. On their return to Wisconsin, more than fifty people gathered on the streets of Shawano, a town southeast of the reservation, to welcome the Bible home (Guthrie 1991). Today, the Bible resides in the Arvid E. Miller Memorial Library and Museum in Bowler, Wisconsin.

Some people say American Indians should be grateful to museums for having saved so many American Indian cultural items. In some cases, some American Indians are indeed grateful. But, in other cases, there has been great disappointment. Numerous mainstream museums have not been exemplary in their care of American Indian materials. In 1978, for instance, the New York attorney general took action against a former curator of the Brooklyn Museum for providing dealers with American Indian artifacts from the museum's collections. Similar travesties occurred at the Museum of the American Indian in New York City, the Southwest Museum of Los Angeles, the Maryhill Museum in Washington State, and numerous other facilities across the continent (Weil 1982). Such materials, falling outside of the guardianship of a protective institution, usually wind up in private hands and often leave the country, denying American Indians the opportunity to view or possess things that could be culturally important to them.

Additionally, many objects were literally poisoned by museums in an effort to deter insect damage. There has been conflict between Native communities and museums about whose duty it is to determine the contamination status of returned objects since the testing can be expensive. Arsenic, which museums had routinely applied to organic materials in earlier times now shows up on leather clothes and wooden masks. The contamination means that such items cannot effectively be returned to ceremonial use for it would be deadly to wear an arsenic-laced mask or to blow a whistle covered with the harmful chemical. And currently there is no effective means to remove arsenic.

The return of objects has instigated a resurgence of ceremonial activities and cultural vitality in many recipient tribes. Further repatriation will see continued elaboration of cultural revitalization. The pride of ownership of materials relating to historical events and cultural activities serves to transmit pride to upcoming generations whose grandparents experienced great loss, deprivation, and injury to their own sense of pride. Material culture is vital to community identities and NAGPRA seeks to redress some of the losses American Indian communities sustained during years of uncertainty and diminishment of their political power.

The next chapter provides more details on the creation of the Native American Graves Protection and Repatriation Act (NAGPRA) as we explore the demands for the return from museums of vast holdings of remains of American Indian ancestors.

6

Demands for Return of
Human Remains

The remains of as many as 600,000 indigenous individuals have been in the possession of museums, universities, federal repositories, and private collectors (Preston 1989, 67). Most of those remains have been, or will be, returned to homeland areas due to the 1990 passage of the Native American Graves Protection and Repatriation Act (NAGPRA). I say "most" because some have no identification and will require special policy if they are to be re-interred. There are also some American Indian nations which decline acceptance of disturbed human remains. But the question looms: How did so many American Indian skeletons become the property of museums in the first place?

The desire to possess American Indian bones has a long history in the United States. Thomas Jefferson, perhaps America's first documented archaeologist, excavated a burial mound on his property in Virginia in 1770 (Braidwood 1983, 350). The first major museum in the United States, Charles Willson Peale's Philadelphia Museum (established in 1786) included an American Indian skeleton in its catalogue of collected materials (Alexander 1983, 62). From the beginning days of museums in North America, there was the accepted expectation that American Indian remains belonged in museum exhibitions. Nearly every historical society and natural history museum exhibited an Indian skeleton. Displaying an American Indian skull or skeleton was not only accepted as appropriate to do, but was considered by many to be a required part of a museum's exhibitions.

In the 1840s, Samuel Morton, one of the first physical anthropologists in America, undertook an exhaustive study of human skulls in an effort to

Figure 6.1. Ishi was known as the last of his tribe when he came out of the seclusion of the California hills in 1911 to ultimately become a resident of the University of California's museum at Berkeley. Upon Ishi's death in 1916, his brain became part of the Smithsonian Institution's collections until a group of California Natives successfully located and reclaimed his remains. The exhibit sign in the photograph says "Yana house built by Ishi."

Courtesy of the Phoebe Apperson Hearst Museum of Anthropology and the Regents of the University of California. Photographer unknown, catalog number 15-5424.

prove that white people were superior to others. After collecting about 600 American Indian skulls (Gould 1981, 50) primarily through military sources, he concluded from his studies that whites were indeed a superior race. It is especially ignominious that the loss of remains of loved ones from battlefields and graves served to support studies to further degrade Native populations. Morton's proclaimed results helped pave the way for the undermining of the rights of non-whites, which included further taking of American Indian lands, relocating Native populations, and encouraging other genocidal activities such as curtailment of supplies, vaccinations, and other humane services.

In 1868, scientific studies found more need for American Indian skulls, and army personnel were directed by the U.S. surgeon general to collect them from bodies on battlefields (Monroe and Echo-Hawk 1991, 57). Some of the studies were concerned with the effects of modern weaponry upon human physiology.

B. E. Fryer, an army surgeon, became an active procurer of American Indian heads. In 1868, he sent twenty-six crania from nine tribes to the surgeon general. From 1868 to 1874, Fryer sent at least forty-four American Indian skulls to George A. Otis, a curator of the Army Medical Museum (Riding In 1992, 106–9).

In 1878, the victims of the Sand Creek Massacre were beheaded to fulfill the ongoing request for Native skulls as issued by the surgeon general (Peerman 1990, 935). The collections amassed by the army were originally accessioned into the Army Medical Museum, which in turn later handed the materials over to the Smithsonian Institution, affectionately known as America's Attic.

In addition to taking bodies from battlefields, great numbers of Native human remains found their way to museum shelves direct from their repose in graves. Surgeon Fryer also collected for the army from graves, and noted in a letter that "a good deal of caution is required in obtaining anything from the graves of Indians, and it will have to be managed very carefully to prevent the Indians from finding out that the graves of their people have been disturbed" (Riding In 1992, 108).

Native graves have rarely received the protection granted to European-American cemeteries. Repeatedly, individuals known as "pot hunters," along with archaeologists (often regarded by American Indians as licensed pot hunters), were free to open graves, gather bones and artifacts, and carry them off as institutional or personal possessions. Joining them were farmers, ranchers, miners, construction workers, ditch diggers, gravediggers, treasure hunters, gardeners, geologists, and any number of other people armed with trowels, shovels, pick axes, or other earth-moving equipment. James Riding In, a Pawnee involved in repatriation efforts, likens the mass collection of Native remains to a "spiritual holocaust" (Riding In 2000, 109).

The *Brooklyn Daily Union* noted on July 17, 1876, that Shinnecock tribal members were indignant on finding that graves on their Long Island reservation had been opened for study. The report noted that further research was halted, but then said it was probable the "relics" would be placed in the museum of the Long Island Historical Society. Native people concerned with protecting gravesites found their task to be like an overwhelmed cat watching too large an array of mouse holes. It could not be known when or where an assault would be undertaken. Graves thought to be in protected areas were often excavated in the middle of the night while graves in remote areas were often excavated in broad daylight.

A human skull could bring a good price at any flea market. Many purchasers thought an Indian skull made a handsome coffee table embellishment or desk ornament. If one had a little business by a roadside, an Indian skeleton might be just the draw you needed to get patrons to linger longer, increasing the odds that they would buy something, or buy more. In fact, if you had an Indian skeleton and a few other tantalizing items in a separate room, you could charge motorists a fee to gawk at the objects in your "museum." Not all collected remains were for scientific study. Many amateur-collected human remains were eventually offered to museums.

In 1916, anthropologist Alfred Kroeber noted that the University of California's Museum of Anthropology, then located at Parnassus possessed "hundreds of Indian skeletons that nobody ever comes near to study" (Rockafellar 2006).

To American Indians, the stories of collecting their ancestors' remains reek of racial bias. American Indian bones and antiquities were definitely targeted and Native ownership and Native thoughts on propriety were absolutely disregarded. These attitudes continued until recent time, and still linger in the minds of some citizens. For instance, during construction of the Tellico Dam in eastern Tennessee, which began in 1965, white, black, and Native graves were disturbed. White and black remains were immediately reburied while Native remains were collected for study (Friends Committee on National Legislation 1986, 2).

In 1965, the District Court of Appeals of Florida failed to find a young man guilty of desecration for removing a Seminole skull taken from a Florida Everglades burial site that was only two years old because the removal was not proven to be wanton or malicious conduct (Rosen 1980, 7–8; Price 1991, 56). While Florida officials protected "cemeteries" as defined by the law at the time, the unmarked burial statute referred to remains that were at least seventy-five years old (Price 1991, 56). Florida's current laws, however, are expected to ensure protection of all burials.

There has been such a long practice in the United States of collecting American Indian remains and objects, that it seems digging up old Indian graves has bordered on being a national pastime. Consequently, there was not much support for protecting Native remains or the objects buried with remains. For many Americans, a Saturday afternoon of collecting or buying or trading American Indian antiquities and bones became a way of life. The existing facts were that American Indian remains were marketable. Native burials were not recognized by the legal system as cemeteries. For scientists, American Indian bones were simply objects of study.

Yet, persistence by the Nez Perce tribe created an arrangement with the University of Idaho in 1967 for having remains turned over to the tribe for reburial after archaeologists completed analysis of excavated bones (Rosen 1980, 15). That was the kind of partnership most American Indians would have been willing to engender if there had been more willing partners. When partnerships failed to materialize, confrontations were bound to flourish.

Anthropologist Franz Boas became interested in the study of people through his interest in ethnographic objects. In 1886, he financed his own initial study of the Northwest Coast where his linguistic skills aided in his gaining information and objects. After only four days in a Kwakiutl village, he gave a potlatch in return for being allowed to view a dance. After spending several months visiting various villages he had amassed sixty-five pieces of cultural material and concluded a study that made him one of the authorities on the region. Near the end of his idyllic visit he picked up skulls from an old burial ground, the first of many skulls he would collect during his long career (Cole 1985, 102–8).

In 1888, Boas was commissioned by the British Association for the Advancement of Science to undertake a survey of the Northwest Coast focusing on language and physical anthropology. The latter would require collecting human remains. Although he acknowledged in notes and letters that it was "repugnant work" and gave him bad dreams, he felt it was a necessary task and noted that it could prove lucrative, as well (Cole 1985, 119).

Boas dug in a burial ground near Victoria while a photographer friend distracted nearby Indians. He bought a collection of seventy-five skulls from two brothers who offered to gather more. While collecting more remains for Boas, they incurred complaints from several groups including people at Fort Rupert and Alert Bay. Cowichan Indians discovered that many of their graves had been disturbed and they obtained a warrant to search the brothers' property. Although nothing was found, the Indians hired a lawyer to pursue the case (Cole 1985, 119–121).

The notes of George A. Dorsey, a curator for Chicago's Field Museum, reveal his willingness to undertake theft and deception in the procuring of human remains. In 1897, he told of scavenging burial caves in the Victoria area and of finding a shaman's remains. As a result, Dorsey was briefly arrested, castigated in newspapers, and publicly reviled by the missionary working with the Masset Indians following a hearing of complaints by the Indians. Dorsey provided partial restitution to end his arrest. A Toronto friend of Dorsey's admitted he could hardly defend Dorsey in light of the news that some of the raided graves were recent burials (Cole 1985, 166–76).

C. F. Newcombe, working for Boas in 1902 on the Northwest Coast, invited an old Indian chief, who was blind, to guide him around the coast to the locations of various caves which served as burial sites. Newcombe noted that he and his assistant were able to rifle through the caves for remains and objects while the unseeing chief remained unaware of their pillaging. In 1903, Newcombe recorded that he was caught in the act of removing bones from a grave, but that he was able to bribe the two witnesses to keep them silent (Cole 1985, 191–97). The collecting practices of pilfering Native bones as done by Newcombe, Boas, and Dorsey were not isolated incidences, but instead represent a widespread practice among collectors of the time. Their secretive thefts were not unobserved by the communities they assailed, and the memories of the members of those communities were enduring, passed on to ensuing generations, and contributed to Native people's disdain of the museum world.

An especially appalling tale began in 1897 when six Eskimo people were brought from Greenland to America by Arctic explorer Robert E. Peary who presented them to the American Museum of Natural History. Peary had enticed the six Eskimo to come with him because he believed Boas could use the individuals in his studies (Roberts 1994, 23). Indeed, upon their deaths from illness, Ales Hrdlicka, a physical anthropologist working for the museum, opportunistically commandeered the remains of the adults and accessioned them into the collections (Preston 1989, 69). Minik, a child accompanying his father Qisuk, survived the illnesses that took the lives of the others and was raised by a museum employee. Minik, thinking he had attended his father's funeral, had instead been shown a mock burial of his father. Instead of having been buried, Minik's father had been provided an accession number, the flesh had been removed from his bones, and his brain had been preserved. The remains had been measured, scrutinized, and stored for decades. When Minik accidentally came across his father's remains in a display case in the museum's storage area, he became troubled and ill. He soon began a campaign to obtain the release of his father's bones. Occasionally the museum would be embarrassed by adverse publicity in area newspapers regarding the remains, but generally the museum chose to ignore the situation, and they were allowed to do so.

The full account of this intriguing and sad story can be found in Kenn Harper's book, *Give Me My Father's Body*, originally published in 1986 and re-issued in 2000 with an update. Minik's efforts to get his father released from the museum's collections were unsuccessful. Harper's book brought attention to the situation again just as repatriation was becoming a hot topic. However, even when repatriation became law, the remains of the Greenland Natives were exempted because they had come from outside the United States. However, in 1992, the museum finally began efforts to return the remains to their homeland and the following year Qisuk and the others were finally buried in Greenland (Harper 2000, 96–239).

Although Minik's story had occasionally been publicized in New York papers, very little else had been written about the frustration American Indians were experiencing with museums and archaeologists. However, much was being done by many American Indians to inform themselves and others about the continuing situation of remains being viewed as museum property. As the pitch of their voices raised, the media began to seek them out. American Indian authors James Nason and Richard Hill began publishing information concerning repatriation in national publications during the 1970s. The word, new to many at first, soon became familiar.

From 1971 through 1972, Bea Medicine charted the main issues of concern to American Indians as seen in issues of *Akwesasne Notes*, a Native paper published by the St. Regis Mohawk and distributed to a worldwide audience. She noted that recovery of human remains (along with other museum possessions) was the issue of most concern during that time (Medicine 1973, 25–26). The writings in Native papers, found in university and museum libraries, and thus read by many sympathetic non-Indians, were sometimes picked up by non-Indian journalists. These writings served to inform and activate many individuals, who, upon viewing inappropriate exhibitions, began to register complaints to museum and historical society authorities. A movement was burgeoning.

In 1970, frustrated that so many non-Indian authorities seemed unable to understand the pain and anger of American Indians regarding the disturbance of American Indian remains, a group of students at the University of Minnesota engaged in a simple action in an effort to put things in perspective. The group, The American Indian Student Association, submitted a written proposal to the National Science Foundation seeking funds to excavate a pioneer cemetery (Hill 1996, 86). The proposal, of course, was not considered as valid, but ensuing publicity helped bring the issue to the notice of influential people.

During the summer of 1971, the Field Museum, Chicago, began an archaeological excavation of a site being eroded by motorcyclists. Nine sets of human remains were located. When the news became public, the Native American Committee of the University of Illinois lodged a protest. The museum responded by inviting the committee to meet with the excavators. The Field Museum, in consultation with the committee, agreed to transport the remains to an Indian cemetery where they were re-interred. The museum issued a statement of ethics concerning human remains, and stipulated that its policy of reburial pertained only to historical remains (meaning after European contact) because they were more easily associated with particular tribes (Lurie1976, 247–48).

In 1971, John Pearson, a construction engineer working on Highway 34 in Iowa inadvertently discovered a turn-of-the-century cemetery during excavation. The state archaeologist was called in and removed twenty-six non-Indian people from their graves, placed them in new caskets, and saw to their reburial at a nearby cemetery. At the same time, the archaeologist took the remains of an American Indian woman and baby from their grave in the cemetery and retained them for study (Monetathchi 2000). Pearson related the incident to his wife, Maria Pearson, Yankton Sioux, who began protesting the desecration of the Native grave (O'Driscoll 1998). The next year American Indians picketed the Iowa Historical Society in protest of an exhibition of American Indian remains. The society removed the remains from view (Hill 1996, 86). As a result of issues raised by the protests, Iowa enacted reburial legislation in 1976 that became a model for other states regarding grave protection (Price 1991, 64). Maria Pearson was appointed the governor's advisor for Indian affairs (O'Driscoll 1998) and held the post for more than twenty-five years.

The quest for legal protection of buried Native relatives spread throughout Indian country from coast to coast. In 1972, the skull of Chief Comcomly, a Chinook Indian who had welcomed the Lewis and Clark expedition to the West Coast, was returned from a local museum, following lengthy negotiations, and re-interred by the Chinook tribe. Following Comcomly's death in the late 1920s, his skull had been sold to an English museum. Eventually Comcomly's skull was returned to his home area, but was placed in the possession of a small non-Indian museum. During discussions between the tribe and the holding museum, one frustrated American Indian negotiator reportedly offered to bring in the skull of a white man if the museum needed something to replace Comcomly's skull (Hopkins 1973, 22). Non-Indians are often stunned by such threats, deeming them abrasive and brash. But, frustrated American Indians hope that by placing "the shoe on the other foot," people might better relate to the situation at hand, and see it from the American Indian experience.

Also in 1972, recently excavated remains were turned over to Onondaga leaders in response to a request made by Onondaga spokespeople (Case 1972). The instance was reported in the *Syracuse Herald Jour-*

nal and soon newspapers across the nation were filing various reports of American Indian dissatisfaction with non-Indian treatment of Native bones.

In 1973, the University of Michigan's Museum of Anthropology gave up remains for reburial (Hill 1996, 86). In 1974, the newly-formed Iroquois Advisory Committee of the Buffalo and Erie County Historical Society requested that human remains be removed from exhibition and be reburied. The museum complied on March 25, 1975 (Gonyea and Hill 1981). In 1976, the Union of Ontario Indians made a citizen's arrest of an archaeologist involved in excavating a burial. The remains were later released for re-interment (Hill 1996, 86). The issue was spreading like wildfire.

American Indian activists staged The Longest Walk, a protest march from Alcatraz to Washington, D.C., in 1978 (Matthiessen 1980, 375). During this cross-country walk, participants visited universities, laboratories, and museums along the way and discovered, according to Jan Hammil, "our ancestors by the hundreds of thousands stored in cardboard boxes, plastic sacks and paper bags." Following the march, American Indians Against Desecration was founded and Hammil became director (Hammil 1985,1). Representatives from the group participated in many protests across the nation.

The American Indian Religious Freedom Act of 1978 was expected to solve many of the problems American Indians faced in trying to protect their buried dead, in retrieving stolen remains, in seeking protection of religious practices, and gaining repossession of, or at least access to, sacred items. But, in practice, the law failed to have effective "teeth." Too much was left for states and courts to conceive and to interpret, and egregious acts were still occurring, while past grievances were not being settled.

In 1979, a Native burial was discovered during archaeological work on Nantucket Island. Following publicity of the find, the Commission on Indian Affairs contacted the state archaeologist for Massachusetts to request reburial of the remains. A burial place was arranged, and following scientific analysis, the remains were re-interred. This was the first cooperative undertaking between American Indians and archaeologists in Massachusetts, and proved to be a valuable one, because later that year, the remains of more than fifty Native individuals were found during a construction project. The Commission on Indian Affairs was immediately contacted and a cooperative arrangement was easily developed which allowed for analysis without time constraints, to be followed by ceremonial burial (Talmadge 1982, 48).

A large number of states were developing new legislative initiatives regarding American Indian burials. The number and size of repatriations began to increase. In 1981, perhaps the largest re-interment at the time occurred when 840 remains were reburied at the request of the Native

American Heritage Commission of California (Hill 1996, 88). In May 1985, the University of Tennessee turned over a large collection of human remains to the state of North Dakota. As a result, the remains of 500 Hidatsa-Mandan and Arikara Indians were re-interred by Native spiritual leaders (Friends Committee on National Legislation 1986, 2).

In 1984, the United South and Eastern Tribes (USET), a consortium comprised at the time of a dozen federally recognized tribes, discussed proposing federal legislation to guarantee rights of retrieval of tribal materials from federally funded institutions, but other projects diverted their energies and they never undertook the project (Floyd 1985, 8). Meanwhile, the National Congress of American Indians (NCAI), the Native American Rights Fund (NARF), tribal governments, and other American Indian organizations continued their efforts across the country on several fronts.

At many American Indian conferences and meetings, repatriation became a theme. A reburial symposium was held at Haskell Indian Junior College in Kansas in January 1986 (Price 1991, 66). Magazine and newspaper articles began appearing with regularity presenting the American Indian point of view regarding the desire to rebury their dead. The issue struck a chord with readers. The balance began to shift in favor of American Indians and in opposition to organizations that appeared to be riding roughshod over admirable sensibilities of Native people.

While nothing was expected to happen overnight, the repatriation pot was simmering and the heat was beginning to change the climate. There had been many successes, and more were imminent. But, the movement also began to focus. It became evident to some of the key players that if the biggest museum could be brought into the fold, the others would follow.

In 1982, Buster Yellow Kidney, representing the Blackfeet tribe of Montana, contacted the Smithsonian Institution for information about Blackfeet remains that had entered Smithsonian collections in 1898. The story of the remains began in 1892, when fifteen Blackfeet skulls and two arm bones were surreptitiously removed from the prairie where they had been placed during the Starvation Winter of 1883–1884 when rations failed to arrive and 500 Blackfeet died. Because there were more deaths than coffin makers could manage, many bodies were placed on a designated area on the open prairie. Army surgeon Z. T. Danial, stationed on the reservation, pilfered and shipped the remains to the Army Medical Museum in Washington, D.C. In 1898, those remains were transferred to the Smithsonian Institution (Robbins 1989).

In March 1986, Blackfeet representatives, including Gordon Belcourt, Mike Swims Under, Buster Yellow Kidney, Curly Bear Wagner, Ken Weatherwax, Marvin Weatherwax, and Thom Whitford, began further inquiries to the Smithsonian Institution's National Museum of Natural History concerning those remains and requesting the return of them (Jacobs 1988, 3).

Initially, the Smithsonian declined to relinquish the remains. Then a letter from the original collector surfaced in which he had discussed how the bones were pilfered in secret so that the Blackfeet would not know he was stealing remains. Rather quickly, for such a behemoth institution, the Smithsonian returned the remains to the Blackfeet tribe, completing the return on September 11, 1988 (Robbins 1989). This was not the first repatriation of human remains from the Smithsonian— Modoc remains had been returned in 1984 (Owsley and Compton 1990, 11–12)—and it would not be the last.

Another Smithsonian repatriation involved Alaskan remains and has been poignantly described by Gordon L. Pullar in *Reckoning with the Dead* (Pullar 1994). In 1987, the tribal council of the Alutiiq village of Larsen Bay, Kodiak Island, Alaska, formally requested the return of remains collected by a Smithsonian Institution scientist fifty years earlier. Although the people had long been angered over the invasive collecting, they had not requested return of the remains until Pullar, as president of the Kodiak Area Native Association, had learned of the excavations and suggested the Alutiiq council seek return. They sent a letter to the Smithsonian Institution and received a response that seemed dismissive. Their second letter requested "the return of all human skeletons taken from our region along with the artifacts" (Pullar 1994, 18).

In 1989, Pullar was in Washington, D.C., and visited the Smithsonian Institution. He was invited to see the storage area of human remains. He remembers being overwhelmed upon seeing rows and rows of drawers marked "Kodiak Island, Alaska." There were 4,000 remains from Alaska with nearly 800 of them from the Larsen Bay area.

"At that moment I was convinced, in my own mind, that they would be brought home where they belonged," wrote Pullar (1994, 20).

The collecting scientist's own notes provide evidence of grave robbing, "just as the parts were all gathered . . . I learned that the old woman claimed the bones to be those of her long departed husband," while another notation said, "the remains are too fresh yet, but secured a good female skeleton." Initially the Smithsonian resisted repatriation of the Alaska remains, but finally, in 1991, the remains of about 1,000 Native Alaska people were re-interred not far from where they had been collected (Pullar 1994, 15).

Meanwhile, many museums, universities, archaeologists, and other organizations, alarmed by the mounting interest in repatriation, were fighting the idea of returning remains. They cited the value of their research and tried to explain their need for vast numbers of skeletal remains for research projects (Preston 1989, 67; Leone 1989). Curators and archaeologists were divided on the issue and sought ways to address their concerns. There was a flurry of articles, seminars, meetings, and presentations at annual meetings and in special committees.

In 1987, the ransacking of an Indian burial ground on Slack Farm in Kentucky by "pot hunters" engaged in artifact poaching captured the attention of the nation. The devastation to the site alarmed both archaeologists and tribal people. The ten perpetrators had paid $10,000 to the farmer for "mining" rights. At least 650 graves were disturbed and remains were scattered about the field. Dennis Banks, American Indian Movement activist, and Leon Shenandoah, chief of the Onondaga Nation, representing a group of gathered Indian activists, claimed the remains under "'friend of the deceased" status, as provided by then-existing laws. Archaeologists agreed to examine remains to gain information for the trials of the "pot hunters," and then to turn the remains over to the American Indian contingent for ceremonial reburial (Arden 1989, 376–92). The story was told in the March 1989 issue of *National Geographic* magazine.

In the fall of 1987, the American Association of Museums, having struggled with developing policy for museums regarding American Indian human remains, appointed a task force that included American Indians as members. Task Force members were Dan Monroe, Oregon Art Institute president; Michael Fox, Heard Museum director; JoAllyn Archambault (Lakota), Smithsonian's National Museum of Natural History's American Indian Program director; George H. J. Abrams (Seneca), North American Indian Museums Association chairman; Rennard Strickland (Cherokee), law school dean of Southern Illinois University; Patterson B. Williams, Denver Art Museum director of education; and Ray Thompson, Arizona State Museum director (American Association of Museums 1988a). Their report, approved by the Association in 1988, said museums should "seek the collaborative resolution of requests for the repatriation of human remains and ceremonial materials" (American Association of Museums 1988b, 4).

Meanwhile, museums contended that as research institutions they had a justified need of remains and a variety of objects to study, and as educational organizations they needed a collection of various materials to exhibit. They often countered Native claims of cultural patrimony by asserting that the contended items were as much a part of America's cultural patrimony as they were of tribal cultures and, therefore, America's museums and universities were proper repositories. They believed museums with staff members who were experienced in collections care were preferred caretakers to American Indian claimants, who, it was deemed, had inadequate training in care of artifacts and lacked proper facilities for the storage of materials. Such dismissals offended American Indians who argued that they maintained traditional methods of care, which had been used successfully for millennia in caring for Native materials. If required to have museum training and museums of their own, their quandary centered on how to obtain the formal training they needed and build appropriate facilities while America's museums and universities continued to be hostile to them and to Native sensibilities. To American Indians, the most important matter concerned appropriate sensitivities for not only Native remains but for all Native material, something that they saw lacking in non-Native institutions.

In March 1988, a contingent from the Pawnee tribe of Oklahoma visited the Nebraska State Historical Society in Lincoln and discovered that 1,000 American Indian remains were in the collections with a large number of them being Pawnee. The tribe began a concerted effort to see that their ancestors would be reburied. However, the director of the NSHS, James Hanson, was adamantly opposed to turning over the human remains and asserted that the museum had appropriate title to the items in its collections. Further, he stated that he considered reburial to be destruction of scientific information that would "be morally and ethically reprehensible" (Echo-Hawk and Echo-Hawk 1994, 60). His attitude was representative of many "old school" museum leaders, who felt a keen sense of entitlement by museums to all things cultural, regardless of sensibilities, methods of ownership, or claims by those regarded as inferior to the intellectual standards of museums.

The historical society even went so far as to block the tribe's access to collections records that would reveal how the society had obtained the remains. The Nebraska attorney general ordered the NSHS to permit Pawnee researchers admittance to files, but the society continued to balk and ultimately, upon losing their case, was ordered to pay for the legal fees incurred by the tribe during the lawsuit. When the files were finally examined they revealed that the permits required to exhume remains had not been obtained by the excavators (Echo-Hawk and Echo-Hawk 1994, 61).

The decision to take legal action was pushed forward by the Pawnee tribe of Oklahoma, with assistance from the Native American Rights Fund (Thiessen and Lynott 1989, 1). The NSHS accrued bad feeling from Nebraska citizens from the use of inflammatory accusations accusing the Pawnee attorneys of using the controversy to gain legal fees and implying that the tribe was hoping to get the valuable collection in order to sell it. Pawnee citizens sent letters to the society in an effort to resolve the issue, but received no answers. When the tribe turned to the state legislature for assistance, they found support, especially from Senator Ernie Chambers. In January 1989, Chambers introduced legislation to force museums in the state to honor Native requests for return of remains, and the bill passed in May of that year (Echo-Hawk and Echo-Hawk 1994, 62–65). Further support was obtained from the American Civil Liberties Union, the Rainbow Coalition, the Bishop of the Lincoln Roman Catholic Diocese, the Association of Students of the University of Nebraska, and the Nebraska Indian Commission (Thiessen and Lynott 1989, 1).

The act was the first general statute adding repatriation to grave protection (Hill 1996, 91). Called the Unmarked Human Burial Sites and Skeletal Remains Protection Act, the law extended burial protection to private as well as state property and provided for ultimate reburial of any disturbed remains and associated grave goods, allowing for a brief period of time for scientific examination. It also required institutions receiving funding or formal recognition by the state to return any American Indian remains and associated grave goods to any affiliated tribe or family upon request (Price 1991, 83–84). As a result of the Nebraska legislation, the Pawnee tribe reclaimed more than 400 remains from the NSHS. The publicity helped propel other institutions to take action.

Chicago's influential Field Museum passed a repatriation policy in 1989 allowing the return of human remains and associated funerary objects to the descendants of specific individuals or Native groups (Haas 1990, 16). The barriers, indeed, were breaking down.

In February 1987 the U.S. Senate's Select Committee on Indian Affairs held a hearing to discuss repatriation. Smithsonian secretary Robert McCormick Adams testified that the Smithsonian Institution held a total of 34,000 human remains in its collections, representing areas around the world. He reported that North American Indian remains numbered 14,523 while another 4,061 remains were Alaska Native. The numbers shocked many listeners. Adams's accounting, it was discovered, had not included South and Central America or Hawaii. The Smithsonian holdings of remains of all indigenous peoples of the Americas totaled about 32,000 (Friends Committee on National Legislation 1986, 1). In 1989, pressured by the National Congress of American Indians, the Smithsonian Institution made a listing of remains available to tribal authorities. Although the institution defended its policy of collecting and holding remains, it agreed to discuss with interested tribes any requests for returns (Hill 1996, 88).

One of the tribes responding to the distributed list included a group of Northern Cheyenne chiefs who were invited to Washington by Montana senator John Melcher. Clara Spotted Elk accompanied the chiefs and later wrote about the visit in "Skeletons in the Attic" for the New York Times Op-Ed page (Spotted Elk 1989). While visiting various capital area sites the visiting contingent learned that the Smithsonian possessed approximately 18,500 North American Native skeletal remains. The dismay the chiefs felt regarding the discovery of such a great number of Native remains was shared by their senator. He immediately began drafting a Native American museum claims act (Preston 1989, 68), soon called the "Bones Bill." The proposed legislation did not require repatriation, but was designed to provide a forum for resolving disputes. It was defeated (Hill 1996, 89). Although Melcher lost his seat, Senator Daniel Inouye carried on with the campaign (Preston 1989,68). All told, six bills regarding repatriation were submitted to Congress (Hill 1996, 91).

As luck would have it, while repatriation was being debated in Congress, the Smithsonian was about to become the possessor of one of the largest collections of American Indian materials. The Museum of the American Indian, New York City, was looking for a new home, and there was interest in making its collections part of the "nation's attic." It would require federal legislation to create the National Museum of the American Indian in order for it to be encompassed within the Smithsonian family of museums. If, American Indian activists and allies realized, the MAI materials, along with the already vast numbers of items in Smithsonian possession, could be made subject to repatriation, then it would stand to reason that the rest of the flock (America's museums in general) would soon have to follow.

In 1989, key players in the development of the National Museum of the American Indian (NMAI)—Suzan Shown Harjo, then executive director of the National Congress of American Indians (NCAI); Smithsonian secretary Robert McCormick Adams; Rep. Ben Nighthorse Campbell (D-Colorado, and later to become a senator), and Walter Echo-Hawk, senior counsel of the Native American Rights Fund (NARF)—hammered out the agreement concerning repatriation of objects from Smithsonian collections (Swisher 1989).

When Harjo was a young woman she and her mother had visited the MAI. There she witnessed the distress her mother suffered when they viewed one particular exhibit. The showcase, to their shock, contained burial moccasins created by Harjo's mother. The moccasins had been made for a deceased member of the tribe and were not intended to be outside the grave. Since that time Harjo has dedicated her life's work to gaining rights for Native people (Harjo 1999).

During the negotiations of the Smithsonian-focused group, Stanford University agreed to return 525 remains to the Ohlone-Costanoan people of California. *The Washington Post* noted that the agreement would put pressure on the Smithsonian to consider repatriation (Mathews 1989).

As a result, the 1989 legislation creating NMAI also served to enact repatriation of certain categories of Smithsonian materials. "It's a victory for America to solve quite a disgraceful situation where Indians are an archaeological resource of the U.S.," noted Harjo upon announcing the breakthrough agreement (Swisher 1989, 1).

In 1992, it was further determined that NMAI, having a strong interest in repatriating to American Indians, would no longer be subject to the Smithsonian's Repatriation Review Committee, but was accorded the authority to independently engage in repatriation according to the decisions of the NMAI Board of Trustees. This finding allows for a more liberal practice of repatriation with the possibility that material found in abundance within the vast collections can be viewed as redundant materials and returned if desired (Hill 1996, 94).

The sum of all these cases and actions, along with hundreds of other incidents of American Indians pursuing, demanding, and fighting for lost property, served to create the climate for the nationwide law known as the Native American Graves Protection and Repatriation Act, which finally became a reality in 1990. Since NAGPRA was passed after the NMAI legislation requiring Smithsonian repatriation, the Smithsonian is exempt from NAGPRA, and instead repatriates appropriate materials according to the earlier 1989 legislation.

The *NARF Legal Review* noted of NAGPRA, "For the first time, Congress has accepted the principle that Indian people are entitled to the return of their ancestors' remains and of the items buried with them. Finally, Congress has mandated that cultural objects stolen from tribes must be returned when asked for, and has recognized that Indian people are not simply the objects of anthropological study, but a people with their own culture and customs that must be accorded the respect that they deserve" (Hill 1996, 94).

As a result of NAGPRA, museums and tribes are currently engaged in dialogues. Additionally, tribes and divisions of tribes, separated for generations, are now forced to negotiate, with mostly positive results. Many repatriation returns have been completed. Others are in process. Some will take more exploration to reach resolution as each case requires research of the information previously gathered about the remains to ascertain that the museum's identification has been accurate. Some requests will lead to dilemmas that will be difficult to solve. There are unidentified remains. There are tribes that do not want to handle disturbed remains. But, generally, NAGPRA is seen as a great victory for the rights of American Indians.

As museums and American Indians complete research on how remains and objects came to reside within museums, there will be much that will shock and anger. Recently it was alleged that the University of Nebraska had engaged in a cover-up of its handling of remains. Although an agreement with more than 50 representatives of tribes from the Central Plains will repatriate from the University's collections a total of 1,702 American Indian remains, it was noted that as many as 20,000 bones had actually been misplaced by the institution. University officials admitted that a number of remains were incinerated during the 1960s and agreed, in compensation for this egregious loss, to place a memorial plaque at the site of the incinerator (*Baltimore Sun*, 1998, 10A). The incineration seems to make hollow the argument many institutions had put forth earlier about the paramount need to retain remains for future research. This particular institution apparently was more concerned with denying American Indians possession of remains than of retaining them for further use.

While Canada does not have a repatriation law, museums there are increasingly engaging in repatriation. One of the first returns of human remains in Ontario began in 1988 when the staff of the Peterborough Centennial Museum determined that remains and associated materials excavated in 1960 should be de-accessioned from the museum's collections. Since 1961, the museum had shown an exhibit replicating Native burial traditions, but closed the exhibit in 1983. Museum officials contacted the band council of Curve Lake First Nation and began negotiations to achieve a transfer of the materials. The memorandum of understanding included provisions for the museum to replicate the grave goods, and determined provisions for the burials including a granite marker at the reburial site (Carter 1994).

Meanwhile, museums continue to display Egyptian mummies and other human remains, even as protests mount from foreign cultures. Museums do not seem to know, or care to understand, that some American Indians, due to their cultural beliefs and practices, cannot enter buildings that house deceased humans, or if they inadvertently enter them, they are filled with anxiety and horror upon discovering remains, and some will require a visit to their spiritual practitioner to restore themselves. For citizens of those respectful tribes, most museums with American Indian collections and exhibitions are off limits, and thus they are effectively denied access to one of the major American institutions of learning.

In 1994, a disagreement in Hawaii during negotiations to repatriate two Native chiefs' remains, culminated in the mysterious disappearance of the *ka'ai*, as the woven-covered bones are called. Shortly after their disappearance from the collections of the Bishop Museum, a telephone caller announced, "Liloa (the name of one of the chiefs) is home." The dispute had centered on where the materials would be interred. Descendants of the chiefs, traditional priests, and other interested parties disagreed about burial locations. During a period of fumigation of the museum storage areas, the materials disappeared. Anthropologist Marjorie Kelly noted, "If nothing else, the incident demonstrates the confusion that can result when cultural traditions are weakened and people conclude that desperate measures are their only recourse" (Kelly 1995, 232).

Anthropology, as a relatively new science (like museology), has adherents of differing theories and practices. The earliest days of human cultures are shadowy and unknown. Various theories about the peopling of the Americas have been put forth. Most evidence points to the idea that Native people have been in the Americas since the last ice age while non-American Indian people appear to have arrived during so-called historic times. But, science is a fluid study. Theories are based on evidence, and as new evidence appears, new theories are developed. Theories are ideas supported by evidence, but they are not fact.

In July 1996, a nearly complete skeleton was found on the banks of the Columbia River near Kennewick, Washington. It was assumed the remains were of a historic person since the remains seemingly had Caucasian features. However, a spear point was lodged in a pelvic bone. The point was of a type representative of multiple thousands of years past. If the skeleton was of an indigenous person before European arrival, it was subject to NAGPRA. If the person proved to be Caucasian, it would not be subject to repatriation, and the discovery would lead to a rethinking of when the earliest European arrival had occurred (National Endowment for the Humanities 2002). Immediately, a conflict arose. Scientist wanted to engage in study; Native people, understanding their ancestors to be the continent's original people, claimed the remains as ancestral and wanted the remains immediately reburied.

After more than two years of inflammatory debate, the National Park Service, which administers NAGPRA, decided to move forth on determining if the remains would be subject to NAGPRA under the law's provisions. Although Native protestors had wanted no further tests to occur, and scientists wanted a broader range of testing, the NPS found it needed tests in order to move the issue toward resolution. Tests concluded the remains dated between 9,510 and 9,320 B.P. (before present), and Dr. Francis P. McManamon, chief archaeologist for the National Park Service, concluded that the bones predated known European arrival, and were subject to repatriation to Native claimants. Laboratories had been unable to extract DNA from the remains due to mineralization of the bones (Department of the Interior 2000).

The remains, having been held by the Burke Museum of Natural and Cultural History in Seattle, were going to be turned over to the Umatilla, Colville, Wanapum, Nez Perce, and Yakama tribes for reburial (Department of the Interior 2000). Scientists, however, sued, contending the remains had not been defined as Native American. Ultimately, the scientists obtained the right to study them and conveners at the American Academy of Forensic Sciences listened to findings in 2006 (Lipske 2006). The entrenched arguing over the remains polarized parties, abraded sensibilities, and continues to provoke pain. Tribal members and scientists are often divided among their own ranks about how to handle unprecedented situations.

The next several paragraphs concern Ishi, the last surviving member of his band in California. Ishi's life is described in a book written by Theodora Kroeber, published in 1961, called *Ishi in Two Worlds*. California Indians suffered a terrifying era when they could be shot without their murderers worrying that any punishment would be forthcoming. For most ranchers, roaming Indians were thought of as comparable to rats or coyotes and potentially harmful to one's enterprise. California Indians, rapidly declining in numbers, were terrified of non-Indians. Early in the twentieth century, one particular Yahi family had become decimated and had been hiding in the hills until all died except Ishi, a young adult, left totally alone. Although he could survive in the hills, life as a lone human hiding from all other human contact was hardly worth living. Maybe Ishi was trying to find other Native people when his lonely vigil ended. In 1911, Ishi came into a populated area, daring possible harm, and luckily was protected by the kind people who found and harbored him until anthropologists could secure Ishi, and provide him with a degree of formal protection. He lived out the short remainder of his life actually living in a California museum, an odd existence whereby he shared his knowledge with museum visitors and with the anthropologists who befriended him (Scheper-Hughes 2001).

When Ishi died in 1916, however, he was treated as a specimen, despite the fact that he had enjoyed a very warm relationship with his caretakers. Although his remains were cremated according to his wishes (and placed at the Mount Olivet Cemetery), his preserved brain was sent to the Smithsonian where it was, after a time, generally forgotten by many amidst a large collection of similar materials (Scheper-Hughes 2001).

Arthur Angle, a Maidu Indian activist who became chair of the Butte County Native American Cultural Committee in 1997, decided it was time to locate Ishi's remains and bring them home for burial (Rockafellar 2006). Initially, the University of California's Hearst Museum of Anthropology told the committee there was no historical information supporting the idea that Ishi's brain had been separated from his body. Yet, further searches by researchers helping with the Maidu inquiry found letters indicating the brain had indeed been sent to the Smithsonian Institution. Still, various calls to the Smithsonian departments obtained reports that the brain was not there. One Smithsonian contact reported that the tale of the brain being at the Smithsonian was "old folklore" (Rockafellar 2006).

However, it was ultimately determined that the brain did indeed reside in Smithsonian collections along with 300 other stored brains (Scheper-Hughes 2001). Large institutions, with multiple collections and multiple storage facilities, make research a challenge for even accomplished researchers since it is difficult to determine which of many departments or units might contain, or know of, what one needs. To obtain information regarding proper contacts can take a dozen or more inquiries. Ascertaining how to get to various inner-city or suburban locations (often in fenced and guarded compounds), obtain a researcher I.D., enter the labyrinth of large museum research hallways, and place call orders for materials are all steps that present a significant barrier for inexperienced researchers, such as are many Native Americans who live in remote locations.

The first visit by the Native California delegation to the Smithsonian left them empty-handed because the Smithsonian insisted it needed to be sure it would be turning the brain over to the correct tribal group (Curtius 1999). Such delays are typical before repatriating an item, as there can be competing claims, but any delay can appear to be a form of bureaucratic posturing. Many institutions are slow to complete their repatriations due to staff limitations and due to the need to conduct quality research to avoid errors in judgment that could lead to legal entanglements. To many American Indians, delays can seem to be a lack of will on the part of museums, and lengthy delays can be interpreted by appealing tribal entities as a failure to prioritize Native needs as important.

On August 8, 2000, Ishi's brain was finally brought to California by a representative of the Smithsonian's repatriation office and presented to authorities of the Pit River tribe. A two-day ceremony of feasting and healing ensued. The burial was completed at a hidden site. The Department of Anthropology at Berkeley issued a letter apologizing for the department's role in "the final betrayal of Ishi" (Scheper-Hughes 2001). The repatriation of Ishi's brain is one of many emotional reunions occurring across the United States at tribal sites annually. For invariably every tribe who experiences these returns, the reunions are suffused with feelings of healing and hopes for a better future.

The next great step in repatriation will be to see how the rest of the world responds to requests for information about American Indian collections and to a growing interest in the indigenous remains held by museums around the world. Great numbers of American Indian materials are held in European museums. Indigenous peoples around the world face the same issues American Indians face. Repatriation has become an empowering tool for many Native groups. It is a word few of us were familiar with in the 1970s. Now, the word *repatriation* is commonplace, especially in the museum profession and in Native circles.

Many museums have been slow to respond to repatriation inquiries and slow to finish their research regarding the identity of the remains in their possession. Many possess materials that are, as yet, unidentified, preventing those materials from returning to wherever they belong. And, regrettably, a few people are still adamant about trying to avoid repatriation altogether, even as they hold obviously returnable materials in their collections.

III

WHOSE HEROES
AND HOLIDAYS

Not only have museums been reluctant to relinquish possession of human remains and sacred objects, they have been equally reluctant to refute long-held myths regarding some of America's so-called "heroes" (a word that usually represents a political point of view). Many of the historic heroes revered in American classrooms, extolled from the podiums of public arenas, and protected by museum exhibits generally have been people who took action in support of a political agenda viewed to start or support the development and continuing progress of what has become the United States. As such, their actions helped Euro-Americans prevail and helped conquer or foil those who resisted, which included the aboriginal inhabitants of the territories under contention. Since American Indians are now loyal citizens of the United States (their military service ranks as the highest percentage of any other ethnic group in the country) and they have the deepest roots in this land, it should be time to reach an accord among citizens of this country about who are national heroes, and who are heroes of error.

In this section we look at protests undertaken by American Indians regarding museum and history site depictions of some of the colonizing entities and of the ensuing Manifest Destiny leaders in American history starting with Christopher Columbus, continuing with the Pilgrims, and culminating with the frontier soldier George Armstrong Custer. None of these entities were friends of Native people; instead, they all took up arms against their Native hosts and intended, ultimately, to dominate them, and if necessary, to eradicate them. Forcing American Indian students (of any age) to sit in classrooms to be told how great these aforementioned

American icons were, and to know how much Americans revered, and still revere, them, has amounted to psychological torture of American Indian populations, who are usually presented as the enemies, even though now claimed as citizens. The depictions of history should present information representing fairly the conflicting sides of the issues under study. Spending public dollars on the building of monuments, commemorative ceremonies, and public programs honoring historical figures known to have perpetrated a holocaust upon indigenous populations is insulting, and harmful, to American Indians. Continuously irritated wounds cannot heal, and American Indian cultures greatly need to heal, and to be embraced, rather than to have irritants added to old wounds, and to be pushed away and held at arm's length.

One of the earlier protests American Indians made regarding memorializing American heroes involved the massive sculptures of the four American presidents on Mount Rushmore in the sacred Black Hills of the Lakota. To practitioners of a naturalistic Lakota belief system, the sculptures defaced what amounted to creator-made temples or cathedrals. But, not all the tribal members agreed, since many embraced Christianity and wanted to be accepted by American society. However, the ownership of the Black Hills, contested since 1920, is still under dispute as the Lakota people have refused, and continue to refuse, to accept payment for the land (Deloria 1993, 442). Early protests of the government's taking of the Black Hills were generally ignored because the protests occurred before the voices of minority cultures were afforded credence.

Indeed, many of the earlier protests were all but invisible to most citizens. Government and corporate public relations departments could always find "good" Indians to "support" such public activities as dam openings (even if the dams flooded Native lands or destroyed Native fisheries), dedications of parks which absorbed sacred sites into their boundaries (and often denied future ceremonial use of those sites), and special events like the dedication of the sculptures on Mount Rushmore. Even though government projects might usurp Native resources and might have been protested by either, or both, the tribal government and tradition-bearers within the tribe, photo opportunities usually found a war-bonneted Indian prepared for a pose. At times the American Indians in the photos were not authorities (unless they were government appointees or were elected chiefs of tribal groups whose majority of members refused to go to the polls and thus "officials" were elected without the blessing of the majority of the tribe). Often the American Indians in the photographs were simply paid performers. Looking at some of the old photographs of dedications occurring across the country, it thus appears that American Indians didn't mind losing their land to public works projects or having treaties overturned. During the first half of the twentieth century, no one seemed interested in hearing any complaints, especially if they seemed anti-American or opposed popular myths, so newspapers and magazines rarely reported any opposing American Indian thoughts or activities. Today a popular t-shirt worn by many Native people, perhaps mostly outside of South Dakota, depicts the Mount Rushmore carvings with four historic Native leaders depicted in bright colors in front of the presidential faces fading into the background.

When it comes to holidays, Native cultures have their own times of celebration. However, they aren't excused from the classroom or workplaces during their most important observances. Columbus Day and Thanksgiving Day are viewed by some American Indians as days that are not appropriate for celebration by America's indigenous people. This seems to surprise other Americans when they first hear of it. But, any thinking individual, giving the matter some thought, would come to wonder why anyone would expect American Indians to praise Columbus or celebrate the Pilgrims. The arrival of Columbus led to the loss of Native dominion over homelands, and an ensuing tortured decimation of Native populations, followed by centuries of continual suffering still lingering through high unemployment, poor health, and continual institutional debasing of the proud heritage of Native people. While America's Thanksgiving Day seemingly celebrates the success of colonization, many of the American Indians who presently live in the area where the Pilgrims landed counter that holiday each year with their own "Day of Mourning."

Although two Wampanoag men initially welcomed the Pilgrims with English greetings they had learned while kidnapped, and they aided the Pilgrims with provisions and lessons about survival in New England, the Pilgrims soon loosed their livestock upon clam beds as well as upon Native gardens, and began to take control of the most fertile land. When the Pilgrims first landed, they were hungry and stole corn from Native caches and dug up Native graves, desperately looking for storehouses of useful materials and foods. Breaking the social rules observed by Algonquians, the Pilgrims eventually invoked laws that were punitive and discriminating to the Algonquians. The Pilgrims and other European visitors also carried catastrophic diseases previously unknown to the Americas, resulting in the decimation of up to 95 percent of Native populations in the area (Stannard 1992, 268), with the probable spread into Native interiors not yet known by colonists. Plymouth Rock, the *Mayflower*, and the Pilgrim's plantation do not tell a story resulting in a thanksgiving to be valued by American Indians, but instead tell a story of loss and pain, supplanting the original Native celebrations of thanksgiving when the wild strawberries ripened and again when fresh corn could be enjoyed.

In September 2004, the commemoration of the exploration of Lewis and Clark was met with Native protests. About twenty-five protesting

American Indians told reenactors to turn their boats around and go home, simulating an action many wish their long-ago ancestors had taken. Most Americans forget that many of America's heroes were expansionists, and thus were adversaries of American Indians. It often comes as a shock to reenactors that American Indians will take the time to protest, loudly and robustly, the honoring of many American heroes. It is often a surprise to uninformed Americans to learn that many of the people they've been taught to view as American heroes were people who harmed American Indians. The colonizing of the Americas and subsequent expansion into the great American West brought disease, disenfranchisement, warfare involving cruel weapons, and subsequent loss of the wildlife, as well as the land, which had sustained Native life for so long.

One of the most dreaded anniversaries, from an American Indian point of view, was the approach of the Columbian Quincentenary, or 500th anniversary of the "discovery" of the Americas by Christopher Columbus in 1492. Many American Indians feared that an American celebration of Columbus's voyage would serve only to aggrandize the explorer, reinforce the idea that colonization had been an appropriate course, and overshadowing any efforts to have a discussion about what Columbus's arrival meant to the inhabitants of the Caribbean and the mainland beyond.

The very uses of the words "discovery" and "New World" illustrate a foreign point of view from which America's history is portrayed. An inhabited land can hardly be undiscovered, and the world of American Indians is an ancient one, not something newly contrived. With the coming of Europeans, there was launched a successive number of "firsts." However, many of those firsts were not actually firsts, and have since been appropriately reworded as "first European" or "first white" regarding houses, births, or cities, in a belated attempt to recognize that American Indians are, after all, fully human and had houses (some of which survive from eras before Columbus sailed), they bore children, and there had been ancient Native cities with populations of more than 20,000 predating the cities that grew up after European arrival in the Americas. It's been slow in coming, but an American conscientiousness has been maturing through the decades.

As the 500th anniversary loomed, many American Indians feared that the centuries-old attitudes of European superiority would dominate public programs and exhibitions during 1992. And, indeed, it didn't take long for a Columbus-focused exhibition worthy of protest to emerge. The following chapters explore American Indian museum-related protests targeting Columbus, the Pilgrims, and Custer.

7

No Celebration for Columbus

The beginning of the myth where Christopher Columbus assumes the mantle of the Discovering Hero (standing in for all others who crossed the Atlantic, some quite a long time before he did) began in a misty era along with the birth of many other American legends. Someone pitched the story of Columbus, it gained momentum, and a following ensued. By 1892 a statue of Columbus was erected in New York City, but it wasn't until 1971 that President Nixon made a federal holiday of Columbus Day. Merchants and federal employees, of course, loved the idea. Columbus, however, represents to American Indians all that has been lost, of untold suffering, and of all that should be protested. As 1992 (500 years after the initial voyage of Columbus) loomed on the horizon, American Indians braced for a blizzard of celebrations. They were especially concerned about how museums might commemorate the anniversary.

"As a Native American, I was fearful of the possible consequences of the national and worldwide focus on the Columbus Quincentenary. Such a focus, I thought, would give rise to renewed white American ethnocentrism to the detriment of Native Americans, Native American issues, and Native American history," wrote Rosebud Sioux author and historian Joseph Marshall III in a National Park Service periodical (Marshall 1993, 39). Most American Indians involved in museum work expected that somewhere in the nation a troublesome exhibition espousing a biased version of Columbus would arise.

In November 24, 1989, Russell Means, a founder of the American Indian Movement (AIM), a national Native activist group founded in Minneapolis (United States Commission on Civil Rights 1981, 4), participated in a

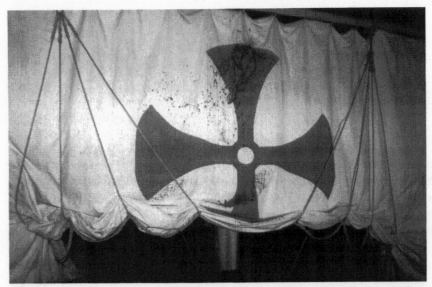

Figure 7.1. Protesting a touring exhibit designed to honor Christopher Columbus, American Indian Movement member Vernon Bellecourt threw a pint of his own blood on the sails of the exhibited replica of Columbus's ship. The bloodstained sails remained on exhibit in 1992 at the Science Museum of Minnesota alongside an in-house exhibit to counterbalance the touring exhibit's information.
Courtesy of the Science Museum of Minnesota.

group demonstration outside the Florida Museum of Natural History in Gainesville concerning the exhibition *First Encounters* (*Museum News* 1990, 11) which had opened six weeks earlier. Jan Elliott, an American Indian Movement activist from Gainesville, initiated the protest (Silva 1992). Many of the protestors were students from the University of Florida who took turns walking a picket line for two weeks (Milbrath and Milanich 1991, 34). One student was arrested for jumping onto the deck of the one-inch-to-twenty-four-inches scale model of the *Niña*, Columbus's favorite ship (Krech 1994, 6). The long-expected Columbus-lauding exhibition had arrived and had been found by Native protestors.

The *Gainesville Sun* reported the protestors cited the exhibition as "racist and degrading to native Americans" (Acle 1989, 1A). Protestors demanded that the exhibition, which was about Spanish contact in the Americas, be dismantled, asked for a formal apology, called for a termination of the celebration of Columbus Day and an end to all quincentenary activities (*Museum News* 1990, 11–12). Although the curators of the exhibition, Susan Milbrath and Jerald T. Milanich, said they designed the exhibition to provide understanding of both European and Native American perspectives, they admitted they had not sought any consultation from living Native Americans. The curators reported, "Despite our efforts to incorporate the negative impact on Native culture, a small number of people perceived our exhibit as a celebration of Columbus." (Milbrath and Milanich 1991, 34). To many interested Native Americans, the "negative impact" was not adequately covered in the exhibition.

The exhibition catalog demonstrates the tenor of the exhibit. Most of the section headings of the catalog are not about Native life, but are about European life: Spain at the Time of Columbus, The Jews and the Moors, Spain's Military Machine, On the Eve of Discovery, Columbus and the Spanish Crown, European Voyages Before Columbus, Columbus Sets Sail, The *Niña*, Columbus the Navigator, Columbus' First Voyage, Columbus Arrives in the New World, La Navidad, Columbus Encounters the Taino, Columbus Returns to the New World, and Those Who Followed Columbus (Milbrath and Milanich 1990). It is not surprising that protestors viewed the exhibition as a celebration of Columbus since his name predominated in the section headings.

The exhibition title, *First Encounters*, seemed to hold out the promise of a two-way exploration, since it takes at least two entities to make an encounter. Yet, the exhibition was disappointingly, and disproportionately, presented from the point of view of one side of the encounter, not both, which would have made a far more appropriate and informative exhibit. The exhibition catalog demonstrates that the curators viewed encounters strictly from the establishment point of view (whether that be mainstream American, immigrant European-American, European explorer, or curator

American). The exhibition, by chronicling the movements and actions of explorers, rarely provided illumination of Native life or of Native experiences before, during, and after their encounter with explorers.

While the exhibition may not have been intended as a celebration of Columbus, it had a biased view, and the bias leaned greatly away from any sensitivity to, or equitable presentation of, Native perspectives. For instance, the catalog says the Spanish colonies were "plagued by ... a lack of Indian support" (Milbrath and Milanich 1990, 18), as if the Native people were stubborn, insubordinate, lazy, obstinate, or in some way guilty of not performing appropriately. Of course, the Spanish explorers had done nothing to earn support and had done everything to cause lack of support ranging from acting rudely to acting savagely, including Columbus's enslavement of 500 Native individuals who were transported to Europe in 1493 (Milbrath and Milanich 1990, 14), a fact which the exhibit catalog does provide.

On page 22, the catalog states, "Gold mining in Hispaniola began in 1494. When Native labor became scarce, colonists began importing African slaves." The statement sanitizes the horrible events that made Native labor "scarce," which was the precipitous death rate of the enslaved and mistreated Natives. There is, from the Native point of view, inadequate description of atrocities enacted upon the Native populations of Hispaniola and the southeastern United States while the difficulties of colonization, and of individual colonists, are more fully studied and presented. The language discussing Native hardships seemed impotent, bereft of power and emotion.

Some incidents are not adequately detailed and become misleading. On page 40, a caption says that a Coosa chief promised to give the explorer Hernando de Soto "many native women." An uninformed reader might assume that it was the custom of southeastern Indians to offer women to men. In this instance, the chief was being required to fulfill a demand, but the text does not make that clear. According to writings of anthropologist Charles Hudson, a scholar of southeastern Native cultures, the chief's seeming agreement to fulfill the request for women was a stall for time to mount a defensive attack (Hudson 1976, 112). The word "defensive," of course, was not utilized in the catalog description. De Soto was simply "attacked."

The catalog even engages in discounting the descriptions of the devastation endured by Native Caribbean peoples as noted by Bartolomé de Las Casas whose published accounts in the sixteenth century sought to obtain redress for the harsh treatment he observed. The catalog states, "The accuracy of his descriptions remains a subject of scholarly debate" (Milbrath and Milanich 1990, 53). Ultimately, the exhibition, *First Encounters*, also became the center of debate about scholarship and authority.

The one catalog section devoted to Native perspectives uses its space to say there is little to report because recorded information is lacking. Modern ethnohistorians, however, find there is much to say about Native actions during initial contacts. Besides interpreting the recorded accounts of the times, which are fairly extensive, and by studying ethnohistories of later times, or of first encounters in other places, much can be understood of the Native people Columbus met.

The exhibition catalog notes that Hernando de Soto used "vicious attack dogs to intimidate native peoples." "Intimidate" is a mild word when it is widely acknowledged that de Soto used attack dogs to tear Native people apart (Hudson 1976, 108). The kinds of words selected for catalog entries are telling of the attitudes of its authors. Possibly, the only usage of the word "murder" by the authors occurs in a caption of Native people killing a Jesuit missionary (Milbrath and Milanich 1990, 57)—this, in a book that covers a period of time when great numbers of Native people were ruthlessly murdered. Instead of being murdered, the Taino "disappeared" (17), southeastern Indians "died out" (52), Florida Natives suffered "violent conflict" (35), and attack dogs "intimidated" Natives, according to the catalog.

"It is disheartening to learn that our society is built upon the graves of millions of Native Americans who lived in the New World in 1492," the curators state (51). On the same page they note that "the Spaniards proved to be . . . sometimes cruel." The term "cruel" does not seem adequate to the range of terrors invoked upon the people Spanish explorers met. The curators close the catalog with a plea to protect archaeological sites (72), yet there is no plea to protect, or to respect, American Indian cultures and peoples.

First Encounters was exactly the kind of exhibition American Indians had feared would develop as a result of the quincentenary. To the general public, it would seem to be an attractive exhibition. To Native populations, it would feel like one more nail in the coffin. And, it was scheduled to crisscross the United States from 1989 to 1992.

Protestors hoped to stop the exhibition, but also were determined to use the publicity they generated to educate the public. An article in *Museum News*, a publication of the American Association of Museums, vilified the demonstrators opposing *First Encounters* by attributing their protest to be a "challenge to an open discussion of America's past" and likening them to Jesse Helms, a senator known to attack the arts and of maintaining a narrow view of American traditions (*Museum News* 1990, 13).

The curators conclude in a statement they made in a later issue of *Museum News*, "And if individuals become frustrated because their voices are not part of the exhibition, the most productive avenue is for them to create their own exhibitions and public forums" (Milbrath and Milanich

1991, 37). This statement is callous and ignorant (reminiscent of "let them eat cake"). How many opportunities exist for American Indians to create exhibitions that will be viewed by a national audience? Even with the new opportunities brought about by the formation of the National Museum of the American Indian (NMAI), Native voices will be filtered through a federal institution's political expediency and conservatism fostered by economic concerns, as well as by the great number of non-Indian museum professionals who are employed by the NMAI, particularly in its exhibitions department. There are virtually no large-scale exhibition venues for unfettered American Indian voices. There is no National Holocaust Museum for American Indian survivors. The attitudes of curators like Milbrath and Milanich serve to drive American Indian protestors to show up at the doors of museums with picket signs and drafted demands in hand. The protestors of *First Encounters* realized their best opportunity for obtaining a national forum for their concerns was in holding the protest itself. Not only did they want to prevent the exhibit from giving viewers a false impression, they seized an opportunity to deliver their own messages.

Milbrath and Milanich defended their point of view and the text of the exhibition by saying, "Like a student in an introductory course on World civilization, the public does not want to deal with too many contradictions and uncertainties when attempting to learn new information" (Milbrath and Milanich 1991, 37). Along with insulting the public's ability and desire to think, this statement suggests that when presenting a point of view new to an audience, a curator would not be able to reveal a complete story. The curators go on to say, "Furthermore, the public has come to see museum exhibitions as expressing the truth as it currently is understood" (Milbrath and Milanich 1991, 37).

Their thinking is exactly why American Indian protestors have been so concerned about the impact of exhibitions upon the public and why they have targeted exhibitions for protest during the past thirty years. The public has been kept innocent and ignorant, to a great extent, of many facts about the United States and its historical heroes, of the Native people of the continent, and of the events and conflicts that have occurred between the two groups. "The truth as it currently is understood," if applied by publications, exhibitions, and other media, would mean that our understanding of past events would be forever frozen until something (perhaps protests) caused a correction. The curators apparently did not believe that museums should be one of the means for advancing new explorations of our nation's truths.

The exhibition began its scheduled travels to several other sites. Tampa's Museum of Science and Industry invited the protestors of *First Encounters* to camp out in a green space immediately outside the museum

(Milbrath and Milanich 1991, 36). In this way, the protest was, in part, treated as a vital part of the exhibition. At the Albuquerque Museum in New Mexico, a handout providing perspectives keyed to exhibition sections was prepared by Richard Hill (Tuscarora), then director of the Institute of American Indian Arts Museum in Santa Fe (Hill 1990). Additionally, Native American speakers were given an opportunity to present their points of view in a scheduled presentation (Milbrath and Milanich 1991, 36). The museum invited Agnes Dill (Isleta Pueblo), a retired teacher; Joe Sando (Jemez Pueblo); Milton Chee, a Navajo scholar; Douglas George (Mohawk), newspaper editor; and Lee Miller, a Cherokee consultant to the Library of Congress, to speak about European colonization (Albuquerque Museum 1990).

The exhibition was canceled in Houston, but continued on to the Science Museum of Minnesota in St. Paul. Science Museum staff had determined that the exhibit they had scheduled for a May 30, 1992 opening contained scholarly research, but they also believed the exhibit had neglected to integrate indigenous perspectives (Science Museum of Minnesota 1997).

The museum incorporated a community advisory team comprised not only of Native Americans, but also including Chicano, Latino, African American, and Euro-American members (Condon 1992). The group was charged with mounting an accompanying exhibition, *From the Heart of Turtle Island: Native Views 1992* to open simultaneously with *First Encounters*. Touted as "the first large-scale attempt by a U.S. museum to provide a forum for other viewpoints on the Quincentennial and the legacy of Columbus" (Prince 1992), the exhibition actually intruded into the space of *First Encounters* with freestanding signs which asked questions like "Why is First Encounters offensive?" and then providing a sentence or two of insight developed by the community group. A diorama of two Native greeters, shown offering de Soto a string of beads, was fronted by a sign noting that the trusting men became captives of de Soto. A statement also noted that while Euro-Americans are accustomed to seeing indigenous people behind glass in museums, "indigenous people do not see themselves as exotic, extinct specimens" (Condon 1992).

Despite the Science Museum's best efforts to deflate reasons for protest, picketers (including Florida's Jan Elliott and Vernon Bellecourt, one of the founders of AIM) protested against the exhibition with demands that it be closed. During a press conference at an exhibition preview, Bellecourt threw a pint of his own blood on the sails of the replica of the *Niña* and dashed the figure of Columbus overboard (Silva 1992). Dan Swan, director of the museum's Native American collections program and exhibitions curator, decided to support Bellecourt's actions and chose not to remove the bloodstains from the exhibition. Newspaper editorials, letters to the editor, and correspondence between the Florida Museum of Natural History and the Science Museum of Minnesota as well as comments by local citizens, Native and non-Native, demonstrated the passions aroused by the destructive act (Science Museum of Minnesota 1995).

Many Native people in the St. Paul and Minneapolis vicinity opposed the intervention of AIM supporters, and supported the work of the local exhibits team that had creatively "corrected" the lapses of *First Encounters*. The Science Museum of Minnesota concluded that the forced dialogue had been beneficial.

> The best evaluation of our program can be found in the anecdotal comments recorded by the public in the exhibit. The comments reflect an awareness of our attempt to promote dialogue and to help people review their opinions during the teachable moment. Arranged chronologically, these comments give a firsthand picture of the transition in the community from outrage on both sides of the issue to some kind of understanding for the need to move beyond ancient hatreds. (Science Museum of Minnesota, Feb. 12, 1993)

In 1993, the Science Museum hosted a conference on the issues of presentation of Indian cultures by museums. The museum filmed the conference as part of a video project documenting the collaboration between the museum and the community planning team during the development of *Native Views*. The video was released in 1997 under the title *Journey: Museums and Community Collaboration* (Science Museum of Minnesota 1997). One could say the protest of *First Encounters* directly led to this and other worthy projects that have served to shape museums and the public who visit them.

To many American Indians, any official recognition of the anniversary of Columbus's voyage to the Americas that didn't emphasize the ensuing trauma to the hemisphere's Native people was tantamount to a celebration of the assault upon American Indians that resulted from Columbus's actions. The effect of the noisy, press-grabbing resistance to *First Encounters* led to an almost silent passage of the remainder of the 500th anniversary of the 1492 voyage. It seems the protests effectively served to truncate any celebratory aspects of the anniversary.

"While I do believe that white American ethnocentrism exists to some extent, my assessment of the Columbus Quincentenary is that it was a bust," reported Joseph Marshall III in his article, "Valuing Cultural Diversity is Cultural Validation." He continued, "It is significant to note that many activities relative to Columbus Day or the Columbus Quincentenary in general were labeled as an observance or observation, instead of a celebration. While there were a number of Columbus Day 'celebrations,' there appeared to be an overall sensitivity to the use of the word celebration; though I suspect in some cases the sensitivity was predicated mainly on the desire to avoid bad publicity or possible confrontation with Native American radicals, and not necessarily on a brotherly concern for Native American feelings" (Marshall 1993, 39).

The Smithsonian Institution's quincentenary exhibition, *Seeds of Change*, at the National Museum of Natural History, focused on things, rather than people and, thus, avoided discussing Columbus. Instead, the exhibition discussed the two-way impact of exchanges of pathogens, foods, and animals between continents.

Atlatl, a national Native arts organization, created a traveling art show designed to provide rebuttal to the general hoopla expected regarding the quincentenary of the 1492 voyage of Columbus. Named *The Submuloc Show/Columbus Wohs*, the participating artists wanted to show the contemporary side of Indian life and teach viewers something about Native feelings regarding the efforts at domination exerted by Non-Natives upon Natives as a result of "discovery" (Harjo 1996). The exhibition was a form of protest, as have been many art pieces created by American Indian artists.

Although the Gainesville museum experienced record-breaking attendance, protestors were as happy about that as were museum officials. "[A] lot of people who went through there read our material," said a protestor (Dupont 1989). One protestor carried a poster stating, "Racism creates political prisoners and exhibits" (*Gainesville Sun* 1990). The one thing the protestors sought but never got was a formal apology from the creators of *First Encounters*. The closest resemblance to an apology is a statement made by Susan Milbrath following the Minnesota incident saying the exhibition "could be considered to be institutionally racist, but I do not put that in the same category as an exhibit that is intending to portray any Native American group in a negative light" (Silva 1992).

Milbrath continued to defend the appropriateness of the exhibition and determined to make known that her efforts had not been intentionally Eurocentric. However, by her failure to apologize or revise the exhibition, her unintentional Eurocentric points of view traveled the nation in a way that said it was the prerogative of curators to be Eurocentric, and that, thus, most exhibitions will continue to be Eurocentric, and therefore, most Americans will be encouraged to continue to be Eurocentric in their point of view. The actions of Science Museum of Minnesota curator Dan Swan, on the other hand, raise hope that future curators will seek to encourage discourse, allowing minority access to opportunities at the podium where they can express their point of view. Swan was courageous in standing fast against an array of condemning editorials and in face of the long-honored preeminence of museum standards of operation, which too often have high-handedly been imposed in preference to the ethical treatment of people and their cultural sensibilities.

A performance art piece, developed as a counter-commemoration to the Columbus Quincentenary celebrations, was performed by Coco Fusco and Guillermo Gomez-Pena and entitled *Two Undiscovered Ameridians*. The two artists pretended to be recently captured Native people being held in a cage. Wearing a jumble of clothing representing tribal motifs mixed with sunglasses and modern equipment, the two spoke in unintelligible phrases. The audience, unsure of what it was witnessing, responded with varying reactions. The presentation traveled to museums in Chicago, London, New York, Madrid, Buenos Aires, and Sydney in 1992 (Butler 1999, 88).

Native protests seeking to prevent Columbus from being treated as a hero moved from museums after the quincentenary to the protesting of Columbus Day parades and the idea of a federal holiday honoring Columbus. Seventeen states do not recognize Columbus Day as a valid holiday.

In 2004, 230 people were arrested while protesting the Columbus Day parade in Denver. Protests over the parade occurred there for more than a decade. In 2005, protestors in Denver staged a mock die-in at an intersection of the parade route, but moved before the parading entourage reached the area, thereby avoiding arrests, which they had experienced in the earlier demonstration (Associated Press 2005). Protests of the parade, however, are expected to be ongoing.

In 2003, the United Confederation of Taino people held a Columbus Day protest in front of the San Juan Capistrano Mission, choosing a mission as a representation of the oppression experienced by California Indians (Bobbitt 2003). Southern California Indians are also engaged in a concerted effort to prevent Father Junipero Serra, the founder of the mission system beginning in 1768, from being named a saint by the Catholic Church (www.californiahistory.net). They view the missions as death camps that overworked and enslaved their ancestors. Maidu artist Harry Fonseca, a prolific artist known for his Coyote series, named one piece *Saint Coyote* to protest any bid for canonization of Serra (Abbott 1990).

In 1998, another Native protest concerning the anniversary of the arrival of a "conqueror" quietly occurred near Santa Fe. A bronze statue of Don Juan de Onate was defaced, or more appropriately, de-footed. An unidentified group of American Indians sawed the right foot off the statue in memory of Onate's decree in 1599 to remove the right foot of each Acoma Pueblo man. An anonymous letter to the newspaper states, "We took the liberty of removing Don Juan de Onate's right foot on behalf of our brothers and sisters of Acoma Pueblo" (Teters 1998, 14). Although the statue was repaired, viewers can discern where the damage occurred.

Meanwhile, across the country, Native Americans and non-Native Americans revere different heroes, reflecting our country's past history regarding American Indians.

Anniversaries will serve to remind American Indians of past injustices and of the tragic necessity of past generations of American Indians to forcibly swallow those remembrances. More recently, memories have been freed and American Indians are airing their bitter regrets in order to mourn and to seek healing and wholeness.

Figure 8.1.   In 1972, American Indian protestors climbed the mast of the Mayflower replica at Plymouth, Massachusetts, to establish Thanksgiving Day as a Day of Mourning for American Indians. Protests at Plymouth began in 1970 when a politely written speech prepared by Frank James (Wampanoag) was rejected by Massachusetts state planners after they had invited him to speak at the 350th anniversary of the Pilgrims' arrival.

8

Thanksgiving Mourned

Recently, people have become familiar with the story of Squanto be-friending the Pilgrims in their time of need. However, the First Thanksgiving feast, as most Americans know it, remains a myth. Only a single eyewitness paragraph written by Edward Winslow describes the event (William Bradford makes only an oblique reference to the event in his later manuscript which provides no details of the gathering). Winslow's description is sparse. He tells us that in the fall of 1621, ninety Wampanoag men, including tribal leader Massasoit, were entertained for three days with feasting and games during the Pilgrim's celebration of their first harvest. Successful fowling and fishing added to the bounty, he notes. The Wampanoag men contributed five deer, he says. There was no reference to *thanksgiving* in Winslow's description (Pilgrim Hall 2007).

Days of official "thanksgiving" during the colonial era occurred in church and did not include feasting or frolic, but were serious affairs of prayers and sermons. As conflicts began to occur between colonial settlements and Native communities, generally due to the continuing arrival of additional settlers and livestock, some "thanksgivings" were noted to commemorate successful skirmishes with Native communities.

Fifty years after the initial friendly harvest celebration, according to colonist Increase Mather, the decapitated head of Massasoit's son, Meta-comet (christened Philip), who had become tribal leader, was "hanged up as a monument" in Plymouth (Society of Colonial Wars in the State of Connecticut 2007). The once amicable relationship between the Wampanoag and the colonists had completely deteriorated. Metacomet's family was enslaved following his death, and the Wampanoag Nation was diminished, both in numbers and in power. It is hard for Wampanoag people to feel affection for the original Pilgrims.

European farmers had long celebrated their harvests with feasting and relaxation, and so, too, had agricultural Native Americans. Such celebrations continued across the land, and soon seemed an American tradition. In 1777, the Continental Congress declared a day of Thanksgiving, and presidential proclamations followed throughout the ensuing years (Pilgrim Hall Museum 2007). In 1841, a historian came across Winslow's early account of the feast at Plymouth and the researcher believed he had found evidence for the origin of the American harvest fest. It wasn't until after the "Indian Wars" ended in the 1890s, however, that the image of American Indians and Pilgrims dining together in peace became popular with non-Indian citizens. Since that time, the story of the "First Thanksgiving" began to be embellished with romantic and false descriptions (Goldstein 2006).

Meanwhile, in 1921, celebrating the 300th anniversary of the first harvest of the original colonists, Plymouth citizens reenacted a march to the church emulating the early practice of "thanksgiving" for God's favor. An annual enactment of a thanksgiving procession, sometimes referred to as Pilgrim Progress or Pilgrim Parade still occurs, with a coterie of Plymouth citizens marching from the Mayflower Society Museum to Burial Hill (Marker 1999). Recalling that colonial thanksgiving treks sometimes had been called to commemorate successful murderous attacks upon Native people, American Indians rankle at the activity.

In 1970, the Massachusetts Department of Commerce asked the Wampanoag tribe to provide a speaker for the 350th anniversary of the Pilgrim's landing. Frank James was selected to represent the tribe. The Plymouth, Massachusetts, ceremony planners asked to see a copy of his speech in advance. After seeing the proposed speech, James was asked to present in its stead a speech provided by the planners. James refused. He did not get to participate as a speaker in the official anniversary celebration (Council on Interracial Books for Children 1971, 368–72). Instead, he went to the statue of Massasoit, the Pilgrim-era Wampanoag sachem, on Cole's Hill overlooking Plymouth Harbor with its replica of the *Mayflower* and presented his speech to a small group of American Indians and other supporters (Pilgrim Hall Museum 1999).

James's soulfully written text told of the losses his people had suffered since the arrival of the Pilgrims. And it noted proudly that the Wampanoag people still had the will to survive and were determined to regain their rightful place in society. No doubt, the intended speech puzzled, rankled, and frightened the ceremony planners, because it described what had happened to the Wampanoag people since their contact with the Pilgrims. It contained no lies, no threats, no invectives, and no call to subterfuge. The words were based on historical happenings, on heartfelt pain, and on proud strength. Two cultures; two stories. Following is the speech presented with its message intact and abbreviated only by the removal of extraneous portions. The reader can see that nothing in the speech was worthy of being denied presentation:

I speak to you as a man—a Wampanoag man. I am a proud man, proud of my ancestry, my accomplishments won by strict parental direction—"You must succeed—your face is a different color in this small Cape Cod community." I am a product of poverty and discrimination, from these two social and economic diseases. I, and my brothers and sisters have painfully overcome, and to an extent earned the respect of our community. We are Indians first—but we are termed "good citizens." Sometimes we are arrogant, but only because society has pressured us to be so.

It is with mixed emotions that I stand here to share my thoughts. This is a time of celebrating for you—celebrating an anniversary of a beginning for the white man in America. A time of looking back—of reflection. It is with heavy heart that I look back upon what happened to my People.

Even before the Pilgrims landed, it was common practice for explorers to capture Indians, take them to Europe and sell them as slaves for 20 shillings apiece. The Pilgrims had hardly explored the shores of Cape Cod four days before they had robbed the graves of my ancestors, and stolen their corn. . . .

Massasoit, the great Sachem of the Wampanoag, knew these facts; yet he and his People welcomed and befriended the settlers of the Plymouth Plantation. Perhaps he did this because his tribe had been depleted by an epidemic, or his knowledge of the harsh oncoming winter was the reason for his peaceful acceptance of these acts. This action by Massasoit was probably our greatest mistake. We, the Wampanoags, welcomed you, the white man with open arms, little knowing that it was the beginning of the end; that before 50 years were to pass, the Wampanoags would no longer be a Tribe.

What happened in those short 50 years? What has happened in the last 300 years? History gives us facts and there were atrocities; there were broken promises—and most of these centered around land ownership. Among ourselves we understood that there were boundaries—but never before had we had to deal with fences and stone walls, with the white man's need to prove his worth by the amount of land that he owned. Only ten years later, when the Puritans came, they treated the Wampanoag with even less kindness in converting the souls of the so-called savages. Although Puritans were also harsh to some members of their own society, the Indian was pressed between stone slabs and hanged as quickly as any other "witch."

And so down through the years there is record after record of Indian lands taken, and in token, reservations set up for him upon which to live. The Indian, having been stripped of his power, could but only stand by and watch—while the white man took his lands and used them for his personal gain. This the Indian couldn't stand, for to him, land was survival, to farm, to hunt, to be enjoyed. It wasn't to be abused. . . .

Has the Wampanoag really disappeared? We know there was an epidemic that took many Indian lives—some Wampanoags moved West and joined the Cherokee and Cheyenne. They were forced to move. Some even went north to Canada! Many Wampanoag put aside their Indian heritage and accepted the white man's way for their own survival. There are some Wampanoag who do not wish it known they are Indian for social or economic reasons. . . .

History wants us to believe that the Indian was a savage, illiterate, uncivilized animal. A history that was written by an organized disciplined people, to expose us as an unorganized and undisciplined entity. Two distinctly different cultures met. One thought they must control life—the other believed life was to be enjoyed, because nature decreed it. Let us remember, the Indian is and was just as human as the white man. The Indian feels pain, gets hurt and becomes defensive, has dreams, bears tragedy and failure, suffers from loneliness, needs to cry as well as laugh. . . .

Although time has drained our culture, and our language is almost extinct, we the Wampanoags, still walk the lands of Massachusetts. We may be fragmented, we may be confused. Many years have passed since we have been a People together. Our lands were invaded. We fought as hard to keep our land as you the white did to take our land away from us. We were conquered, we became the American Prisoners of War in many cases, and wards of the United States Government, until only recently. The necessity of making a living in this materialistic society caused us to be silent. Today, I and many of my people are choosing to face the truth. We ARE Indians! . . .

What has happened cannot be changed but today we work towards a more humane America, a more Indian America where men and nature once again are important. . . .

You the white man are celebrating an anniversary. We the Wampanoags will help you celebrate in the concept of a beginning. It was the beginning of a new life for the Pilgrims. Now 350 years later it is a beginning of a new determination for the original American. . . .

We still have the spirit, we still have a unique culture, we still have the will and the determination to remain as Indians. We are determined that this is only a beginning of the American Indian to regain the position in this country that is rightfully ours. (James 1971, 368–72)

In following years, the November gathering by Native people and their supporters at Massasoit's statue continued, formalized by a group known as United American Indians of New England (UAINE). The annual gathering became known as the National Day of Mourning. Skits and presentations were developed to discuss feasting and fasting. Other minority groups joined in the effort. The media, including large newspapers representing various areas of the United States as well as wire services, have steadily covered the event (Pilgrim Hall Museum 1999).

Representatives of AIM, including Russell Means, have also joined the local protestors. Throughout the following years, the protestors have variously rallied at the living history facility of Plimoth Plantation, or commandeered the replica of the *Mayflower* and climbed its mast, they have ripped flags in the community, and they have kicked sand upon, and spat on, Plymouth Rock (Hertzberg 1988, 319; Burnette and Koster 1974, 273).

In 1996, four hundred Native participants and friends confronted the Pilgrim procession, causing the Pilgrim portrayers to alter their course, and ultimately to retreat to their headquarters, followed by UAINE participants chanting, "Pilgrims progress, we say no; racism has got to go." The Native group then proceeded to Plymouth Rock and invited children to break a piñata filled with symbols of oppression: money, police badges, toy soldiers, handcuffs and chains, and alcohol advertisements. The items were then thrown upon Plymouth Rock (Workers World 1996).

The next year, Plymouth police were out in force. Twenty-five protestors were arrested in 1997, after a disturbingly physical encounter with the police. Later, Plymouth dropped the charges and agreed to budget for two large, bronze plaques providing a short history of area Native people and of Thanksgiving Day. One plaque was placed at the statue of Massasoit, on Cole's Hill. It partly reads, "Many Native Americans do not celebrate the arrival of the Pilgrims and other European settlers. To them, Thanksgiving Day is a reminder of the genocide of millions of their people, the theft of their lands, and the relentless assault on their culture." The other plaque was placed in the town's Post Office Square and commemorates Metacomet (Haskell 2001).

Plimoth Plantation, a living history museum, has long celebrated the survival of the Pilgrims with its reconstructed settlement and first-person interpretations. Portraying the plantation, however, without interactions with the Pilgrims' neighbors and oft-time visitors, the Wampanoag, meant the settlement was not actually being portrayed accurately or fully. Southern New England Indians had steadily called for the addition of an American Indian presence at Plimoth, pointing out that the Pilgrims would never have survived without the friendship and aid of Squanto, Massasoit, and other Native advisors. Plimoth Plantation first hired American Indian staff people in 1973 (Nanepashemet 1995), three years after James's speech and after members of the American Indian Movement participated in the National Day of Mourning. The protests in the town of Plymouth, and across the nation, most likely contributed to the difficult effort toward integration of Plimoth Plantation's interpretive staff.

Instituting an American Indian component into the successful Pilgrim-focused living history museum proved perilous. The new Native staff members were expected to acclimate to being referred to by Pilgrim impersonators as "savages" (the word savage derives from sylvan, meaning "of the woods" and that is the meaning of the Pilgrim's usage of the word *salvage*). The Pilgrims viewed the Wampanoag people as unnaturally natural. Even if the word was less offensive in the early days of the Pilgrims, modern-day Native people felt the sting of the word, which had acquired very negative meanings through time. The use of it was hard to ignore and painful to their modern ears. Pointedly, what effect would the use of the word to describe American Indians have upon visiting children? Stereotypes supporting racial bias would be too easily reinforced through use of period-appropriate language, when some of the words, like savage, had taken on different meanings through the evolution of the English language.

Plimoth Plantation currently tries to prepare visitors by explaining that the Pilgrims were intolerant of many cultures and of Christian practices different than their own. Their Web site for the *Mayflower II*, a replica of the original vessel, advises, "Although the English write of their admiration for Massasoit and other Wampanoag leaders, there are also passages that betray a deep cultural prejudice against the Wampanoag and other Native People. You may hear this common 17th-century-perspective reflected in comments made by role players. Please remember that these comments are made 'in character' as a means of teaching you about English colonial attitudes" (Plimoth Plantation 2007).

One can only worry that children and many adults who don't bother to read, or to pay attention to such advisories, do not understand the context of what they are exposed to during their visit to the Plymoth sites, and may either learn that derogatory talk directed at American Indians is acceptable, or that there are no longer authentic American Indians to offend by such talk. Perhaps it would be more appropriate to forego role-playing (first person interpretation) in exchange for third-person interpretation.

Since the Wampanoag language has been lost through centuries of repression, it became impossible to create and inhabit a comparable Wampanoag village site filled with Native people communicating as they did in 1627, the date used by the re-created plantation. Even if the Wampanoag enactors were to learn another Native language, how would that help them communicate with visitors? Wanting to have a Wampanoag presence as accurate and spectacular as the long-vaunted recreated plantation itself proved frustrating. The losses the Wampanoag had suffered through the centuries became ever more poignant to the Native people who were trying to develop a successful Wampanoag counterpart to the plantation reconstruction of the past.

The Wampanoag Indian Program tried a variety of interpretive formats including coming out of character and responding to visitors in modern

American English and, alternatively, using American-English speaking guides to interpret the tasks being undertaken by silent enactors. Some years, the Wampanoag village site was closed to visitors and was available only for scheduled school group visitation. Currently, the program enacts the lives of one particular English-speaking Wampanoag man and his family who, records reveal, were known to live adjacent to the plantation serving as an ambassador of sorts for the tribe's interests. Additionally, visitors entering the plantation area are provided with an orientation to prepare visitors with information, which hopefully prevents their heaping insults upon American Indians during their visit. I served as a museum educator for a dozen years in a New England museum and experienced people feeling my hair, using the word "squaw," questioning my Indian-ness, and suggesting that Americans Indians should just forget the past (this said while visiting a history museum). I often experienced emotional fatigue from hearing again and again demeaning and aggravating comments. Working at Plimoth Plantation, because of the nature of the setting, would expose Native interpreters to greater abuses than I had experienced.

By choosing not to stay in character, Native staff people at Plimoth are able to address some of the stereotypes emanating from tourists, answering such questions as why there are no tipis at the sight, what sort of horsemen were the Wampanoag, how did they hunt buffalo, what were missionaries like, and other questions that beg attention, but blur time and place.

During a job interview I underwent at Plimoth Plantation in the 1980s, I was asked if I were familiar with some of the challenges the Wampanoag Indian Program faced. I admitted that I had heard a few tales about the difficulties of the program. Of course, when I talked to Native staff members, they expressed a different set of problems than did the non-Native administrators. Some of the difficulties had to do with friction between white administrators and Native interpreters; some had to do with friction between insensitive visitors and Native interpreters. In the views of the Native staff, they were sandwiched between two groups of insensitive non-Indians. The executive staff, of course, saw a different set of problems which they called personnel issues. I was asked what I might do, if I were selected to work there, to address some of the "problems." During this discussion, I was asked how I would handle Native personnel who were found working on their automobiles during employment hours.

I replied that I would ask the employee to defer car repairs to after work hours when I would then be glad to provide whatever assistance I could in resolving this person's transportation problems. The question made me uncomfortable. It seemed tinged with an insensitive, challenging undertone (there are jokes about "Indian cars," described as held together by wire coat hangers, duct tape, and bailing twine). Poverty has been the experience of many Native families. No doubt, the museum's managers at that time were perplexed at the social and cultural differences they had to navigate after adding the Wampanoag program to their already successful Pilgrim endeavor. It is likely, as the Wampanoag employees experienced policies and attitudes unfriendly to their way of life, and due to their vulnerability in working in an institution where the balance of control rested securely in the hands of another culture (one that had severely punished their ancestors), they quite likely pushed back in a passive/aggressive mode designed to serve as cultural resistance, to gain attention, and, hopefully, to result in dialogue and action that would rectify or adjust the imbalance they were painfully experiencing.

The museum administrators at Plimoth had long been working with European-American descendants who had been taught that Pilgrim and early American histories were something of which to be proud. Those non-Indian citizens lived in a history-soaked area (a history totally friendly to them). They were comfortable and adept at socializing in a workplace comprised of several layers of the prevailing social strata of the community (including upper income levels). They often had the leisure and means to engage in time-absorbing studies of Pilgrim-focused topics. The subjects they were portraying had been thoroughly studied by scholars, and information was plentiful and particular.

On the other hand, few scholars until recent times had engaged in comprehensive studies of Wampanoag life in colonial days. Wampanoag people living in the area had been instructed through many avenues that their ancestors' stories were secondary to the importance of the Pilgrims' stories. The history touted in New England villages was not kind to its Native residents. As a result, in the 1970s, Native New England people who chose to continue following Native values and traditions had not experienced a life in which the study of history in white institutions was centrally important, comfortable, or even available to them. The readily found information about Wampanoag life in popular literature was so limited as to appear cartoon-like. And, yet, Native people strongly wanted the opportunity to learn more about their history and to interpret and relate their own stories, but on their own terms, not through the veil of white propriety about who was civilized and what could be said about the white heroes and heroines.

The problems Plimoth Plantation encountered in staff relations were due to several factors. Included among those factors is a long history of conflict between the two cultures (and the ensuing repercussions and fallout from the resulting animosity and jealousies) and a contemporary unwillingness to amend patterns of interaction between employee and employer (insisting instead that one culture completely abandon its patterns to conform, without support and guidance, to the imposed standards of another). As time progresses, the results of deeper research into Wampanoag history and culture, the long presence of Native staff people, many of whom have gained respect and admiration from their fellow non-Native historians and interpreters through their own accomplishments as living historians, will serve to lessen the gap between Native and non-Native employees.

Currently, Linda Coombs (Wampanoag) serves as associate director in charge of the Wampanoag Indigenous Program at Plimoth Plantation. The Plimoth exhibit, *Thanksgiving: Memory, Myth & Meaning*, addresses Thanksgiving myths and uses historic voices to tell the story of how two cultures lived their lives side by side.

The lessons obtained from Plimoth Plantation can aid other living history programs in incorporating Native presence into their venues. Colonial Williamsburg, Jamestown, St. Marie Among the Iroquois, Fort Frederick in Maryland, and other sites are struggling with how to appropriately depict early Native life. Without those depictions, such sites are not accurate and create, or support, their own inappropriate myths.

The challenge of myth busting is also experienced by the National Park Service at many of its historical sites throughout the nation. The next chapter examines some of the same issues in another venue.

Figure 9.1. The Custer Battlefield National Monument was established in 1946 and immediately began to offend Native populations. Following decades of protests and negotiations, the site was renamed the Little Bighorn Battlefield National Monument in 1991. In 2003, Spirit Warriors, by Lakota artist Colleen Cuschall, depicting Native horsemen, was dedicated to American Indians who fought on either side of the conflict at the Little Bighorn.

9

꿇

The Custer Chronicles

In 1879, a congressional decree established Custer Battlefield National Cemetery to honor the gravesite of the fallen soldiers of the Battle of the Little Bighorn, located east of Billings, Montana, in the midst of the Crow Indian Reservation. The Crow Nation, it should be noted, were allies of the U.S. military at the time of the Battle of the Little Big Horn. In 1946, President Harry S. Truman named the site Custer Battlefield National Monument and soon a museum and visitor center were opened and began to interpret the story of the June 25, 1876, battle in which Lt. Col. George Armstrong Custer led 220 soldiers, Indian scouts, and civilians to their deaths (Turner 1997).

Although well informed by his own scouts, Custer had insisted in pursuing a superior force. There may have been as many as 2,000 fighting men in the Indian encampment reportedly populated with as many as 15,000 people (Turner 1997). In an attack on one edge of the village by Major Marcus Reno, two of Gall's wives and three of Gall's children were killed. Gall later noted that in his fury he attacked soldiers with a hatchet. The fighting in the village lasted not much longer than an hour. Little is known of the losses the Indians experienced. The surviving Native warriors, in turn, quickly mounted an attack on Custer's forces and soon killed all they found.

To support the Park Service site, the Custer Battlefield Historical and Museum Association was founded in 1953. To raise funds, the organization operated the bookstore at the site (and reportedly declined carrying the popular *Bury My Heart at Wounded Knee* by Dee Brown which conveyed a pro-Indian perspective) (Turner 1997). Members of the association were generally non-Indians and were considered fans of Custer (note that the word fan derives from fanatic). They were dedicated to honoring his memory. It was not surprising that the interpretation at the Custer-named site tended to glorify the fallen leader and his cavalry. On the 765-acre site, the fallen military soldiers were accorded marble headstones and the U.S. Congress raised two marble markers in honor of the white soldiers (Bartimus 1990). One monument to soldiers offended Indians. It noted that the soldiers were "clearing the District of the Yellowstone of hostile Indians" (Jordan 1986, 803). If the Cheyenne and Sioux had been given the authority to write the text, they could easily have described the cavalry as a hostile force. From the Native point of view, American Indians were defending their homeland and the military was invading Native lands.

Edward T. Linenthal, author, historian, and museum expert, remembers a visit to Little Bighorn while working on his book *Sacred Ground*. A local historian took him down to the site of the Indian village. "[S]tanding in the Indian village is a completely different experience and alters the terms under which you experienced the battle (while visiting Custer Hill) because now you're not with Custer and the remnants of the 7th—you're down in the Indian village with women and children and thousands of warriors—and here's Major Reno riding into the village intent on doing some harm. You look at the battle with different eyes" (Linenthal 1999, 8).

There was no monument provided to honor the besieged Sioux and Cheyenne. There was no monument to the winners of a battle that has captured the American imagination more than had many Civil War battles where more lives were lost and where engagement raged for longer periods of time. Custer's only notable military "accomplishment" was a previous attack on a Cheyenne settlement where he killed 11 warriors and 92 women, children, and old men, plus 875 Indian horses (Turner 1997).

In 1972, American Indian Movement (AIM) activist Russell Means came with a group of protestors and demanded greater recognition of the embattled winners of the conflict, Northern Cheyenne and Teton Sioux. The demonstrators came mainly from the nearby Crow Reservation. They installed a temporary plaque honoring the Indians who had fought and prevailed. Means called for a permanent Indian monument (Turner 1997). Clifford Long Sioux (Cheyenne) participated in the unsanctioned memorial, noting that American Indians had "tried to ask for a memorial to their grandfathers who died there, but it had always fallen on deaf ears" (Bone 2003).

In 1976, the bicentennial year of the United States's Declaration of Independence and the centennial year of the Battle of the Little Big Horn, another demonstration took place. The park service had arranged for an array of notable speakers including U.S. Army Colonel George Armstrong Custer III, who would lay a wreath to honor his ancestor. AIM protestors arrived with an upside-down American flag as a signal of distress. Means took over the microphone and again demanded the installation of an Indian memorial (Turner 1997).

In 1988, American Indians arrived on horseback to protest the Custer Battlefield National Monument's museum exhibitions. Sixteen exhibits focused on the military combatants while half that number discussed American Indians. Why, protestors wanted to know, was the site named after a soldier who had failed in his mission and wasted the lives of the soldiers he commanded? Why was it dedicated to the loser of the battle, and not to the winners? The obvious answer seemed to be "prejudice." Means and a group of AIM members dug earth from the burial site of the enlisted soldiers and placed a plaque there honoring those who fought against Custer and his soldiers. There were some who were aghast at what they considered to be a desecration of graves. Of course, the protestors chose their action precisely because Native graves have time and again been desecrated without outcry from non-Indian quarters. The irony could not be overlooked. The National Park Service, and various citizens were waking up to the understanding that the site had long harbored an imbalance of information. NPS formed a committee to select a site for an American Indian memorial. NPS promptly received a letter threatening to destroy such a memorial should it ever be built (Linenthal 1999, 9).

"This is the only place where all the monuments are to the losers," noted Barbara Booher (now Sutteer), appointed by NPs in 1989 as the first American Indian named to superintend the site (Bartimus 1990). Her appointment was met with protests from the Custer Battlefield Historical and Museum Association, in conjunction with one of the former superintendents of the site, along with other Custer aficionados (Bartimus 1990). Her detractors questioned her ability, the appropriateness of her appointment, and her desire to change the focus from Custer to one with greater inclusion of the American Indian story.

In 1991, legislation was passed, under the sponsorship of Senator Ben Nighthorse Campbell, a Cheyenne from Colorado, changing the name of the site to the Little Bighorn Battlefield National Monument and ensuring that a monument would be installed to acknowledge the American Indians who fought at the site (Turner 1997).

Also in 1991, the Associated Press wrote a piece about sixty-four Crow warriors who were involved in Operation Desert Storm in the Persian Gulf. The writer also noted the tribe's military involvement including their service with Custer and, before they were allowed to vote in 1924, their service with Theodore Roosevelt in the Spanish-American War. Four hundred Crows served in World War II. Accordingly to John Pretty-On-Top, who can count more than forty relatives who have served in the military, the Crow have fought for the United States continuously because they can't imagine going through a takeover from another country—again (Associated Press 1991). The juxtaposition of the AP account with the battle for Indian recognition at Little Big Horn provides an enigmatic view.

American Indians of different tribes played a part in both sides of the conflict at Little Big Horn, while Custer was serving just one side. American Indians have served in the U.S. military in higher proportion of their population than any other group in the United States (United States Department of Defense 1996). The American Indian side of the Little Big Horn story has constantly been diminished, while the opponents to including the Native side of the story suggest they have no interest in hearing any more history unless it will glorify their own familiar stories.

Gerard A. Baker, a Mandan-Hidatsa National Park Service professional, was the second American Indian to be named superintendent of the site. Again, he came under fire from Custer-focused contingents because of his attempts to be inclusive of Native history and to embrace the local Native community, and perhaps, too, because he was Native American.

According to Logan Curley Sr. in a conversation with writer Frederick Turner, "with Gerard, things are kind of blooming for Native Americans. Prior to that, we felt like we could never set a foot inside that entrance gate. We sure wouldn't have had access to the office we just met in" (Turner 1997), he noted after leaving a meeting with Baker.

However, anonymous threats were periodically telephoned to Baker's home. At his request, with his young family's safety in mind, Baker was transferred to a different Park Service position in Oklahoma. Later, he managed the Lewis and Clark Trail commemoration, and is now superintendent at Mount Rushmore National Monument, where he is expected to introduce Native interpretation of the Black Hills.

The construction of the Little Bighorn Battlefield National Monument Indian Memorial began in 1999. The attractive memorial uses a see-through panel to create images of past warriors riding across the flat land, unfettered and free of the painful past. Since Congress did not provide the funds for the memorial, entrance fees were increased to help raise the needed funds.

On June 26, 2001, a marker to commemorate the battle's 125th anniversary was dedicated to Long Road, a San Arc Lakota Sioux, who died, according to the marker, "while defending his homeland and the Sioux way of life" (Gildart 2001, 62).

The change in the monument's name represents a major opportunity for a future lessening of the grip "Custerphiles" have consistently held over the site. Then again, a recent resurgence of white supremacy activities in the United States may mean that Custer will serve as an endangered white hero, a sort of mascot for all that is threatened in the myth that was America's history which so many of us were shamelessly taught. Currently, Custer aficionados are using Internet Web sites to convey their dissatisfaction with American Indian involvement in the national monument.

What happens at the battle site, as well as at Mount Rushmore and other similar sites, will serve as a bellwether for the future of American Indian and mainstream-American relations in the field of interpretation.

IV

CLAIMING OUR
OWN PLACES

The concept of museum does not fit easily into traditional American Indian practices (hoarding is not a desirable trait, written labels stand in opposition to oral traditions, self-description does not fit a life of humility, intervention in the life cycle of material opposes the Native idea that nature's cycle is best, etc.). The closest analogy to a museum in Native life is reverence for elders as holders of knowledge, but elders are not a place or a thing.

American Indian protests of museums aided Native communities in gaining back rights and gaining back lost cultural materials. Additionally, the protests had taken Native people inside museums and had brought them face-to-face with curators and museum directors. Serving on advisory committees for large or local museums gave American Indians the opportunities to push their agendas for museum reform. The opportune time for Native Americans to be able to tell their own histories through a museum vehicle in their own communities had arrived. Transitioning from a wariness of museums to embracing them has led many Native communities to examine carefully each step toward developing museums, and invariably Native communities want to do so in a way that suits their own needs.

As we saw in the beginning of this book, museums can serve as part of the nation-building process, allowing its owners to define themselves, to tell their stories in their own way, and to protect national patrimony (the symbols of nationhood and origin). Toward this goal, Native communities in North America have developed more than two hundred facilities that operate as museum-like institutions.

By converting museums, by creating new institutions in their own image, American Indians continue their protest of museums. Such communities often name their museum-like places heritage center, cultural center, history center, people's center, visitor's center, or they use words in their own language to capture the meaning they intend. By their reluctance to apply the word museum to their counterpart institutions, Native communities are protesting museums, exhibiting their disdain for institutions that have so scourged them they cannot bear to apply the word to their facility. And, yet, of course, there are many Native communities who do use the word museum for their institutions. Often it is the best way to attract tourists, who will understand that a museum is a place where visitors are welcome, while tourists might be reluctant to stop at a reservation building called a people's center or cultural center. Even while using the word museum, many communities seek to change the institution, in quiet protest regarding the inadequacies of the past. All of these efforts represent continuing struggles of great consequence.

Two Native museum-like places, Ak-Chin Him Dak (Maricopa, Arizona) and the Makah Cultural and Research Center (Neah Bay, Washington), undertook their transforming work with great success. So, too, have the creators of the National Museum of the American Indian who worked to change museum approaches to Native exhibits, so much so that most non-Native exhibit reviewers failed to appreciate the exhibition presentations, while most Native attendees and reviewers endorsed and praised the museum. It is obvious that Native modes and preferences are different than those of the non-Native. While Native museum attendees have hardly found it easy to decipher non-Native museums, the change-about offers non-Natives an opportunity to gain insights into Native priorities.

In addition to opening centers as a way to help preserve Native life and culture, many communities fight to regain control over and access to holy sites and historical places. It is essential that these cultural places be reconnected to Native people in order for the fabric of Native community to be whole again.

Many sacred sites, usually beautiful and unusual tracts of land, were confiscated to serve as U.S. or Canada parklands, while, at the same time, many historical sites important to various indigenous tribes were studiously ignored by non-Natives who perhaps thought it preferable to not dwell on parts of their own pasts that now seem unsavory.

Some sites important to Native cultures were enclosed behind military boundaries, consequently keeping religious practitioners at bay. Fort Sill, an artillery military installation in the state of Oklahoma, grew around Medicine Bluff, a sacred site of the Comanche. Unable to engage with a community's ceremonial sites, the Native knowledge of practices often faded away from common experience or left the practitioners with a heavy sense of loss and betrayal.

How important are historic sites and cultural icons? If the United States did not possess Mount Vernon, Ellis Island, the Statue of Liberty, Gettysburg, Boston's Freedom Trail, Fort McHenry, and a myriad of other touchstones of history spread throughout this land, the nation would be a nation without memory. Additionally, it is the Grand Canyon, the Great Lakes, Window Rock, Niagara Falls, Yellowstone, salt flats, endless grasslands, mountain peaks and ranges, caverns, and mighty rivers that make our country a land worthy of awe. Americans would be a people less awesome, less grounded, less inspiring without these historical places and natural wonders. By taking equivalent places away from Native people, federal and state governments have been guilty of larceny on the grandest scale. American Indians, tied so strongly to land and ancestors, have not been indifferent to these thefts. They protested from the beginning, when they were most vulnerable and ignored, and they continue to protest. Recent protests include a struggle to protect petroglyphs in New Mexico, a resting place of massacred ancestors in South Dakota, a revered lake in New Mexico, a spiritual mountain in South Dakota, a quarry in Minnesota, and an imposing ceremonial site in Wyoming.

Countless important Native sites have been lost, and some have been forgotten because their keepers, or an entire people, were lost or ignored, along the way. Many known sites are still threatened. On June 20, 2003, the first National Prayer Day for Native Sacred Places was held on the steps of the U.S. Capitol to impress upon Congress the need for legislative protection. In 2006, about fifteen different sites across the United States simultaneously hosted the day of prayer. The events are coordinated each year through the Morning Star Institute, founded by Suzan Shown Harjo (Cheyenne and Hodulgee Muscogee) (Morning Star Institute 2006).

Although meaningful sites are not museums, they can be related to them. And, often, a museum-like interpretive center springs up to orient tourists to the site. While sacred sites are not museums, and Native people would rather have such sites off-limits to nonpractitioners, as population growth occurs and unexplored lands decrease in the Americas, more and more visitors are attracted to increasingly rare opportunities to commune with natural beauty. To most Americans, if something is natural and out-of-doors, they consider it akin to parkland and will seek to visit it. Sacred sites on public lands need visitor centers to help control access and to appropriately inform visitors, with the hope of deflecting tourists from interfering with Native religions and practices.

The National Park Service has experienced many protests involving American Indians. Most of the protests have occurred due to the close proximity of parkland to Native land, making protest events more accessible to Native people. Most of the larger Park Service lands either border, surround, or are surrounded by tribal lands and many have either taken land or swapped for Native land during the development of the various Park Service properties. Most parks were, of course, Native lands at some point in time.

The 1998 book *American Indians and National Parks* by Robert H. Keller and Michael F. Turek details some of the troubles the Park Service has inflicted upon Native groups. They cite that, "the list of Indian/Park Service conflicts and disputes is long: boundary lines, land claims, rights-of-way, hunting and wildlife management, grazing permits, water rights, employment preference, craft sales, cultural interpretation, sacred sites and the disposition of cultural artifacts, entrance fees, dams, the promotion of tourism, commercial regulation, 'squatting' in parks, relations with tribal parks, and resentment over past injustices" (Keller and Turek 1998, xiii–xiv).

Despite the contentiousness of past interactions, the Park Service is considered by many to be among the best of federal agencies when it comes to developing policies and interactions involving American Indians. That is largely due to the depth and numbers of interactions, and thus experience, that has occurred between the Park Service and Native groups. Currently, the Park Service is one of the largest federal employers of American Indians, along with the Bureau of Indian Affairs and the military.

Some of the Park Service-American Indian interactions include the following. The Pima and Zuni tribes successfully blocked the formation of authorized parks destined for their homelands in 1971 and 1988 (Keller and Turek 1998, 29). In 1925, Ute Mountain Ute protestors blocked roadway repairs to protest ongoing problems at Mesa Verde Park where vast portions of their land had been taken over (39). In 1915, a delegation of Blackfeet citizens went to Washington, D.C., in order to protest the renaming of sites in Glacier National Park, which had been part of their home territory. They requested that their Native language site names remain in use (51–52). Yankton Sioux have long demanded that Pipestone Quarry be returned to them since it is a sacred site (254). Mount Rushmore remains a perennial aggravation since Lakota people refused to accept payment for the Black Hills. In 1980, the Supreme Court found that the land had been essentially stolen from the Lakota and awarded them a $117 million settlement. However, the Lakota want the land, not the money (Klein 2001). For many Lakota, the carving of sacred hills is a travesty that can never be righted.

These are just a few of the protests directed at National Park Service sites by American Indians. In most cases, Native people would not have forfeited or exchanged lands for the development of parks, except that they were tricked, pressured, and sometimes not even consulted when the land conversions were enacted. Keller and Turek's book informs the reader that much Indian land was taken from Indians during recent times, and land grabs can still be a reality for Native communities.

These final chapters explore how Native peoples seek to claim places of their own by either transforming museums so that they become comfortable institutions or by maintaining or retrieving access to areas of cultural significance.

Figure 10.1. In August 2006, Lakota protestors gathered near Sturgis, South Dakota, during a biker rally to encourage motorcyclists to avoid using Route 79, which runs beside Bear Butte, a sacred site. Bear Butte defenders want a buffer area around the mountain so that ceremonies and prayers are not disturbed by noise and commotion from bars, campgrounds, and outdoor music.
Courtesy of Amanda Takes War Bonnett/*Lakota Country Times.*

10

Native Cultural Sites

Many of the spiritual and natural wonders within state and national parks have been, and still are, cathedrals to Native people. Sacred places are beyond time; they are meditative places where silence is holy and communion is riveting. The Grand Canyon, for example, cannot be witnessed without awe, without a soulful and humble drinking in of the beauty and majesty of something grander than the human realm.

This section will explore protest efforts to maintain protective control and use of not only sacred places, but historic and other culturally related sites as well. American Indians are no less devoted to sacred or culturally significant sites than any other culture, and possibly are more devoted than many. The loss of access to and use of such important areas through time changed and challenged the Native peoples who were forced to vacate such sites as those found in Yosemite Valley, in Yellowstone, and at Devils Tower National Monument, Bear Butte, Pipestone, and a host of other places.

Land shapes people; it informs them. In turn, people gain a sense of duty to homelands. The sense of duty becomes even more powerful when the landscape contains a place of awe, or when an event happens upon the land that strengthens the people's commitment to each other, and to the site (consider the site of the former World Trade Center of New York City, or Ellis Island and the Statue of Liberty to immigrant Americans). The concept of hallowed ground (whether it be cemeteries, battlefields, places of birth or death or miracles, or of holy or momentous events) endures in all cultures.

Regrettably, much powerful Native land wound up within parklands in the United States, often turning spiritual places into recreational areas. Native people once freely accessed natural and spiritual areas, but when those lands were taken from them, they were reduced to fee-paying park visitors (today free access is often extended to qualifying Native entrants). Natural resources important to cultural practices (plants, minerals, and animals used in ceremonies, or for religious object production, or for ceremonial foods) became lost to many Native Americans, most often without choice or compensation. It some cases, money was offered, and not accepted, but the land was still forfeited. American Indians generally were not consulted concerning the establishment of parks. In many cases, they didn't even have the right to vote as citizens, or to pursue legal protections, when important sites and home territories were taken from them.

Access by American Indians to many precious Native cultural sites has often been denied by the Bureau of Land Management, by military installations, and by various other federal and private entities. Due to protests, some of these restrictions are loosening.

This chapter provides a survey of some of the special sites where Native protests have occurred. Much of the information for this chapter comes from National Park Service Web sites and the book *American Indians & National Parks* by Robert H. Keller and Michael F. Turek (1998). For similar information in Canada, see the *Report of the Royal Commission on Aboriginal Peoples*, volume 3, chapter 6, published in October 1996, found on the Indian and Northern Affairs Canada Web site (www.ainc-inac.gc.ca). The Canadian report discusses Native philosophy and issues, relaying similar stories of dispossession, disregard, and current anger as found in the United States.

The United States National Park Service (NPS), created in 1916, also manages national monuments, national cemeteries, and national battlefields. Some of the parks the service now manages were formed as parks before the service itself was developed. National forests are managed by the Department of Agriculture, while the Bureau of Land Management falls under the Department of the Interior. Projects of the U.S. Army Corps of Engineers have also harmed Native Americans. Tribes concerned with land issues must wage their battles on many fronts, and in early days bureaucracies were in no mood to listen to Native pleas. The limited resources of Native communities have often delayed or derailed protests, and unresolved issues continue to fester.

American Indians find themselves in the quandary of trying to pry loose NPS control over some lands, while trying to gain protection for other lands of Native concern, such as sites where Native people were massacred, battlefields significant to Native communities, Native burial sites and cemeteries, Native prayer and ceremonial grounds, and other sacred places, such as places of tribal origins. The human-built structures of Canyon de Chelly, Casa Grande, Serpent Mound, and countless other mounds and stone works must be protected from looters, plunderers, or agricultural, mining, and industrial concerns. The century or older historic homes of influential chiefs and Native leaders and other historic buildings also merit protection. Striking a balance between preservation and physical and spiritual use, between autonomy and partnerships, between Native and non-Native concerns continue to challenge American Indians, the courts, legislatures, and various bureaucracies.

BLUE LAKE

One of the central cases leading to the creation of the American Indian Religious Freedom Act of 1978 involved Blue Lake, New Mexico. In 1906 the federal government had placed Blue Lake (known as Ba Whyea to the Taos Pueblo) under the control of the U.S. Forest Service. The pristine lake is a significant religious site for the community, and the lake's water flows directly into the village. Initially the leaders of Taos Pueblo believed the Forest Service would preserve the remote lake, and accepted the federal decision. Tribal members were substantially shocked when the lake and surrounding land was proclaimed a multiple-use area by the government with plans to increase access to it (McLeod 2006).

As the Taos people protested, the government considered its options. In 1924, the Pueblo Lands Act awarded the tribe compensation for Blue Lake, thinking that money could resolve the conflict, but money was not what the tribe wanted. In 1933, the Senate Indian Affairs Committee, pressured by Taos leaders, recommended that title be restored, but the Department of Agriculture simply responded by issuing a permit for Native use rights. In 1951, the Taos filed suit with the just formed Indian Claims Commission. Repeated attempts fell short of the goal, but the Taos would not be deterred (McLeod 2006).

Paul Bernal spoke for the Taos community in testimony before Congress in 1969: "Our tradition and our religion require people to adapt their lives and activities to our natural surroundings so that men and nature mutually support the life common to both. The idea that man must subdue nature and bend its processes to his purposes is repugnant to our people" (McLeod 2006).

In 1970, after more than sixty years of struggle, Blue Lake was finally restored to the Taos Pueblo (Taos Pueblo 2006). The case, and others like it, served to make it clear that American Indian religious beliefs and practices had not originally been given adequate understanding, tolerance, and protection. Ensuing laws like the American Indian Religious Freedom

Act began to redress those earlier shortcomings, but tendencies of a resource-hungry economy will always threaten sacred places, and bureaucratic complications make it extremely difficult to wage battles to protect those places. Laws concerning religion are subject to interpretation, and courts are not always well-versed in Native beliefs and practices.

The Zuni Pueblo struggled to preserve Zuni Salt Lake, which was threatened by a nearby mining project. Since the early twentieth century, the Zuni tribe fought to regain control of the lake where they have held their purification rites. In 1977, it was returned to the tribe, and the Zuni thought their struggles were over. However, in 1986 they learned that an adjacent mining project would lower the aquifer by four feet, endangering the lake and threatening 500 burial shrines. In July of 2002, protesting Hopi, Acoma, Taos, and Laguna people engaged in a reenactment of the ceremonial pilgrimages to Zuni Salt Lake. After several lawsuits, the mining proposal was abandoned in 2003 (Neary 2003).

PETROGLYPH NATIONAL MONUMENT

One of the hardest categories of ancient Native creations to protect is rock art. Ancient petroglyphs and pictographs are so widespread and numerous that it seems impossible to protect them all. Over 20,000 etchings in volcanic rock exist in Petroglyph National Monument, bordering Albuquerque, New Mexico. One could seemingly expect that once a site is placed within the confines of a national preserve, there would be permanent and rigorous protection. However, Petroglyph National Monument, a sacred site still used by today's area Pueblo people, proved assailable by proponents of highway development. The highway project was designed to relieve street congestion by running across monument land.

More than 400 Native protestors and their allies participated in a gathering November 20, 2005, in Albuquerque. Winona LaDuke, an Ojibwe woman and former Green Party vice-presidential candidate, spoke at the meeting. Participants represented Indigenous Environmental Network, Gwich'in Steering Committee, Colorado AIM members, and the Indigenous Youth Coalition. The All Indian Pueblo Council, the Navajo Nation, and the National Congress of American Indians all expressed opposition to the highway project, known as the Paseo Extension, an addition to the Paseo Del Norte Road (Colorado American Indian Movement 2005).

The struggle at Petroglyph National Monument began in 1992 when the freeway plan was first announced. Eight and a half acres were promptly removed from federal jurisdiction by federal legislation and placed in the hands of Albuquerque (Norrell 2005).

During study stages of the road enhancement project, other locations for a roadway were found to be acceptable, yet the route through the federal land was ultimately selected by the city and approved for its use. The only concessions made to those protesting the use of the monument's land were that five engraved rocks in the path of the highway would be moved and preserved in a new location. After threatened lawsuits, the highway was to be greatly reduced in width to decrease further disruption to the site of the antiquities. Such compromises, however, are not satisfactory for cultural preservation concerns, and ignore and offend Native sensibilities.

DEVILS TOWER NATIONAL MONUMENT

The rock formation at Devils Tower National Monument, in northeastern Wyoming, rises 867 feet into the air. Its starkly sheer walls dominate the landscape. President Theodore Roosevelt proclaimed it the first national monument in 1906 (Schneider 2001). Looking like a giant stump of a tree, or a place where a giant grizzly used its claws, the stone formation has long been regarded by all American Indians who came within sight of it as a place of power. The Arapaho, Kiowa, and eighteen other tribes maintain reverence for the place, possess oral traditions about it, and have their own separate names for the unique formation. The tower has been used, and is still used, by Native people for religious practices including vision quests and sun dances. Prayers given in the tower's presence are thought to have stronger power.

But, the vertical rise of the formation also attracts rock climbers, whose numbers are growing in this era of increased leisure time, compounded by a current avidity for extreme sports. In 1973, 312 climbers were recorded, but in the year 2000 more than 6,000 climbers were counted at the tower (Schneider 2001). The two groups, American Indians and rock climbers, were increasingly getting in each other's way, and the practices of each appeared to be regarded as loathsome by the other. While American Indian visitors left prayer bundles, climbers left climbing bolts in the Tower's stone face. American Indians decried the defacements as well as the lack of privacy during ceremonial intervals.

Although named a monument in 1906, it wasn't until the 1930s that the Civilian Conservation Corps built access roads to the previously almost inaccessible tower, and a newly built visitor center beckoned visitors to come. American interest in the tower increased when it was shown in Steven Spielberg's 1977 film, *Close Encounters of the Third Kind* (Schneider 2001). A formerly quiet location was transformed into a busy destination site.

In the early 1990s, the NPS convened a working group to address the issues between the rock climbers and American Indian constituents. NPS learned that the summer solstice was considered the most important time for American Indian ceremonies at the tower. If climbing could be controlled at that time, NPS planners reasoned, it would greatly facilitate Native use of the site. A voluntary ban was sought, and there was an 84 percent reduction in climbing activity during the summer solstice after the ban went into effect in 1995 (Schneider 2001). Even so, climbers filed a lawsuit maintaining the ban conflicts with first amendment rights regarding separation of church and state. The lawsuit failed and the U.S. Supreme Court declined to hear the appeal, citing that a voluntary ban did not conflict with the amendment's purpose (Schneider 2001).

Multicultural education increased at the site in an effort to aid climbers in understanding the importance of the landform to American Indian cultural practices and beliefs.

In the spring of 2006, Dorothy FireCloud, a member of the Rosebud Sioux Tribe, was appointed superintendent. American Indian groups also protest the monument's name, saying it is disrespectful of Native beliefs. Bear Lodge has been proposed as an improved name (Bleizeffer 2006). Meanwhile, conflict continues at the site.

YELLOWSTONE

"When a contemporary, traditionally minded Crow arrives at the shores of Yellowstone Lake today, it is not uncommon for him to light a cigarette, puff four times, and pray," according to authors Peter Nabokov and Lawrence Loendorf in *Restoring a Presence: American Indians and Yellowstone National Park* (Nabokov and Loendorf 2004, 52). The magnificent geysers and steaming springs were regarded as sacred ground to Native people. But, the park was established when Natives in the area were viewed as combatants, and there was little effort by park authorities to befriend area Natives, or in fact to care much at all about them, or their relationship to that curious environment.

Yellowstone National Park was created in 1877, when the West was still considered wild. Two of the first tourists traveling to the new park were killed by Nez Perce scouts in retreat from military forces hot in pursuit of them. Many different tribes had seasonally passed through Yellowstone and considered parts of it as their own; some lived there continuously. With the establishment of the park, it was no longer Indian land.

While the park was intended to preserve wildlife within its boundaries, by 1889 only 200 buffalo survived in the park, out of an estimated 1,091 surviving in North America. Upon learning of the impending extinction, Congress passed a federal law protecting buffalo in 1894. Still, in 1902 buffalo had plummeted to only 25 in Yellowstone. However, importing fresh breeding stock from two sources (one of them a Native American source) served to rebuild the Yellowstone herd and they eventually were thriving in the Park (Nabakov and Loendorf 2004: 115).

There was hardly any park relationship with the surrounding Native populations. An occasional dance for public audiences and some selling of Native crafts was the extent of interaction. Often it takes a catalyst to transform an uneasy truce into a pitched battle, which then, in the best of situations, can often lead to fruitful conversations.

News of increasing deaths of buffalo being struck by vehicles, falling prey to hunters when they left the protection of the park, and being sent to slaughter when brucellosis struck, brought American Indians to the park to protest. In 1997, when the one thousandth animal wandering outside the park was killed, a National Day of Prayer for the Buffalo was held at three locations. One was at the northern entrance to Yellowstone, another at the Montana Capitol Building, and another in Washington, D.C. (Nabokov and Loendorf 2004: 125).

The buffalo crisis appeared to turn the tide in relations between the park and area Natives. Park management began working with area tribes to develop a bison management plan, and also began informing area tribes about archaeological projects. An arrangement was developed to allow affiliated tribes to enter the park for traditional purposes without paying the recreation fee. Twice-a-year consultation meetings with twenty-five area tribes has been enacted by park authorities, and the service cooperated with the Confederated Salish and Kootenai in producing a film about pre-1870 Salish presence in the park lands (Nabokov and Loendorf 2004: 302).

The painful truth, however, is that the Native relationship regarding access to and use of Yellowstone, and other such sites, can never be fully restored, it can only be mended.

PIPESTONE NATIONAL MONUMENT

Pipestone National Monument, Minnesota, a site heavy with a reddish-hued stone often used for making ceremonial pipes, was established in 1937 with the mandate to continue to allow quarrying by Native Americans in the traditional manner. The stone has long been regarded as sacred material by American Indians of the area. Oral traditions explain that the blood-red stone represents the blood of ancestors. The information provided here has been taken from the administrative history of Pipestone and can be found on the NPS Web site at www.nps.gov/pipe/adhi/adhi6 .htm (Pipestone National Monument 2004).

The Park Service regarded the continuation of quarrying as a valuable interpretive opportunity. Limited to Native quarriers obtaining permits and using hand tools, the expected impact on the resource appeared minimal. But, determining which American Indians should be allowed to quarry soon became an issue. American Indians residing in the immediate area seemingly came to regard the stone as a commodity, while descendants of earlier Sioux residents who had migrated west to the Great Plains regard the stone as sacred material.

In the past century, local Ojibwe natives quarried and carved in an effort to either make a living or to supplement meager incomes. But during the off-season when few tourists were around, they found it necessary to sell underpriced carvings to non-Native merchants in the area, who later raised the prices as the season returned. The quarrying by American Indians was unduly benefiting non-Native merchants.

The Pipestone Indian Shrine Association (PISA) was formed in the 1950s to develop a sales counter at the park's visitor center in an effort to counter the advantage area merchants had realized and to aid area Native craftspeople. By 1989, the entire PISA staff was Native. The park enjoyed the support of non-Native volunteers as well as the coming and going of Native stone carvers.

In the early years of the park, non-Native supporters developed a pageant, *The Song of Hiawatha*, based on Henry Wadsworth Longfellow's romantic epic poem, written in 1855. The pageant became a traditional summer offering (pageants appeared in other parks and in various communities across the continent). As time passed, the stereotypical dialogue became a discomfiting sound to sensitive ears. In 1970, American Indian Movement protestors visited a show and disrupted it by shouting and stamping their feet. However, the pageant continues since it represents a strong tie to the local community and is not viewed as mean-spirited, but simply as anachronistic. It will possibly fade away as public interest wanes.

The AIM activists, during their 1970 visit to Pipestone, conducted an assessment of the operations of the monument and were surprised to find there was strong American Indian participation in park activities. Even so, exhibition narratives were found to be outdated, emphasizing Anglo-American explorers and using past tense to refer to American Indians of the area. Changes were needed, but the national site was at least on good terms with local Native populations, mostly due to the enduring quarrying relationship.

At one point, some visiting American Indians expressed concern about the display of pipes in the visitor center; some were especially upset that many displayed pipes were connected to their stems (when not in use, pipes should be disengaged, or unconnected, since engagement is a status reserved for spiritual practice alone).

Conflict about which American Indians should be using the quarry continues. NPS determined to allow all card-carrying Native Americans access, but some interested parties felt only local Minnesota American Indians should be there, while others believed the Yankton Sioux, last official owners of the quarry, should be the only Natives to have access.

Another issue for some was whether pipes, considered inherently sacred by some American Indians, should be among the carvings offered for sale. In 1986, the National Congress of American Indians (NCAI) passed a resolution calling for the prohibition of the sale of objects and pipes made of pipestone. They held that treating pipestone as a commodity instead of religious material was sacrilegious. Adelbert Zephier, a former cultural interpreter at the monument, wrote a letter protesting sales of pipestone materials. He noted, "[W]e know people who buy pipes don't use it right."

In June 1988, about fifty American Indians from South Dakota began a march to Pipestone to protest sales of pipestone materials. The local Native community viewed the marchers as interlopers. No resolution of the conflict occurred while the South Dakota visitors were in the area. In 1989, the Spiritual Run for the Sacred Pipe was held, again bringing protestors from South Dakota. That same year the NCAI asked Congress to prohibit the sale of pipestone. The Spiritual Run became an annual event and the issues continue to be debated.

BADLANDS AND THE STRONGHOLD

When a federal government entity needs land for some use such as storage or military operations, they find it easiest to look at land already under federal jurisdiction, such as Native lands held in trust. It is much simpler to transfer the land from one federal entity to another. In 1942, a bombing range was quickly located on a section of the Pine Ridge reservation, rapidly dislocating residents within ten days. The need for the bombing range passed and, in 1968, it was proposed that the same land become part of Badlands National Monument (Norrell 2004). However, the Oglala Sioux, fierce about not giving up land, resisted and held out for maintaining ownership while allowing the park to expand onto the reservation in exchange for jobs and concessions rights. Like the Black Hills, the Badlands continue to be sacred land.

In 1890, Lakota people surviving the Wounded Knee massacre fled into a Badlands area known as the Stronghold, trying to preserve their lives, as well as their right to practice the Ghost Dance. The South Dakota Home Guard pursued the fleeing families and killed seventy of the dancers, eventually throwing their frozen bodies off the top of the plateau into canyons below (Norrell 2004). According to Oyate Lakota (as the traditional practitioners are known) the site of the remains should be protected.

The area containing the Stronghold, known as the South Unit of Badlands National Park, is officially owned by the Oglala Sioux, but has been managed by the National Park Service since the 1970s. When the Park Service announced plans in 2000 to launch a three-year excavation project to remove dinosaur bones in the area of the Stronghold, Lakota protesters set up camp and reasserted their ownership of the area. Determined to protect the site where kinsman's bones reside, the protestors began to promote the idea of removing the NPS from control of the South Unit. As a result of the conflict, the dinosaur excavation was terminated (Gease 2002).

The South Unit Visitor Center is at this time managed by the Oglala Sioux Parks and Recreation Administration. New exhibitions are being planned to help relate the significance of the Badlands to Native people of the area.

Meanwhile, the Black Hills, taken from the Lakota in 1868, remains in dispute. In 1980, the Supreme Court awarded eight Sioux tribes $106 million for the stolen land (based on the 1877 value of the land plus interest). The money sits untouched, collecting more interest, in a special account because the Lakota, although enduring economic deprivation, want the land, not the money (Frommer 2001).

SAND CREEK

In Colorado, on November 29, 1864, the troops of Colonel John M. Chivington, the "Fighting Parson," positioned four howitzers on a hill overlooking a Cheyenne camp inhabited by 500 people 200 miles southeast of Denver (Anton 1995; Archaeological Institute of America 2003). Although an American flag flew over the peaceful camp, the howitzers were fired, and 163 people died. Survivors ran for their lives while others dug into the creek's sandy cliffs. Captain Silas Soule refused to let his men join the attack, saying he had been horrified at seeing children beg for their lives while soldiers beat them to death (Anton 1995).

Denver city authorities declared the day Chivington returned to be a holiday. In the Opera House, the scalps of 100 Native people, including those of children, were strung across the stage while the crowd rose with a standing ovation (Anton 1995). Chivington, and his role in the Sand Creek Massacre, was investigated three times, and court-martial was attempted, but Chivington resigned, exempting him from further prosecution. A treaty with the Cheyenne was enacted, promising them compensation for their losses, but was never fulfilled. Historians note that the Sand Creek massacre sparked twelve years of warfare, culminating in the Battle of the Little Big Horn (Archaeological Institute of America 2003).

In the 1960s, anti-Indian sentiment crushed an attempt to make a section of Sand Creek a National Monument (Anton 1995). By the 1990s, finding no evidence of the massacre on a site thought to be where the onslaught occurred, people realized no one knew exactly where the event had happened. In 1998, President Bill Clinton signed the Sand Creek Massacre Site Study Act, sponsored by Senator Ben Nighthorse Campbell, a bill designed to determine exactly where the massacre site had been. Finding a fragment of a howitzer shell, the original site was finally pinpointed (Archaeological Institute of America 2003).

In November of 2000 land consisting of 12,480 acres in Kiowa County, Colorado, was ordained the Sand Creek Massacre National Historic Site, but the designated land remained in private hands. In 2002, the offering of 1,465 acres was made available by a potential donor/dealmaker to possibly join 920 acres already obtained for the site's use. Little development of the site has occurred, but planning is underway. In 2002, a plaque was dedicated at the Colorado state capital to honor the victims of the Sand Creek Massacre. The placing of the plaque was a giant step in improved relations between Native people and non-Native people in Colorado (Archaeological Institute of America 2003).

BEAR BUTTE

Bear Butte, a 4,422-foot landmark in South Dakota, is managed by the state's Division of Parks and Recreation. New Age spiritualists began using the site for ceremonies, offending Cheyenne River Sioux, Cheyenne, and Arapaho, who liken the incursion as tantamount to someone going into a Christian church and holding mock ceremonies and leaving behind false idols. The Butte has been a traditional vision quest site for Northern Plains tribes for centuries. Local Native Americans held a rally of 200 protesters during summer solstice in 1994, and carried their demands for limiting New Age use of Bear Butte to the park manager. The park has since increased its efforts toward educating visitors about the importance of Bear Butte to Native practitioners in hopes that respectful New Age visitors will limit their use of the site (Young 1994).

"This is a problem that's happening to Indian people all over the country," noted John LaVelle (Santee Sioux), working for SPIRIT (Support and Protection of Indian Religions and Indigenous Traditions), located in San

Francisco (Young 1994). The ongoing battle continues to frustrate traditional Native Americans whose only recourse is to protest and keep the issues alive.

In the case of Bear Butte, disturbances occur beyond the borders of the
property. In August of 2006, hundreds of Native Americans showed up to
protest at the 68th Annual Sturgis Motorcycle Rally, asking cyclists to
avoid use of Highway 79, which goes past Bear Butte. Protesters have
been fighting the application for a liquor license for a bar adjacent to the
Butte. They are seeking a five-mile buffer zone around the mountain so
that the peaceful nature of the butte will not be disturbed and so prayers
can be conducted without disturbance (Black Hills Pioneer 2006).

Not only have parks and historic sites often denied Native people access to significant cultural sites that had been theirs for millennia, but
other federal properties and agencies have also excluded American Indian religious practitioners. Native Americans have had to pressure many
visitor centers at sites to improve their interpretations and to include
American Indians in decision-making activities. While some laws have
served to restore some rights, there are still many ongoing struggles in the
effort to assure continuation of Native ceremonies and practices integral
to particular land sites, and to ensure that Native sensibilities are not forgotten in the management of sites relevant to American Indians.

11

Transforming Museums

Many Native museum-like facilities refuse to use the word museum in the name of their facility, and often their museum-like centers operate differently than museums have typically done. Native communities often develop people's centers, history centers, friendship centers, or cultural centers, and sometimes these places are like museums, or have within their complex a museum, or something like a museum. Some communities use words from their own language to identify their exhibition facilities. This refusal to use a word that visitors would readily understand represents a subtle protest, an act caused by aversion, directed at the institution known as museum.

There are more than two hundred Native museum-like institutions in North America (Cooper and Sandoval 2006). The reported numbers of such institutions can vary depending on one's definition of Native American museum, which could include any museum having a Native collections and exhibitions, or could, if tightly defined, include only those that are Native-managed. The term *tribal museum* signifies Native ownership, but some Native nations prefer to avoid the term tribal, believing that non-Indians perceive the word to imply a simple society (but that's only because most non-Indians don't know the complexities of tribal societies).

While most Native-managed museums do pattern themselves after mainstream museums, a significant group of them, in one way or another, resist such a template. In such cases, these recalcitrant Native institutions' alternative practices can be seen as a form of protest against the mainstream museum model.

Figure 11.1. The Native American Center for the Living Arts, 1978–1995, was housed in an innovative structure built in the shape of a turtle and located near Niagara Falls. The building has remained empty for more than a decade since the center closed, but it is remembered for launching the careers of many artists and Native museum professionals.

Courtesy of Mike Hudson/*Niagara Falls Reporter.*

Janine Bowechop (Makah), director of the Makah Cultural and Research Center (MCRC), in Neah Bay, Washington, notes, "The way in
which tribal collections are stored, managed, and accessed may have profound significance to their host communities as agents of preservation
and support or as agents of change" (Mauger and Bowechop 2006, 63). In
other words, if a Native museum organizes its collections in the same way
that a mainstream museum does, it is possible that a ripple of change will
infect the community. Change, of course, is inevitable since Native societies are not stagnant or existing in total isolation, but Native communities are constantly engaged in a struggle to determine which parts of
change they should embrace, and which must be resisted. And, they must
constantly discern how tradition can be supported in the face of change.

The adoption of museums in Native communities lies within the con-
fusing morass of change offered to Native communities. The earliest Native museums began early in the second quarter of the twentieth century,
so it is only recently that Native museum-like centers have come to serve
as tools for Native communities. The Native communities that consider
having them must consider whether museums represent useful, or destructive, tools.

While many Native museum-like centers were developed with the
hope they would serve as economic development ventures, very few
achieve that goal. Some Native centers, however, aspire solely to save
what can be saved and to facilitate community interactions and learning.
Such centers hope to strengthen familiar social structures such as honoring elders, warriors, and spiritual leaders; educating youth in community
practices; and informing citizenry about local issues. These centers don't
aspire to become trendsetters or to be renowned throughout the world.
Some communities might expect their own center to continue the Native
understanding that every natural thing has life, which leads to the idea
that artifacts require care in a different manner than mainstream museums have provided. Some want their facility to further their community
arts and crafts, not only keeping those traditions alive, but also offering
an opportunity for citizens to make a living in traditional ways. While
some Native communities may seek to avoid creating something like a
mainstream museum, others seek to create museums that are especially
Native-like and, thus, hope to engage in changing, or indigenizing, the institution known as "museum." Either way, whether remaining insular or
hoping to transform the concept of museum, their choices represent a subtle protest of the institution known as museum.

I will explore in the next several pages two Native centers that chose
unique paths in opposition to mainstream museum styles. They are the Ak-
Chin Him-Dak Ecomuseum (an ecomuseum is a neighborhood museum
focusing on the life of the community) established in 1991 in Maricopa,

Arizona (Ak-Chin Him Dak means "our way of life") (Fuller 1992, 328–59) and the Makah Cultural and Research Center, Neah Bay, Washington, which opened in 1979. I'll also take a look at the largest Native-managed museum, the Mashantucket Pequot Museum and Research Center in Connecticut.

"Indian people will not create the types of museums that have made the untimely announcement of their demise; instead they are creating living, dynamic, community-based organisms, often modeled on the EcoMuseum concept," noted Carla Roberts, writing for *Akwe:kon Journal*, a product of Cornell University's American Indian program (Roberts 1994)

MAKAH CULTURAL AND RESEARCH CENTER

The Makah Cultural and Research Center (MCRC), was founded in 1979. Its history began in 1969 with community concerns about erosion at the remote site of the 300-year-old, landslide-covered village of Ozette (Erikson 2002, 122). Perfectly preserved for centuries, erosion was beginning to expose materials. Oxygen would begin its destructive decay, and the exposed material was becoming easy targets for pot hunters (non-trained excavators who typically shovel up items, ignoring and destroying the contextual information, and often selling what they find).

The uncovering of the buried village brought the Makah community opportunities. These were opportunities that might have been wrested from them, but instead the Makah seized them and would not let go. The tribe negotiated excavation agreements with archaeologists and demanded to participate in the excavations, to have their young people and elders involved in the project of discovery. They also insisted that the collection would be theirs, not the property of a university or museum remote from their village. They became determined to build whatever sort of facility might be deemed necessary for the collection and for ensuing exhibits (Erikson 2002, 124–25).

The local school developed class work concerning the ongoing excavation. Dialogues between students and elders increased, and the Washington University archaeology students began to be steeped in ethnology as well as archaeology. The excavation jarred older people's memories about cultural practices they had not discussed since childhood (Erikson 2002, 125–29). The excavation continued for eleven years (Erikson 2002, 140) during which time the Makah planned their exhibition center.

The retrieved materials represent a fantastic collection of ordinary Makah life captured like a snapshot, a moment frozen in time. Household items along with treasured materials were all sealed tightly in mud, which had prevented oxygen from deteriorating the organic materials (Erikson 2002, 21).

In 1979, the Makah Cultural and Research Center opened, displaying the best of the trove of materials from Ozette. A replicated house, complete with salmon smells, and murals abetted by ocean and gull sounds augment the collections to help tell the story of Makah life as it used to be, and as it is still honored. In 1993, the center completed its curatorial facility and received the remainder of the Ozette collection into the storehouse sitting behind the exhibitions facility.

The materials found at Ozette had been made and used in a time period which followed social traditions that separated men's work materials from women's work materials, and which stipulated that men and women not touch, and consequently contaminate with opposite powers, each other's materials. Clan divisions of property were also important. Makah sanctions would determine the groupings of materials in the collections facility, meaning certain materials would have to be together, while some materials would not be near other materials. The very practice of organizing the collections began to reinforce cultural knowledge and practice (Erikson 2002, 182–84).

Instead of organizing the collections by the typologies museums would typically use, MCRC staff members decided to organize the collections by Makah cognitive categories. In some cases Makah language roots would determine affinities. Since the Ozette people had never spoken English, using the Makah language to identify items in the collection seemed most appropriate. By doing so, the MCRC staff began to see what importance earlier Makah people placed on the uses of some objects versus methods of manufacture or the raw materials comprising the objects (Erikson 2002, 182–85; Mauger and Bowechop 2006, 57–63).

The MCRC maintains the community's confidence and is viewed as the appropriate voice of the community. During the 1999 whale hunt, conducted by the Makah tribe as a revival of their ancestral practices, the small, isolated community of Neah Bay was inundated by animal rights activists and environmental protectionists. The museum was selected by tribal authorities to serve as the authoritative voice of the community, handling press conferences and journalists' queries (Erikson 2002, 205–9). It makes sense that a Native museum like the MCRC, practiced in interpreting cultural life, would be most likely to smoothly handle probing questions about a community's practices, beliefs, and habits. It is hard to imagine a non-Native community's officials selecting the town museum to serve as the official voice during a crisis.

Author Patricia Erikson, in her ethnography of the Makah Cultural and Research Center titled *Voices of a Thousand People* (2002), extensively explores the concept of indigenization of museums, and maintains that the MCRC represents a Native culture re-inventing museum processes. Janine Bowechop, director of the MCRC and one of the youngsters involved in the excavation of Ozette, later educated at Dartmouth, writes (with coauthor Jeffrey Mauger) of her experience in indigenizing collections management for the MCRC in the book *Living Homes for Cultural Expression* (Cooper and Sandoval 2006).

AK-CHIN HIM DAK ECOMUSEUM

While undertaking archaeological work in the 1970s in the Maricopa area in preparation to installing irrigation canals, 700 boxes of cultural material providing evidence of 15,000 years of continued occupation were taken by the federal government. The Ak-Chin people asked for the return of the material, but only the human remains were offered to them since, at that time, the federal authorities insisted on suitable storage for artifacts (Simpson 2001, 159).

In 1986, a room in the Ak-Chin community center began to serve as a temporary museum. Carol Antone and Eloise Pedro began learning about museum practices and installed an exhibit demonstrating the changing landscapes of the reservation and informing residents about the statewide system for delivering water, a critical situation for the reservation's future. The two women observed that residents enjoyed the interactive portions of the exhibits. To learn more about what the community would like, they interviewed families about their expectations for a museum (Fuller 1992, 346–47).

A planning grant was obtained from the Administration for Native Americans and advisors were sought to help the tribe establish a facility. Among the advisors was Nancy Fuller of the Smithsonian Institution, whose work with the International Council of Museums led her to suggest the French-Canadian concept of ecomuseum (a grassroots, community-based concept first occurring in 1982) as a model that might suit the Arizona tribe. In their search to find what suited the Ak-Chin Indian Community, more than thirty residents participated in field trips to more than a hundred facilities, including archives, historical societies, and museums of all sizes (Fuller 1992, 349).

In 1989, selected Ak-Chin Him Dak staff members began a museum certificate program at Central Arizona College. At times, a specially developed class was open to other members of the community, strengthening bonds and community readiness. Many classes were held at the local community center to accommodate the students. Other classes involved field trip experiences and internships. Meanwhile, the local museum project board was developing plans for the facility and settled on an 8,000-square-foot building to be located deep within the confines of the community (Fuller 1992, 353–57).

Groundbreaking occurred in November 1990. During the process of development it was decided that the museum should foster community growth and development by discerning and exhibiting shared community motivations. The work accomplished by the Ak-Chin Indian Community replaced typical museum hierarchical patterns of decision making with new community processes (Fuller 1992, 359).

Exhibits at Ak-Chin Him Dak are self-produced (no exhibition consultants with contracted fabrications are required) and focus on community people and the life of the community. Such a facility is more easily sustainable for any resource-limited community than the model of today's modern museum with big-show emphasis. Although tourists are welcome at Ak-Chin Him Dak if they make the journey, they are not the targeted audience of the museum. Community member Elaine Peters has served as the director since its earliest days.

The MCRC and the Ak-Chin Him Dak Ecomuseum are both unique examples of Native museums engaged in the process of indigenization. Although both centers seemingly operate on a small community scale, both have been written about extensively in museum publications and both museum directors have been active participants in presentations at national and regional museum conferences.

MASHANTUCKET PEQUOT MUSEUM AND RESEARCH CENTER

One of the largest Native museums, the Mashantucket Pequot Museum and Research Center in Mashantucket, Connecticut, opened in 1998 and is a 300,000-square-foot facility. During the more than twenty years that I lived in Connecticut (1967 to 1989), I watched the struggles of the Pequot after the last residents of the Mashantucket reservation died. If the reservation had been deemed abandoned, it would have been vulnerable to confiscation by the state, so descendants of the previous residents moved into a drafty old trailer and embarked on seemingly futile attempts to establish an economic base in hopes of drawing more Pequot members home. They tried projects like maple sugaring, hog-raising, and greenhouse lettuce production.

While textbooks, dictionaries, and encyclopedias had as recently as the 1970s defined the Pequot as an extinct tribe, and museums in the state had failed to inform Connecticut citizens about Pequot history or about the tribe's contemporary presence, it became the dream of tribal members to build their own museum. "The museum was always something that the tribe wanted to establish," according to Theresa Hayward Bell, the founding director of the museum (Maxwell 2005).

Without a likelihood of succeeding in a fund-raising effort, the small tribe knew it had to find its way to wealth and independence. They needed federal recognition as an existing tribe and they needed enterprises to guarantee jobs on the reservation to tribal members. During the lengthy process of making application for federal recognition, the Mashantucket Pequot lined up foreign investors (U.S. investors are reluctant to invest in tribal properties because reservation land has been uniquely protected from seizure). The Mashantucket Pequot Tribe prepared to launch a casino and resort at the first opportunity. The subsequent success of their venture allowed the development of their large and modern museum.

The Pequot Massacre of 1637 had been an especially traumatic and defining event for Pequot people, and it continues to resonate in the memories of the survivor's descendants. To tell the story, the Pequot Museum developed a film about the attack on a sleeping Pequot village. While finally able to tell the tragic side of their history, the Pequot community also wanted to tell about their ancestor's lives. With cool air wafting over them, visitors ride an escalator along a glacial wall, representing the last ice age when Native people first moved into what is now southern New England. A room-filling hunting diorama, ringed by artifact cases on the outer walls, tells of early life. Inside one large gallery, a recreated village with mannequin residents can be toured with handheld recorders telling of life just before contact with Europeans. Historical events and recent times are detailed in continuing galleries. An array of public programs, entertainments, lectures, and workshops are available, too. A handsome seasonal calendar and a membership newsletter are produced and distributed. Poor just a generation ago, the Pequot had long dreamed of righting the wrongs done to their ancestors. They have done so with a vengeance, albeit a warmhearted one.

As the Pequot people began developing their museum, some seasoned museum professionals scoffed at the idea that the tribe could succeed. After all, the detractors thought, the tribe had no collections, nothing left of their nearly annihilated culture.

"Most people think that museums are about artifacts," Bell noted. "There's more to being native and understanding native people than an artifact. It's what's in your heart, the way you were raised. It's what you're about" (Stoll 1998). Archaeological work was welcomed on the reservation and resulting artifacts created a basic collection. With newfound wealth, the Pequot tribe acquired some artifacts, received others as gifts, and replicated whatever was missing. They challenged the idea that a wealth of artifacts must be the foundation of a museum. The museum represents the Pequot intention to tell the world the Pequot story, to honor their ancestors, and to protest, intellectually, past mistreatments.

NATIONAL MUSEUM OF THE AMERICAN INDIAN

One early effort to reach a national audience through a museum-like center was undertaken in Niagara Falls. The Native American Center for the Living Arts, expecting to draw a large sustaining audience, perhaps an international one, on the American side of the honeymoon capital, opened in 1978 in a wonderful structure designed by Dennis Sun Rhodes. The two-story building was shaped like a turtle, with the shell providing a carapace for a huge open arena and exhibitions area, while the legs provided stairwells, and the head housed a restaurant. The exhibition center provided invaluable museum experience for a few of today's successful Native museum professionals (Richard Hill, Fred Nahwooksy, and Tim Johnson, for example). Opened as a privately funded center having tapped into the largesse of granting agencies of the time, it wasn't long until the center ran into financial trouble. Income expectations didn't bear out during an economic downturn. The Turtle, as the center was affectionately called, died a slow and agonizing death. At its end, staff had drifted away, the lights went out due to unpaid utility bills, and ultimately, since the facility was not on reservation lands, the IRS seized the collections in 1995 (Native bidders, at least, were able to obtain the collection). One dream sadly ended.

The idea held by American Indians in the United States of reaching a national audience with their own voices as primary speakers in museum exhibits never died. As one such museum passed on, another took on an excited reality following legislation establishing the National Museum of the American Indian (NMAI) in 1989, as part of the Smithsonian family of museums. By the time NMAI was coming into being, there was quite a number of seasoned Native museum professionals to help guide the development of the new national museum.

NMAI traces its beginnings to 1897, when George Gustav Heye, son of a Standard Oil executive, was managing a railroad project in Arizona. He bought one of his Navajo foreman's buckskin shirts, after being intrigued that the foreman's wife undertook chewing the leather seams during the making of the shirt. With that purchase, Heye soon became an avid collector of Native materials, collecting at a time when older members of Native communities not only recalled earlier ways of life, but also still possessed a number of pieces relating to those earlier times. Still trying to adjust to a cash economy, the Native Americans Heye met provided a market of cultural riches for his interests. He collected so many items by 1916 that he eventually established the Museum of the American Indian (MAI), locating it at 155th and Broadway in a then-wealthy neighborhood of New York City. By 1922, he had also built a collections and research facility in the Bronx. The museum became one of the leading institutions of Native materials and continued with a fine reputation into modern times when it invited Native artisans to demonstrate their talents during programs and festivals. The museum instructed visiting school groups and published studies. Heye died in 1957, but the museum continued (Force 1999, 9–18).

One of the museum's major bumps in the road occurred in 1975 when its director Dr. Frederick J. Dockstader and the board were investigated regarding the museum's financial and de-accessioning practices. Ultimately, Dockstader was dismissed, and the New York State Attorney General demanded an inventory of the collections. Meanwhile, a new board was formed, which included, for the first time, Native members. George H. J. Abrams (Seneca) and Vine Deloria Jr. (Dakota) took the first American Indian seats on the board in 1977. Native Americans N. Scott Momaday (Kiowa), John C. Hunt (Cherokee), and Harold Pruner (Delaware) were added the following year, while Dr. Clara Sue Kidwell (Choctaw and Chippewa) and Dr. Robert E. Powless (Oneida) were added in 1979 (Force 1999, 466–67). The new director, Roland W. Force, undertook the inventory, and upon getting through that crisis, tackled the museum's greatest challenge, that of finding a new, larger home. Force's 1999 book, *Politics and the Museum of the American Indian: The Heye & the Mighty* describes the intricate process the MAI director and board engaged in while finding the future of the institution.

Almost a century after Heye had begun his collection, the museum had outgrown its exhibition space as well as its storage space, and was experiencing the deterioration of its once elegant neighborhood, thereby diminishing the number of visitors, and making it increasingly difficult to raise the operating money required for such a large museum. The museum board began looking for more support and a new home to properly house its premier collection of more than 800,000 pieces. Many proposals were explored, including one from H. Ross Perot (Force 1999, 266–67), but the MAI board found none exactly to its liking.

Senator Daniel K. Inouye of Hawaii and chairman of the Senate Select Committee on Indian Affairs, had just started conversations with Smithsonian leaders concerning the great number of Native human remains being held in the Smithsonian's repositories when he became aware in 1987 that MAI was searching for a better location and was considering sites outside of New York. While New York City officials were struggling to keep the MAI in New York by encouraging a merger with the American Museum of Natural History, MAI didn't favor such a merger, believing that any deal that could be forged would see the MAI collections and mission being lost within the larger institution. A struggle ensued involving the New York State Attorney General, New York City's mayor, various senators, and other influential people. Ultimately, the Smithsonian came up with an appealing deal in 1988, guaranteeing New York City that exhibitions and programs would continue in the city, if the city could provide the proper venue. The Custom House in lower Manhattan was offered up (Force 1999, 406). The deal was set.

On Capitol Hill, Senator Inouye was joined in the process of passing legislation to establish the National Museum of the American Indian with Senator Ben Nighthorse Campbell, a Northern Cheyenne silversmith from Colorado, who, of course, took great pleasure and interest in paving the way for the founding of the new museum (Force 1999, 441).

From the beginning, American Indians hoped that the new National Museum of the American Indian would have Native leadership, Native voice, and Native sensibilities, things that would not have seemed possible in a Smithsonian museum just a decade earlier. American Indians yearned to bring their stories to a national audience, to embrace the nation and be embraced by it. The impending development of the NMAI made such a goal tangible, albeit the museum's development would be within the confines of the Smithsonian Institution system, encumbered with federal regulations, and primarily dependent on various sources of non-Native money (although more than $30 million was ultimately donated from Native sources during the fund-raising drive to support the establishment of the museum) (Trescott 2004).

The 1989 legislation establishing NMAI decreed that more than half of its trustees be Native American (Jacknis 2006, 534). W. Richard West Jr., a Capitol Hill lawyer and son of a successful Southern Cheyenne artist, was named director, and was partnered with Smithsonian workhorse Douglas Evelyn, formerly of the National Museum of American History, who was picked to serve as NMAI's deputy director. Together they built a highly competent team of talented staff members comprised of a mix of Native and non-Native professionals, and they husbanded the process of Native community participation in the workings of the museum as it was formed.

Those charged with creating the new museum devoted much time and effort to developing its policies, planning its multiple buildings and grounds treatments, along with an ambitious exhibitions program, which came to involve more than thirty Native communities from various points of the Americas. NMAI staff members and consultants traveled to various Native places and held twenty meetings with Native leaders and community representatives to discern Native expectations regarding the museum and to learn how they thought it should feel and look, and what it should do (Evelyn 2005). Native people involved on behalf of the museum in the community consultation processes of the earliest days of formation were Pablita Abeyta, Arthur Amiotte, George Horse Capture, Suzan Shown Harjo, Richard Hill, Lloyd Kiva New, Rina Swentzell, and Dave Warren (Gurian 2005, 17).

An 80-page document titled *Way of the People* was compiled to serve as a guide of how to incorporate the consultations with Native communities into the planning of the facilities, grounds, exhibitions, and programs. Never before had a large museum asked American Indians what they wanted to happen in a museum yet to be designed.

The piece of property eventually selected for the new museum lay between the U.S. Capitol and the popular National Air and Space Museum. It was touted as the last available museum space on the National Mall. Currently, windows of some staff offices, museum classrooms, and the resource center look out upon the Capitol Building, and the ironic symbolism is not missed. American Indians want to be visible to the nation's lawmakers, never to be forgotten again, and Native people also want to keep an eye on U.S. government.

To house the enormous collections, the NMAI Cultural Resources Center was constructed in Suitland, Maryland, and nearly five years was spent in transporting the collections from the old storage building in the Bronx to resettling them into their new home. The building has an especially constructed space where smudging (using sage, cedar, or tobacco smoke for blessings) can occur. The building entrance faces the East and the entry foyer is round, with much wood and stone and light.

In New York City, the spaces of the George Gustav Heye Center in the old Custom House, an incongruous Beaux Arts building, have been designed to focus primarily on Native art exhibitions, or ethnography as art, in order to appeal to the New York City museum audience.

In Washington, D.C., seeking to evoke feelings of spirituality through use of awe-inspiring space and natural elements such as prism-induced rainbows, sunlight, circles, natural materials, and curvilinear shapes, the building on the National Mall is monumental in Native, and natural, terms. It appears to be a multistory stone cliff, surrounded on one side by water, on another by Native horticulture, on yet another side by a marsh with a forest springing forth on the perimeters of the property.

With director W. Richard West Jr. and Senator Ben Nighthorse Campbell, both in full Cheyenne regalia (West is Southern Cheyenne while Campbell is Northern Cheyenne), and with possibly 30,000 American Indians from throughout the hemisphere in attendance (and requiring three hours for all to march in a processional from near the Washington Monument eastward to the museum grounds), the museum's opening day on September 21, 2004 clearly demonstrated that the museum represented more than just a museum to Native constituents. Native people had come from all quarters of the Native world, some staying with friends in the area, others in hotels, and others in campgrounds. To accommodate the flood of people, the museum stayed open around the clock. I came to work at the museum in 2003, just in time to be included in some of the planning of events celebrating the museum opening.

As one visitor noted, "The outcome is a place in which Native peoples can feel safe," referring to an absence of exhibits offensive to American Indians (Smith 2005). Many of the attendees felt enormously empowered and valued, believing that now, in their national museum, their cultures will receive the respect and admiration, and the involvement of their people in future projects, which is often missing from their experiences with other American institutions.

"It was experienced Indian activism that led to the establishment of the new museum, and the activists had an idea or two about content, about approach and about ultimate purposes" noted a writer logged in as Accomac on September 22, 2004 on a forum site managed by the Brothertown Indian Nation.

The writer continued, "People of established reputations as scholars and cultural interpreters, such as Suzan Shown Harjo, W. Richard West Jr., Drs. Dave Warren, Charlotte Heth, Vine Deloria Jr., among many others, had challenged the disrespect and disdain shown by museums and science in general to Native human remains, as well as to Native cultural and religious objects." (Accomac 2004).

Certainly, for many Native Americans, NMAI's opening served as a protest directed at past museum injustices perpetrated upon Native Americans. Indeed, the vital voices of the museum's Native staff members, Native board members, Native consultants, and those from Native communities had pushed, and continue to push, for the museum to be different, to not conform to existing museum models.

Every step in planning the multipronged museum involved paying heed to Native sensibilities, leading to the new buildings expressing Native preferences, and exhibitions that are heavy with Native voices. Through Native consultation, the buildings and exhibitions were created in a way that seemingly stumped many of the practiced museum reviewers who were able to get an early peek before opening day. Many of the reviewers, non-Indians in the case of major publications, hardly knew what to make of an indigenized museum.

"Almost all the exhibits have been designed by Native peoples themselves, with a minimum of curatorial oversight, and it shows," noted one wire service writer (Adams 2004). Reviewers from many major newspapers found fault with the museum's premiere exhibits. However, writings in the Native press generally lauded the museum's new approach to museum work and found the exhibits pleasing. Is there a cultural divide when it comes to museum exhibitions? It would seem so. American Indians view their stories, histories, and material culture differently than non-Indians choose to see the information. While the process of turning a message into an exhibit may be relatively new to some Native communities, most of them have definite ideas about what they want those messages to be. The biggest Native complaint regarding the NMAI exhibits usually centered on the fact that one's particular tribe's time had not yet come to be presented in the museum's exhibits (sections of the major exhibits will be rotated, offering the opportunity for great numbers of tribes to be represented in some section of the exhibits at some future point in time).

Director W. Richard West Jr. noted in an interview in 1992, "For too long, we've been outside of the process, voiceless in the business of telling our own story" (Dorris 1992). Under his leadership, the museum has given Native voices a forum by employing community-curated processes.

Some detractors contend the forum is a constrained one, shaped by NMAI exhibit handlers (who were mostly non-Native during the production of the opening exhibits) and by West's contention that only five percent of the Native story involves war, disease, and exile, and thus, such controversial topics merit the briefest of attention in the museum's exhibits. Amy Lonetree (Ho-Chunk), writing in an *American Indian Quarterly* special issue devoted to the National Museum of the American Indian, writes, "[E]ven though the last five hundred years may be only a short period of time, it has had a disproportionate impact." She notes that if the museum were seeking to equitably address sections of time from the past, one could say that it had failed to devote adequate space to the tens of thousands of years prior to European arrival (Lonetree 2006, 638).

"There are certainly days when I am downright angry about the missed opportunity to truly challenge the American master narrative—a narrative that has silenced or even erased the memory of the genocidal policies of America's past and present. The museum falls short in telling the hard truths of America's treatment of Indigenous people," writes Lonetree (Lonetree 2006, 636–37).

The vigilant American Indian Movement, in a statement signed by Floyd Red Crow Westerman, Dennis Banks, Clyde Bellecourt, and Vernon Bellecourt, and published in various newspapers on September 27, 2004, registered their disappointment regarding NMAI's exhibits. "The museum falls short in that it does not characterize or does not display the sordid and tragic history of America's holocaust against the Native Nations and peoples of the Americas," they contended (Rave 2004).

No museum has ever been praised by everyone. As the first large-scale museum, largely by and for Native people, NMAI proves to be a landmark in the relationship between American Indians and museums, and serves as a validation that American Indian efforts in the museum world (whether as protestors or as consultants or as employees) have moved their various agendas forward. While not pleasing everyone, the museum has greatly advanced Native hopes and desires regarding change in museums.

Ira Jacknis sums it up in his piece in the *American Indian Quarterly*, "In some ways, one may view the NMAI as a kind of national tribal museum" (Jacknis 2006: 534). And *Washington Post* writer Jacqueline Trescott noted in a newspaper piece heralding the approaching opening of the museum, "Its planners have created what they call a 'museum different' that might make it very hard for museums on the drawing board ever again to tell a story about people from a detached, third-person point of view" (Trescott 2004).

As a "museum different" or a "national tribal museum," NMAI represents a gigantic, and successful, protest directed at the previously established museum culture and its supportive contingents (from mainstream exhibition reviewers, powerful museum associations, and museum anthropologists to the leaders and exhibit and program producers of museums, large and small, in North America).

The following final chapter sums up all the protests and their outcomes, providing an impressive array of Native-induced steps toward progress in American Indian and museum relationships.

Conclusion

Achievements Gained by Protests

A protestor may or may not realize the success of his or her own individual achievement, but rarely does a protestor know how the effort serves as part of a bigger picture. Each protestor is like one of the many instruments in a large orchestra. The culmination of decades of protests creates a symphony of triumph. The protests that readers encounter within these pages are part of a groundswell of change that has occurred, and is assuredly still sweeping across the land, and affecting the minds of museum leaders to come. Let us recap and tally some of the directly attributable outcomes of the various American Indian protests against the damaging policies and practices of museums and parks.

Protestors in Calgary, Alberta, Canada, obtained support from a variety of museums throughout the world in the form of some museums declining to loan objects to the exhibition, *The Spirit Sings*. Further, the protest led to a major symposium, the formation of an active task force, the publishing of a report, and a study on Native artists' relationship to exhibitions along with the published report of that study. Museum seminars still hear discourse about the aftermath, outcomes, and products of the protests regarding *The Spirit Sings*.

Protestors in Lewiston, Illinois, succeeded in getting an exposed gravesite covered and removed from exhibition. Tribal representatives protesting the display of sacred objects succeeded in getting many items, including medicine masks and Zuni War Gods, removed from exhibition. The Nevada State Museum abandoned plans for an exhibit about Spirit Cave Man after Native people in Nevada lodged complaints; instead the museum engaged in a collaborative exhibit about Nevada's Native people.

171

A lone artist challenged the Philbrook Art Center and succeeded in causing that museum, and consequently other museums, to be less confining of the contemporary arts of American Indian artists. The center broadened the categories of art acceptable in its annual show and, no doubt, other art museums paid heed. Additionally, the Association of Art Museum Directors in the United States released guidelines in 2006 regarding treatment of sacred objects and asked its members to take special consideration when dealing with sacred materials (Eakin 2006).

Cultural items important to tribal functions and human remains have been, and are being, returned to American Indian communities, especially in the aftermath of the passage of national repatriation laws in the United States, which came about due to American Indian protests and pressure on lawmakers.

Museums are listening to American Indians and are hiring and training Native museum personnel. A national monument's name was changed and the stories of national icons offensive to American Indians are being more effectively arbitrated in museum settings. Parklands are finding ways to restore access to sacred sites by Native ceremonial practitioners, and are increasingly protecting historical sites valued by American Indians.

When viewed collectively, the protests can be seen as part of a movement seeking autonomy, self-definition, respect, dignity, human rights, and protection of religious freedom—all necessary ingredients for a people's cultural continuation. The protests were against paternalism, hegemony, ignorance, callousness, appropriation of another people's material culture and human remains, and disregard for laws regarding American Indian rights.

One has only to surmise the underlying meaning of the actions of the museums and related institutions to realize what sparked the protests. What was the meaning of the Glenbow Museum's acceptance of Shell Canada as a benefactor for *The Spirit Sings*? What was the meaning of Philbrook Art Center's allowing only its defined style of art in a nationally celebrated annual Indian invitational art show? What do museums mean when they exhibit things that are sacred, private, or displayed in a manner offensive to Native Americans? What did it mean when the viewing of bones of American Indians was a common experience in museum displays and when museum ownership of Native remains was commonplace? What did it mean to have a national monument named after a man revered because he attacked and killed American Indian men, women, and children and who died in the midst of effecting another attack? What did it mean for a museum to portray the explorations of Christopher Columbus without exploring the horrors he brought to Native people of the Americas?

The meaning of these events, when viewed together and interpreted by American Indians, is seen as institutional disregard for American Indian people and their cultural practices. The protests in museums and parks, each focusing on specific issues, when combined with the more general protests of American Indians concerning economic and empowerment issues, and linked with protests by other minorities and women, can then be seen as part of a unified attack on the paternalistic contempt for others which mainstream institutions had long practiced, and which must still be guarded against. While each protest achieved particular goals, together as a group, they achieved successes that had tremendous effects and which are multiplying and growing tentacle-like into various recesses of American institutions.

In addition to the directly attributable results of the protests, there are also results that are either indirectly related, or partly attributable, to the protests. For instance, in 1990, W. Richard West Jr. (Cheyenne) became the first American Indian director of a Smithsonian museum, the new National Museum of the American Indian. In 1999, he became the first American Indian chairman of the board of the American Association of Museums, which has a membership of 3,000 institutions and 15,000 individual members. In 2006, West was designated as one of 100 U.S. museum champions of the past 100 years (American Association of Museums 2006). There is an increase in the number of American Indians appointed to high museum positions in non-Native museums. In recent years, Hartman Lomawaima (Hopi) was named director of the Arizona State Museum, while Eric Jolly (Cherokee) has been selected as president of the Science Museum of Minnesota. And the National Park Service has appointed several American Indians to head park operations.

There is an increased sensitivity found in modern exhibitions, more sensitivity in museum policies, more outreach directed to American Indians, an improved tone of writings about American Indians in museum publications, more funds and programs available to American Indian museums and museum people, and, of greatest consequence, enforced return of cultural materials and human remains. If protests had not publicized Native concerns about the actions of museum scholars and scientists and of the vast holdings within museums of Native remains and materials, repatriation laws would not have been enacted.

Symposia and sessions exploring American Indians and museums have risen in numbers. In October 2006, Arizona State University held a two-day Museums and Native American Knowledges Symposium in Tempe. The majority of the speakers were Native Americans. In September 2004, the National Museum of the American Indian held a similar event in Washington, D.C., and others have occurred across the United States and Canada.

There have been no comprehensive studies concerning the effects of American Indian protests in museums. In an effort to obtain some statistical information for this study, questionnaires were mailed to thirty-three large North American museums in 1995. The mailing resulted in eleven responses. Although the number of responding museums is small, their answers demonstrate that changes did indeed occur in the responding museums and that those changes coincide with the timing of American Indian protests. Although other factors may have contributed to change, 82 percent of the respondents admit that museums would not be as responsive to Native concerns without the occurrence of numerous protests. It is possible this percentage would have been even higher, except that 36 percent of the respondents could not recall any specific protests (with the exception of those occurring in the respondent's museums). This lack of awareness of Native protests means that many uninformed museum professionals (perhaps due to youth, coming from other fields, or general ignorance and apathy in the field itself) are creating exhibitions and policies without the benefit of knowledge about the American Indian struggles that have brought museums and Native people to the juncture where they now intersect. Indeed, during the research for this study, it was noted that many of the incidents explored here had not been mentioned in museum journals and were more likely to be explored in anthropology or American Indian studies publications. With the arrival of the National Museum of the American Indian, there has been an increase in American Indian-focused articles appearing in museum publications, but most of them, of course, are about the new museum.

The survey finds that of the replying group, only one of the museums had engaged in consultation or collaborations with Native people prior to 1960. During the 1960s, one more museum began using Native consultants and / or engaging in collaborations. During the 1970s, two more museums followed suit, and in the 1980s another five joined the others in using American Indian consultants or collaborating with Native groups.

While the use of consultants and engaging in collaborations does not demonstrate that Native voices are being accorded authority, this step serves as a natural "early stages" step in becoming more integrated. Sharing authority, or power, has been one of the most difficult hurdles for museums. Of the museums surveyed in English-speaking North America, the number of museums implementing advisory committees doubled and the number appointing Native people to governing boards more than doubled following the protest of *The Spirit Sings*. The survey results (see below) demonstrates that the general protest era of the 1960s propelled many changes, followed by greater changes in the 1970s when large-scale American Indian protests were occurring. Yet, the 1990s show the greatest growth (with only five years of that decade available for this report since the survey was conducted in 1995). When looking at the information below, remember that the numbers noted in a decade indicate when uses/appointments were initiated, and, in most cases, the appointments/uses continued through the ensuing decades. Compare the post-1959 column to the pre-1960 column in table 12.1. Each museum did not provide information in every category.

Table 12.1. Museums Involving American Indians

	Pre-1960	1960s	1970s	1980s	1990s	1960s–1990s
Board	0	1	2	0	4	7
Staff	2	2	2	1	2	7
Advisory Group	0	0	2	2	4	8
Consulting/ Collaborating	1	1	2	5	0	8
Totals	3	4	8	8	10	30

Although the survey results cannot conclude with any certainty that any particular protest, or even all the protests together, caused museums to add Native staff members or to make American Indian board appointments, the increase in such actions do indeed coincide with the time periods following protest events.

Gerald T. Conaty, senior ethnologist of the Glenbow Museum wrote when he was curator of the Native Peoples Gallery at the Saskatchewan Museum of Natural History, "There are . . . pragmatic reasons for wanting native involvement in the gallery. First, we would like to avoid an unnecessary confrontation with the native community" (1989, 410). Many directors and curators have echoed the same sentiments. Some resent what they term as "walking on eggshells" regarding trying to appease their American Indian constituents. American Indian ancestors, on the other hand, spent more than a century walking on eggshells in the shadows of museums. Once all the issues are clarified and addressed, perhaps the eggshell analogy can fade away.

The Buffalo and Erie County Historical Society had offended area Iroquois with exhibitions of human remains, false faces, and other offenses. However, by developing and working with an advisory committee, "stereotypes of both museums and Indians have dissolved," reported Richard Hill, Tuscarora museologist (1977, 44). His statement reflects the notion that learning is a two-way street. The advent of advisory committees offers museums an avenue for not only learning, but also provides the opportunity to educate a segment of the public (in this case, American Indians) about the value of the museum to that community and to the world at large. In addition, collaborations prove to incite new creativity as well as obtain greater depth and accuracy. For example, the exhibition *A Tribute to Survival* at the Milwaukee Public Museum opened in 1993 with the help of the area's Native community. The exhibition utilizes life casts of real people to create a contemporary powwow scene that mechanically rotates before gathered viewers (Uebelherr 1993, 16D). It has caused an unprecedented number of Native people to visit the museum and has been cited for the realism it has brought to all viewers.

Increasingly, museums across the country are reporting greater contact with area Natives. The Old Capitol Museum, Jackson, Mississippi, reported in August 1995 that it was working with members of the Tunica-Biloxi, Choctaw, and Chickasaw tribes during planning for their new permanent exhibition (Southeast Museum Conference 1995, 12). The Peabody Museum of Archaeology and Ethnology in Cambridge, Massachusetts, utilized Native people as curators for its most recent exhibitions including *The Children of Changing Woman*, curated by Native American Ernestine Cody Begay in 1995. The numbers of consultations with American Indians are so many that they cannot be noted and described here. Effectively, any museums doing anything of consequence regarding American Indians are presently consulting with Native authorities.

Working with American Indian advisors has caused some museums to question their collecting (and collections care) habits regarding other cultures. The Field Museum, which began collaborations with American Indians as early as 1975, has increased its relationship with American Indians by adding a Native staff member in 1990 and a Native board member in 1993. In 1990, it began asking Native advisors to review exhibitions and collections and has promised to address the problem areas reported by these advisors. During this process, the museum entertained discussions about whether their collections and exhibitions should contain mummies from Egypt, shrunken heads from South America, a Neanderthal skull piece, or tools from China made of human bones (Haas 1990, 17). These questions, and other questions regarding text and cultural patrimony, have needed to be asked for some time.

James D. Nason (Comanche), curator of New World ethnology at the Thomas Burke Memorial Washington State Museum in Seattle, reports that the Burke Museum began changing its method of operation in the early 1970s when it began to recognize "mutual responsibilities that exist and should exist between curators and specialists within Native American communities." He states that "change in . . . traditional museological culture came during the Native American social and political activism of the 1960s" (1994, 57).

Perhaps a collaboration of singular importance has occurred in South Dakota. Reported as a "step toward racial reconciliation," the South Dakota State Historical Society worked with a nine-member Sioux advisory committee to create the exhibition *Oyate Tawicoh-an: The Ways of the People*, which opened in 1994 in the society's Cultural Heritage Center Museum in Pierre. The advisory committee succeeded in "offering their advice, objecting to some . . . characterizations of beliefs or objects, and helping . . . locate craftspeople and other consultants," reported J. R. Fishburne, society director (American Association for State and Local History 1995, 4). "The shape, feel, texture, and direction of the exhibition benefited" from the collaboration according to Claudia J. Nicholson, curator at the museum (Nicholson 1995, 13).

As museums strive to shake loose the past mental shackles that have impeded cross-cultural progress, one method some have utilized is to invite innovative people to create new exhibitions that force museums and their audiences to look at collections in new ways. In 1986, the Museum of Man in San Diego invited Luiseno artist James Luna to create such an exhibition. His exhibition was a protest piece itself, but this time a museum had invited the protest. Luna exhibited himself in a display case with labeling that described scars and other physical details. His aim was to show the objectification of Native people and to question museum practices when exhibiting cultures. An accompanying exhibition case displayed his record collection and family photographs, while another showed his ceremonial objects. Visitors could clearly see that very little knowledge about Luna could be obtained from viewing a few of his possessions (Roberts 1994, 24), and probably realized that an opportunity to converse with Luna could be more illuminating. Other similar performance art presentations, designed to illuminate ignorance and past offenses toward indigenous people, have occurred in museums, not just in North America, but have been presented around the world.

Museums have realized their own shortcomings regarding minority issues, and some have taken innovative risks to aid themselves and their public in better understanding the issues. Fred Wilson, an African-American artist, was invited to use the collections of the Maryland Historical Society to explore minority issues. The exhibition called *Mining the Museum* opened in 1993 and immediately set the museum world on edge. In one section, Wilson selected marble busts of Thomas Jefferson and other notables and displayed them beside empty pedestals labeled with the names of historic important African-Americans, for which there were no classic busts. Finding several cigar store Indians in the collections, he placed them with their backs to viewers and facing a wall with photographs of contemporary American Indians. Throughout the exhibition, he placed familiar objects in unfamiliar positions or with telling juxtapositions, such as a Ku Klux Klan headpiece displayed in a baby carriage, with the implied message that hate is taught from birth (Corrin 1994; Maryland Historical Society 1993). Installations like those of artists Luna and Wilson challenge museums and their visitors to view life from the vantage point of others whose experiences of American history have differed from that of the more popularly distributed accounts found in textbooks, films, literature, and, yes, museums.

Glenbow Museum's senior ethnologist Gerald T. Conaty, writing in a museum journal, conjectured about future Native demands and guessed that they might include repatriation (not legislated in Canada), privileged access to gallery and collections space, employment and training opportunities, and greater voice in interpretation. Surprisingly, and pleasantly, he ended his article by saying that it is "our challenge to identify the emerging needs and wants and to adapt the Museum to meet them" (1989, 413). This represents a change in attitude from that of museum curators and directors of a half-century ago who maintained that they had the privilege of demanding others to adapt to their restrictions and demands.

There are many museum people looking forward to the challenges of welcoming more Native methodologies into the realm of museology. These changes are part of the indigenization of museums, which shouldn't alarm museum professionals. What is intended by most American Indians is not to wrest museums from their influential positions, but to integrate pertinent American Indian practices and beliefs into museums in order for Native people to see their ideologies reflected in museum policies and practices, and thus being more appropriately represented in exhibitions and collections. To know that a continent's museum visitors, which includes all forms of citizens such as writers, teachers, students, politicians, entrepreneurs, and, hopefully, Native people from all walks of life, were being appropriately informed regarding Native cultures would represent a great, and important, victory for Native people. It is a terrible pity that it took such wrenching efforts to get us to this point of entry.

Although protests are not pleasant, they have their place in the scheme of progress. Where dialogues did not exist, dialogues have been forced. Today's museum visitors are the beneficiaries of those who would not tolerate injustice in museum exhibitions and policies. However, it is important to remember that whatever the achievements of past protests, it does not follow that future protests will achieve the same, or similar, results. Each museum and situation is different; each era is different; every cause has its own resonance. If the dialogues that have been forced remain active and sane, there will be little future need for the kinds of protests that have embarrassed museums in recent decades.

However, large museums, due to their unwieldiness, are vulnerable to being targets for protests. While one department may be engaging in dialogue with American Indians, too many mid-level administrators and too many other departments will be unaware of the conversations and will not benefit from the dialogues, meaning the museum, overall, can still err and offend. One museum, lucky to have escaped the onus of public American Indian protests, has been the National Museum of Natural History (NMNH), Washington, D.C., where fifty-year-old, or older, American Indian exhibits presented some old-style thinking and fell short of informing people about the continuance (and subsequent transitions) of Native people. The *Washington Post* referred to the exhibits as "embarrassingly antiquated" (Thompson 2004). Old dioramas, a stenciled silhouette of American Indians burning a frontiersman, artifacts made of human remains, burial items, and outdated storylines told ineffective stories and outraged some Native visitors.

Although it might be easy for large museums to believe they haven't irked anyone, poor exhibits (lacking sensitivities and failing to correct people's misconceptions) do offend and are noted. Large institutions are often out of touch with small communities, and complaints from distant places don't always find their way to the appropriate museum authorities. If the complaints get delivered to the museum at all, they unfailingly don't reach the same eyes and ears in the labyrinth of offices that occur in large museums, and thus the complaints are diminished in power from failing to accumulate in large numbers upon one desk. American Indians may not always officially register their distaste of an exhibit, but they will voice their concerns and complaints to others back home, and to any Native they might know in the museum field. My ears were fed with complaints about NMNH's American Indian exhibits during the decade I worked with Native communities in an office across the National Mall from the museum, and I passed the more particular complaints along to various people at NMNH. I registered my own disappointment in the exhibits as well.

During a long, inactive period whereby many cultural exhibits at NMNH lay fallow, African Americans more effectively protested the offensive, outdated Africa hall. The museum responded by putting together an advisory group and finding the funds to close the old Africa galleries, replacing them with a large, updated and comprehensive exhibit with much contemporary information, called *African Voices* (Arnoldi, Kreamer, and Mason 2001).

Although many American Indians did not like the aging American Indian exhibits at NMNH, no public protest action was initiated or coordinated. Most of the American Indians living in the area, or who were traveling in and out of the area, were generally either working for the federal government, or appealing to federal agencies, and would therefore feel reluctant to stage a protest against a federal entity. While the Africa hall was replaced with a modern exhibit, the American Indian exhibits languished.

Dr. JoAllyn Archambault (Lakota) had been hired by the museum in 1986 to tackle the planning of a sweeping new American Indian hall, which had last received a partial upgrade in the 1950s (Jacknis 2006, 528). She developed extensive plans soon after coming to her position. However, budget cuts kept her plans at bay until exhibit space reductions due to other expanding projects in the museum ultimately rendered her original plans impossible to execute. Then, the birth of NMAI silenced her effort entirely, as Smithsonian funding directives regarding American Indian projects focused on the new museum. Her attractive plans (I viewed them) never came to fruition and she was able to enact only minor changes in the dreary exhibits by interjecting a few bright new exhibit cases.

While some of the causes for the long delay in updating the American Indian hall at NMNH can be attributed to budget concerns, there was an apparent lack of institutional will regarding the museum's failure to tackle the problems with the American Indian exhibits sooner, or more comprehensively. Museum professional Ira Jacknis wrote of the NMNH delay in exhibit hall replacement in *American Indian Quarterly*, "The reasons for this inaction are unclear, and are probably multiple." (Jacknis 2006, 528).

Ultimately, realizing the National Museum of the American Indian would be joining the Smithsonian family of museums with modern American Indian exhibits, NMNH decided to eliminate its American Indian exhibits, even though it possesses one of the world's major American Indian collections. It is hard to know whether being left out of NMNH is a good, or a bad, occurrence. On the one hand, American Indians have resented being showcased in natural history museum exhibits because such exhibits generally have not provided context for understanding contemporary Native people. On the other hand, being absent from the museum means there is a missed opportunity to inform visitors about Native people. Meanwhile, with the old exhibits finally gone, Archambault reports the museum intends to install a new American Indian exhibit, depending, of course, on the availability of funds.

Meanwhile, the Smithsonian's National Museum of the American Indian (NMAI), newly launched in 2004, will be challenged to be responsive to more than 500 tribal entities in the United States, as well as the tribes of the hemisphere, all of which hope to be represented in the museum. Additionally, American Indian artists will look to the museum to provide exhibition exposure. And, American Indian museum professionals will be applying for positions, and those who don't get them will be disappointed.

Not every Native person can have their voice heard, and the more who are heard, the more excluded those who are not heeded will feel. Still, W.

Richard West Jr., Southern Cheyenne from Oklahoma and director of NMAI, has marshaled the creation of one of the most community-inclusive and culturally responsive museums in the United States. Pragmatically, not everyone can be pleased. Can NMAI escape protests? Native expectations for the museum will be high, making the likelihood for future conflicts possible.

Richard Hill, Tuscarora museum professional, spoke about museums in general during a presentation on September 20, 2004, the eve of the official opening of the National Museum of the American Indian. He said, "[M]useums may have a stifling effect on the vitality of indigenous life because of the need to minimize the expression of the culture to fit the needs of the museum" (Gurian 2005, 20).

Indeed, it remains to be seen if any museum can ever do justice to interpreting and presenting information to a largely uninformed, generally misinformed, public. Visitors to museums are standing while reading. Consequently, they are not interested in lengthy reading material. The effectiveness of museums in teaching people remains to be fully measured and analyzed. But, it is for certain that bad information in museums can cause great damage and should never be tolerated.

There are more than 200 Native museums in North America and the number continues to grow. In some ways, the growth of tribal museums, especially those museums that reject standard museum models, can be seen as a protest against mainstream museums. The development of museums, as undertaken by most Native entities, represent precious investment of resources and great devotion of effort, comparatively exceeding that of many museums found in small towns across America, partly because American Indians often have started their museums without frameworks to guide them as they have not been afforded a feeling of fraternity with museums in neighboring communities (assuredly, some of those communities feel rebuffed by American Indians, but generally such instances are repercussions from previous injuries leading to mistrust, or are due to missteps taken when approaching Native communities).

America's museums can benefit from flourishing Native museums. From Native museums can spring new ideas about organizing museum structures and policies. Additionally, shared knowledge will enrich surrounding communities. Information provided in tribal museums will represent a wealth of thought and ideas that has long been untapped. Their museum interpretations may include their own origin stories and their history presentations will present their points of view. There will be portraits of the tribal council, community military veterans, and information about their own heroes. As Native museums undertake research, collect archives, support language preservation, obtain oral histories, develop interpretive programs, and address care of sensitive materials, they could potentially alter the face of the museum field. Fewer mainstream museums will be able to ethically sustain their old-crony exhibition teams, superficial storylines will be unacceptable, collections will need to become more accessible leading to greater knowledge about items, and curators will begin to honor Native ideas about objects as living entities.

Protests in the future will occur only when museums fail to be flexible in responding to Native priorities and views. Museums of the twenty-first century are learning to be both responsive and responsible.

The most difficult protest-prone area to fix is that regarding American Indian artists and art museums. Complaints by American Indian artists regarding lack of museum attention given to Native art echoes across the land. Without museum recognition, an artist has a harder time being financially successful. Art museums are often questioned regarding ethics. To avoid charges of favoritism of certain artists or art styles, one small museum's response has been to restrict their art shows to only deceased artists' works, but application of a policy like that would leave contemporary Native artists without venues. The art world is a rarified world beyond the usual museum milieu. There is plenty of room for protest to occur there, but such protests rarely evoke substantive change. Art is more arbitrary than history, and people prefer that it remain so. Protesting art prerogatives, therefore, is like herding cats. Art cannot be corralled. Yet, art museums should always be called to task for any limitations they create that harms American Indian art and American Indian artists.

Corralling history has also proven to be difficult, but there are certain events and facts that cannot be ignored. While interpretation can vary, some points cannot be denied. But, even as some points may be agreed upon, there will always be points of contention. As long as museums are dynamic, and as long as American Indians are dynamic, protest by American Indians in museums is a probable event. Dynamism is nothing less than exuberant energy.

While protests may be inevitable, we hope future generations will be wise. There is much to be gained through protest, but there is also much to lose. Yet, seeing how much has been gained through past protests, and knowing there are still advances to make, we can only hope that future encounters between museums and American Indians continue to be spirited.

Works Cited

Abbott, Larry. 1990. A time of vision (interview with artist Harry Fonseca). www.britebites.com/native_artist_interview. Viewed 1995.

Abrams, George H. J. 1994. The case for wampum: repatriation from the Museum of the American Indian to the Six Nations Confederacy, Brantford, Ontario, Canada. *Museums and the making of "ourselves": The role of objects in national identity*, ed. Flora E. S. Kaplan. London and New York: Leicester University Press.

Accomac. 2004. Time of the Indian. Brothertown Indian Nation forum Web page. www.network54.com/Forum. Posted September 22. Viewed February 12, 2007.

Acle, Ana. 1989. Columbus protests continue. Student jailed for climbing on exhibit ship. *Gainesville Sun*, December 12.

Adams, Jim. 2004. National Museum of the American Indian reviews: Ceremonies were nice but critics pan content. *Indian Country Today*, October 8.

Albuquerque Museum. 1990. Press release and fact sheet regarding First Encounters exhibit.

Alexander, Edward P. 1983. *Museum masters*. Nashville, TN: American Association for State and Local History.

American Association of Museums (AAM). 2006. Centennial honor roll. www .aam-us.org. Viewed March 1, 2007.

———. 1994. *Code of ethics for museums*. Washington, D.C.

———. 1978. *Museum ethics*. Washington, D.C.

———. 1988a. Task force on repatriation of Native American Ceremonial Objects and skeletal remains. Attachments to letter sent to members, August 12.

———. 1988b. Towards an AAM position on repose for and transfer of cultural property. *Aviso* (membership newsletter) (June).

American Association for State and Local History (AASLH). 1995. Faces and places. *History news* 50, no. 1 (January/February).

American Indian Museums Association. 1979. First National Conference. Transcript distributed by Center for Museum Studies, Smithsonian, Washington, D.C.

American Indian Ritual Object Repatriation Foundation. 1996. Iroquois combs and rattle returned. *News & Notes* (Spring/Summer).

Ames, Michael. 1991. Biculturalism in exhibitions. *Museum Anthropology* 15:2 (May).

———. 1988. Boycott the politics of suppression: Museums and politics: The Spirit Sings and the Lubicon boycott. *Muse* 11:3 (Fall).

Anderson, Lisa. 1996. Telephone conversation to New York State Museum, Albany, June 6.

Anderson, Tim. 2002. Museum prepares to unveil "Under One Sky." *Reno Gazette-Journal*, May 14.

Anthropolog. 2006. E-newsletter for the National Museum of Natural History, Smithsonian Institution, Washington, D.C.

Anton, Mike. 1995. The echoes of Sand Creek. Excerpts from an article in the *Rocky Mountain News*, December 3, posted at www.canku-luta.org. Viewed January 31, 2006.

Archaeological Institute of America. 2003. A sight which can never be forgotten: The Sand Creek massacre. www.archaeology.org, posted September 16, viewed January 31, 2006.

Archuleta, Margaret and Dr. Rennard Strickland. 1991. *Shared visions: Native American painters and sculptors in the twentieth century*. Phoenix: The Heard Museum.

Arnoldi, Mary Jo, Christine Mullen Kreamer, and Michael Atwood Mason. 2001. Reflections on "African Voices" at the Smithsonian's National Museum of Natural History. *African Arts* 34.

Assembly of First Nations and the Canadian Museums Association. 1992. *Task force report on museums and First Peoples*, 3rd ed. Ottawa: AFN and CMA.

Associated Press. 1991. 64 Crow Indians ready for battle. *Danbury News Times*, January 28.

———. 2005. Columbus protesters stage die-in. *The Daily Times-Call* October 9.

Association of Art Museum Directors. 2006. The Association of Art Museum Directors releases report on the stewardship and acquisition of sacred objects. Press release. New York City, August 9.

Association on American Indian Affairs, Inc. 1993–1994. The legislative history of tribal reburial programs. *Indian Affairs* (newsletter of the association) (Winter).

Atlatl. 1977. Final Report. Indian cultural coordinators meeting, Phoenix.

Baltimore Sun. 1998. University agrees to return American Indian remains, September 3.

Barber, Dan. 1996. Telephone conversation, Rochester Museum, New York, May 31.

Bartimus, Tad. 1990. At Little Bighorn, a new battle rages over Custer's last stand. *Danbury News Times*, August 5.

Berlo, Janet Catherine and Ruth B. Phillips. 1993. Vitalizing the things of the past: Museum representations of native North American art in the 1990s. *Museum anthropology* 17:3 (October).

Berlo, Janet Catherine, ed. 1992. *The early years of Native American art history: The politics of scholarship and collecting.* Seattle: University of Washington.

Bilger, Burkhard. 1995. Life after museums. *Federal Archeology* 7:3 (Fall/Winter), excerpt from May/June 1993 *Oklahoma Today* article of same name.

Black Hills Pioneer. 2006. Sacred sites are human rights. www.zwire.com/site/ news. Posted August 6. Viewed February 13, 2007.

Blair, Bowen. 1979. Indian rights: Native Americans versus American museums— a battle for artifacts. *American Indian Law Review* 7:1.

——. 1979a. American Indians vs. American museums. A matter of religious freedom. To preserve relics and destroy culture? Part one. *American Indian Journal* 5:5 (May).

Bleizeffer, Dustin. 2006. Devils Tower gets new supervisor. *Casper Star-Tribune,* May 24.

Bobbitt, Melissa. 2003. Protesters decry Columbus Day. *Daily Titan* issue 20.

Bone, James. 2003. Indians finally get recognition at Custer Battlefield. *London Times,* June 25.

Bower, Bruce. 2000. Ishi's long road home. Science news online. www.sciencenews .org/articles/20000108/bob8ref.asp. Posted January 8. Viewed February 13, 2007.

Braidwood, Robert J. and Gretel Braidwood Manasek. 1983. Archeology. *New Book of Knowledge.* Danbury, CT: Grolier.

Breen, Lise M. 1991. The Osage of Oklahoma. *Objects of myth and memory,* ed. Diana Fane, Ira Jacknis, and Lise M. Breen. New York: The Brooklyn Museum with University of Washington Press.

Brooklyn Daily Union. 1876. Shinnecock bones. New York, July 17.

Buchanan, Susy. 2006. Indian blood. *Intelligence Report* issue 124 (Winter).

Burnette, Robert and John Koster. 1974. *The road to Wounded Knee.* New York: Bantam Books.

Butler, Shelley Ruth. 1999. The politics of exhibiting culture: Legacies and possibilities. *Museum anthropology* 23, no. 3 (Winter).

Carpenter, Carole Henderson. 1981. Secret, precious things: repatriation of potlatch art. *Artmagazine* (May/June).

Carter, John. 1994. Museums and indigenous peoples of Canada. *Museums and the appropriation of culture,* ed. Susan Pearce. London: Athlone Press.

Case, Richard G. 1972. Opinions divided on collecting, displaying Indian remains. *Syracuse Herald Journal,* October 4.

Center for American Culture Studies. 1986. Museums and the American Indian: a question of artifact management. *The Dispatch* 4:2 (Spring).

Chandler, James M. 2001. *Mammoth Trumpet* (December).

Clifford, James. 1988. *The predicament of culture.* Cambridge: Harvard University Press.

——. 1991. Four Northwest Coast Museums: Travel Reflections. *Exhibiting cultures.* Washington, D.C.: Smithsonian Institution Press.

Cole, Douglas. 1985. *Captured heritage. The scramble for Northwest Coast artifacts.* Seattle: University of Washington Press.

Colorado American Indian Movement (AIM). 2005. No roads through sacred land. www.coloradoaim.org. Posted November 20. Viewed November 2006.

Conaty, Gerald T. 1989. Canada's First Nations and museums: A Saskatchewan experience. *International journal of museum management and curatorship 8*, no. 4 (December).

Condon, Catherine. 1992. Culture. Rethinking History. *Skyway News* (St. Paul,
MN), June 16.

Cooper, Karen Coody. 1998. *Tribal museum directory*. Washington, D.C.: Center for
Museum Studies, Smithsonian Institution.

—— and Nicolasa I. Sandoval. 2006. *Living homes for cultural expression*. Washington, D.C.: National Museum of the American Indian.

Corrin, Lisa G., ed. 1994. *Mining the museum: An installation by Fred Wilson*. Baltimore: The Contemporary Press.

Council on Interracial Books for Children. 1971. *Chronicles of American Indian
protest*. Greenwich, CT: Fawcett Publications, Inc.

Council for Museum Anthropology. 1970. Letter by the Committee on Anthropological Research in Museums. *Museum anthropology*. (CMA is a subcommittee of
the American Anthropological Association, Arlington, Virginia.)

Curtius, Mary. 1999. Smithsonian denies request to return brain of the last Yahi.
seattletimes.nwsource.com/html/home/index.html. Posted March 25.

Davies, Bruce. 1979. *Museums and Native American rights*. Published proceedings of
the Mountain-Plains Museum Association annual conference.

de Borhegyi, Stephan F. 1968. A new role for anthropology in natural history museums. Section papers: 63rd annual meeting. Washington, D.C.: American Association of Museums.

Deloria, Philip J. 1993. *The twentieth century and beyond, The Native Americans*. At-
lanta: Turner Publishing, Inc.

Dockstader, Frederick J., ed. 1982. *Oscar Howe. A retrospective exhibition catalogue
raisonne*. Tulsa, OK: Thomas Gilcrease Museum Association.

Dorris, Michael. 1992. His mission? An Indian museum like none other. *New York
Times*, September 13.

Doxtator, Deborah. 1988. The home of Indian culture and other stories in the museum. *Muse* (Autumn).

——. 1993. *Fluffs and feathers* (exhibit catalog). Brantford, Ontario: Woodland Cultural Centre.

——. 1994. The implications of Canadian nationalism on Aboriginal cultural autonomy. Curatorship: Indigenous perspectives in post-colonial societies: symposium papers. Victoria, British Columbia: University of Victoria.

DuPont, Ronald Jr. 1989. Heavy picketing of exhibit ends. *Gainesville Sun*, December 16.

Eakin, Hugh. 2006. Museums establish guidelines for treatment of sacred objects.
New York Times, August 10.

Echo-Hawk, Roger and Walter R. Echo-Hawk. 1994. *Battlefields and burial grounds:
The Indian struggle to protect ancestral graves in the United States*. Minneapolis:
Lerner Publications Company.

Echo-Hawk, Walter. 1979. *American Indian Museums Association conference transcript*. Washington, D.C.: Museum Studies, Smithsonian.

——. 1985. The concept of sacred materials and their place in the world. Transcript
of Plains Indian Museum's ninth annual Plains Indian seminar, September.

Erasmus, Georges. 1992. We want to turn the page: Museums and First Peoples in Canada. *Museum anthropology* 16:2 (June).

Erikson, Patricia Pierce, with Helma Ward and Kirk Wachendorf. 2002. *Voices of a thousand people*. Lincoln: University of Nebraska Press.

Evelyn, Douglas E. 2005. Launching an international institution of living cultures —the Smithsonian's National Museum of the American Indian. *History News* (Summer).

Fenton, William N. 1989. Return of eleven wampum belts to the Six Nations Iroquois Confederacy on Grand River, Canada. *Ethnohistory* 36:4 (Fall).

Ferguson, T. J. 1990. The repatriation of Ahayu:da Zuni war gods. *Museum Anthropology* 14:2 (May).

Ferguson, T. J. and Wilfred Eriacho. 1990. *Ahayu:da* Zuni War Gods: Cooperation and repatriation. *Native peoples* 4, no. 1 (Fall).

———. 1991. Return of War Gods sets example for repatriation. *Zuni History. Victories in the 1990s*. Zuni, NM: Zuni Tribe.

Ferguson, T. J., Roger Anyon, and Edmund J. Ladd. 2000. Repatriation at the Pueblo of Zuni: Diverse solution to complex problems. *Repatriation reader*, ed. Devon A. Mihesuah. Lincoln and London: University of Nebraska Press.

Fikes, Jay C. 1996. *Reuben Snake. Your humble serpent*. Santa Fe: Clear Light Publishers.

Finster, David. 1975. Museums and medicine bundles. *The Indian Historian* 8:2 (Fall).

Fisher, Jean. 1992. In search of the "inauthentic." Disturbing signs in contemporary Native American art. *Art Journal* 51, no. 3 (Fall).

Floyd, Candace. 1985. Repatriation blues. *History News* (April).

Force, Roland W. 1999. *Politics and the Museum of the American Indian: The Heye & the mighty*. Honolulu: Mechas Press.

Franke, Judith A. 1995a. A new view of the past: the renovation of Dickson Mounds. *The Living Museum* 57:1.

———. 1995b. Interview by the author via telephone, August 24.

Freshour, Jon. 1999. Electronic correspondence with chief registrar regarding Museum of New Mexico, March 25.

Friends Committee on National Legislation. 1986. Native American inheritance: Rights to lifeways, land and treaty guarantees. *FCNL Washington Newsletter* (November).

Frommer, Frederic. 2001. Black Hills are beyond price to Sioux culture: Despite economic hardship, tribe resists U.S. efforts to dissolve an 1868 treaty for $570 million. *Los Angeles Times* bulldog edition, August 19.

Fuller, Nancy. 1992. Ak-Chin Indian community ecomuseum project. *Museums and Communities: The Politics of Public Culture*. Ivan Karp, Christine M. Kreamer, and Steven D. Lavine, eds. Washington, D.C.: Smithsonian Institute Press.

Furst, Jans Jorg. 1989. Material culture research and the curation process. *Museum Studies in Material Culture*, ed. Susan M. Pearce. London and New York: Leicester University Press.

Gainesville Sun. 1990. Columbus exhibit protest (heading of photo with caption showing protestor with sign). January 2.

Gallo, Eliza. 1993. Museum director convicted. *Archaeology* (September/October).

Garfield, Donald. 1989. Chronicling the collision of the Old World and the New. *Museum News* (September/October).

———. 1993. Notes. *Museum News* (January/February).

Gease, Heidi Bell. 2002. South unit fossil dig on hold until spring. *Rapid City Journal*, September 25.

Gibson, Daniel. 1993. Hidden transactions. *ARTnews* 92:7 (September).

Gildart, Bert. 2001. History revisited at the infamous Little Bighorn. *Native Peoples* (July/August).

Gilman, Carolyn and Mary Jane Schneider. 1987. *The way to independence. Memories of a Hidatsa Indian family, 1840–1920*. St. Paul: Minnesota Historical Society Press.

Goldstein, Karin. 2006. As American as pumpkin pie. Plimoth Plantation, www.plimoth.org.

Gonyea, Ramon. 1977. *Indian artists, 1977* (exhibit catalog). Washington, D.C.: American Indian Society of Washington, D.C.

——— and Rick Hill, eds. 1981. *Regional Conference of Historical Agencies* newsletter 11:4 (April).

Gonyea, Ray W. 1993. Give me that old time religion. *History News* (March/April).

Gould, Stephen Jay. 1981. *The mismeasure of man*. New York: W. W. Norton & Co.

Grand Council of Chiefs. 1980. Policy statement on Medicine masks, reprinted in 1981 *Regional Conference of Historical Agencies* newsletter 11:4 (April).

Graves, Mary and Andrew J. de los Angeles, eds. 1980. *United Indians of All Tribes Foundation: A ten year history*. Seattle: United Nations of All Tribes Foundation. March 8.

Green, Richard G. 1988. Sacred wampum returned! *Turtle Quarterly*.

Guillory, Dan. 1990. The dilemma of Dickson Mounds. *Illinois Issues* (December).

Gulliford, Andrew. 1992. Curation and repatriation of sacred and tribal objects. *Public Historian* 14:3 (Summer).

Gurian, Elaine Heumann. 2005. Coming full circle. *The Native universe and museums in the twenty-first century*. Washington, D.C.: National Museum of the American Indian.

Guthrie, Margaret E. 1991. The return of a pious gift. *Milwaukee Journal Magazine*, June 2.

Hall, Nancy. 1987. Note from the editor. *Muse* 5:2 (summer).

Haas, Jonathan. 1990. Repatriation at the Field Museum. *Museum Anthropology* 14:3 (August).

Hammil, Jan. 1985. Statement at American Anthropological Association symposium: The protection of Native American burials: Cultural values and professional ethics in the treatment of the dead, Washington, D.C. December.

Harjo, Susan Shown. 1996. Contemporary arts. *Encyclopedia of North American Indians*, ed. Frederick E. Hoxie. New York: Houghton Mifflin.

———. 1999. Keynote address, American Indian Museum Association program, American Association for State and Local History annual meeting, Baltimore, September 29.

Harn, Alan D. 1980. *The prehistory of Dickson Mounds: The Dickson excavation*. Springfield: Illinois State Museum.

Harper, Kenn. 2000. *Give me my father's body: The life of Minik, the New York Eskimo.* South Royalton, VT: Steerforth Press.

Harrison, Julia D. 1993. Completing a circle: The spirit sings. *Anthropology: public policy and native peoples in Canada.* Noel Dyck and James B. Waldram, ed. Montreal: McGill-Queen's University Press.

Harrison, Julia. 1988a. Coordinating curator's statement: Museums and politics: The Spirit Sings and the Lubicon boycott. *Muse* 11:3 (Fall).

———. 1988b. The Spirit Sings: Artistic traditions of Canada's First Peoples. *American Indian Art Magazine* (Summer).

———. 1988c. The Spirit Sings and the future of anthropology. *Anthropology Today* 4:6 (December).

Haskell, David D. 2001. Revising history in Plymouth. United Press International release dated June 7. Posted on members.aol.com/algonkuin/press/thanksgiving .html June 8. Viewed February 15, 2007.

Hennessy, Jefferson. 1995. The Tunica triumph. *Acadiana Profile* 17, no. 1.

Henry, Jeanette. 1970. The Iroquois Wampum Controversy. *Indian Historian* 3, no. 3.

Hertzberg, Hazel Whitman. 1988. Indian rights movement, 1887–1973. *History of Indian-white relations: Handbook of North American Indians,* vol. 4.

Highwater, Jamake. 1976. *Song from the earth: American Indian painting.* Boston: New York Graphic Society.

Hill, Richard. 1977. Reclaiming cultural artifacts. *Museum News* 55, no. 5 (May/June).

———. 1980. Indians and museums: A plea for cooperation. *History News* 34:7 (July).

———. 1990. Exhibit commentary. Some observations on this exhibition from an Indian perspective. Albuquerque Museum.

———. 1995. The battle over tradition. *Indian Artist* 1:1 (Spring).

———. 1996. Reflections of a native repatriator. *Mending the circle. A Native American repatriation guide.* New York: American Indian Ritual Object Repatriation Foundation.

———. 2000. The Indian in the cabinet of curiosity. *The changing presentation of the American Indian: museums and native cultures.* Washington, D.C.: National Museum of the American Indian, with Seattle: University of Washington Press.

Hill, Tom. 1988. First Nations and museums. *Muse* 6, no. 3 (Autumn).

HistoryLink.org. 2005. Fort Lawton military police clash with Native American and other protesters in the future Discovery Park on March 8, 1970. Online encyclopedia of Washington state history, viewed July 2006.

Hoebel, E. Adamson and Karen Daniels Petersen. 1964. *A Cheyenne sketchbook by Cohoe.* Norman: University of Oklahoma Press.

Hopkins, Kenneth R. 1973. Finders keepers? *Museum News* (March).

Horse Capture, George. 1994. From the reservation to the Smithsonian via Alcatraz. *American Indian Culture and Research Journal* 18, no. 4.

Houle, Robert and Clara Hargittay. 1988. The struggle against cultural apartheid. *Muse* 11, no. 3 (Fall/October).

——— and Carol Podedworny. 1993. *Mandate study. An investigation of issues surrounding the exhibition, collection and interpretation of contemporary art by First Nations artists.* Ontario: Thunder Bay Art Gallery.

Howe, Oscar. 1969. Theories and beliefs—Dakota. *South Dakota Review* 7:2.

Hudson, Charles. 1976. *The Southeastern Indians.* Knoxville: University of Tennessee Press.

Hume, Stephen. 1988. The spirit weeps. *Edmonton Journal,* February 14.

Illinois State Museum. 1992. Biennial report. Springfield, Illinois.

Indians of All Tribes. 1970. Proclamation. Alcatraz. *Indians of All Tribes Newsletter* (January).

Isaac, Barbara. 1995. An epimethean view of the future at the Peabody Museum of Archaeology and Ethnology at Harvard University. *Federal Archaeology* 7:3 (Fall/Winter).

Jacknis, Ira. 2006. A new thing? The NMAI in historical and institutional perspective. *American Indian Quarterly* 30, nos. 3 & 4 (Summer & Fall).

Jacobs, Madeleine. 1988. Ceremony at Natural History marks return of remains to Blackfeet. *The Torch* (December). Staff newsletter. Washington, D.C.: Smithsonian Institution.

James, Frank. 1971. Speech: Our beginnings, an Indian's view. *Chronicles of American Indian protest.* Greenwich: Fawcett Publications.

Jensen, Jens Jorgen. 1995. Silent witness. *Federal Archeology* 7:3 (Fall/Winter).

Jonaitis, Aldona. 1992. Franz Boas, John Swanton, and the new Haida sculpture at the American Museum of Natural History. *The early years of Native American art history,* ed. Janet Catherine Berlo. Seattle: University of Washington Press.

Jones, Schuyler. 1994. Crossing boundaries. *Museums Journal* (July).

Keller, Robert H. and Michael F. Turek. 1998. *American Indians and national parks.* Tucson: University of Arizona Press.

Kelly, Marjorie. 1995. Native Hawaiians and Bishop Museum: Negotiating ownership of the Island past. *Curator* 38:4.

Klein, Julia M. 2001. At the interface. *Harvard Magazine* (March/April).

Krech, Shepard III. 1994. Museums, voices, representations. *Museum Anthropology* 18:3.

Kroeber, Theodora. 1961. *Ishi in two worlds.* Berkeley, Los Angeles, and London: University of California Press.

Kwagiulth Museum and Cultural Centre. 1994. Museum brochure. Quathiaski Cove, British Columbia, Canada.

Lawton Constitution. 1992. Indian remains exhibit closes amid controversy, June 28.

Linenthal, Edward T. 1999. From America's battlefield to the Holocaust Museum and the Oklahoma City bombing memorial: The problems and promise of museum interpretation. *Musenews* 29:1 (Winter).

Lipske, Michael. 2006. Scientists release results of first studies of Kennewick Man. *The Torch* (July). Washington, D.C.: Smithsonian Institution.

Lonetree, Amy. 2006. Missed opportunities. Reflections on the NMAI. *American Indian Quarterly* 3 & 4 (Summer & Fall).

Lowe, Truman T. 2005. The art of the unexpected. *Emendatio.* Washington, D.C.: National Museum of the American Indian.

Lumbee Petition for Recognition. 1987. Lumbee Tribal Enrollment Office and Lumbee River Legal Services.

Lurie, Nancy Oestreich. 1976. American Indians and museums: A love-hate relationship. *The Old Northwest* 2:3 (September).

Lynch, Bernadette. 1993. The broken pipe: Non-native museums and native culture. *Muse* (Fall).

Mahoney, Laura. 1999. Correspondence between author and national NAGPRA office, February 12.

Marker, Sherry. 2007. Travel advisory; Thanksgiving at Plymouth, 377 years later. *New York Times*, January 21.

Marshall, Joseph III. 1993. Valuing cultural diversity is cultural validation. *CRM (Cultural Resources Management)* 16:11.

Martza, Barton. 1991. On the trail of the Zuni War Gods. *Zuni History. Victories in the 1990s.* Zuni, NM: Zuni Tribe publication.

Maryland Historical Society. 1993. Exhibition brochure, *Mining the Museum.* Baltimore.

Mathews, Jay. 1989. University to return ancestral bones to tribe. *Washington Post,* June 23.

Matthiessen, Peter. 1983. *In the spirit of Crazy Horse.* New York: The Viking Press.

Mauger, Jeffrey E. and Janine Bowechop. 2006. Tribal collections management at the Makah Cultural and Research Center. *Living homes for cultural expression.* Washington, D.C.: National Museum of the American Indian.

Maxwell, Steve. 2005. Native places, Native stories. *National Museum of the American Indian* (member magazine). Washington, D.C.: National Museum of the American Indian.

McKeown, Tim. 2007. Correspondence between author and national NAGPRA office, March 1.

McLeod, Christopher. 2006. Sacred land film project. Earth Island Institute, Lahonda, California, Web site: www.sacredland.org.

McDonald, George F. 2005. Native voice at the Canadian Museum of Civilization. *The Native universe and museum in the twenty-first century.* Washington, D.C.: Smithsonian Institution.

McLoughlin, Moira. 1993. Of boundaries and borders: First Nations' history in museums. *Canadian Journal of Communication* 18:3 (January).

McManus, Greg. 1991. The crisis of representation in museums: the exhibition "The Spirit Sings." *Museum economics and the community,* ed. Susan Pearce. London: Athlone.

Medicine, Bea. 1973. Finders Keepers? *Museum News* (March).

Merrill, William. 1995. Interview by author via telephone to National Museum of Natural History, Smithsonian Institution, June 1.

Milbrath, Susan and Jerald T. Milanich. 1991. Columbian conflict. *Museum News* (September/October).

———. 1990. *First encounters: An exhibit guide.* Gainesville: Florida Museum of Natural History.

Monetathchi, Dusk. 2000. Tribes host first Native American Repatriation Summit. *Chickasaw Times,* July.

Monroe, Dan L. and Walter Echo-Hawk. 1991. Deft deliberations. *Museum News* (July/August).

Morning Star Institute. 2006. June 21 set for 2006 national prayer day for Native sacred places. Press release, Washington, D.C.

Mullen, Frank X. Jr. 2002. Nevada mummy draws international attention. *Reno Gazette-Journal,* January 8.

Museum News. 1990. M Notes. This "New World" exhibition sets the stage for an old debate. (March/April).

Nanepashemet. 1995. Presentation at American Association of Museums annual meeting, Philadelphia.

Nason, James D. 1973. Finders keepers? *Museum News* (March).

—— and Robin K. Wright. 1994. Sharing heritage: Native American exhibits. *Museum News* (May/June).

National Endowment for the Humanities. 2002. Kennewick man: Science and sacred rights. Edsitement lesson plan at edsitement.neh.gov. Posted April 8, viewed February. 15, 2007.

National Native American Graves Protection and Repatriation Program. 2006. Program brochure. National Park Service, U.S. Department of the Interior. July 31.

Native American Graves Protection and Repatriation Act. 1990. P.L. 101-601, November 16.

Nabokov, Peter and Lawrence Loendorf. 2004. *Restoring a presence. American Indians and Yellowstone National Park.* Norman: University of Oklahoma Press.

Neary, Ben. 2003. Utility drops plans for coal mine. *The New Mexican,* August 5.

Nevada Division of Museums and History. 2006. Under One Sky, http://dmla .clan.lib.nv.us/docs/museums/cc/UnderOneSky.

Newsom, Barbara Y. and Adele Z. Silver, eds. 1977. Indian art—"living with the political realities," *Artnews* 78, no. 10.

Nicholson, Claudia J. 1995. Advisors to partners: bridging the cultural gap. *History News* (Autumn).

Nilsen, Richard. 2006. Anatomy exhibit using cadavers spurs controversy. *The Arizona Republic,* July 11.

Norrell, Brenda. 2004. Keepers of the Stronghold dream. *The Native Press.* thenativepress.com/stronghold.html. Viewed January 31, 2006.

——. 2005. Petroglyph lawsuit filed against city of Albuquerque. *Indian Country Today,* February 28.

O'Driscoll, Patrick. 1998. Law to return Indian remains bogged down. *USA Today,* March 9.

Owsley, Douglas W. and Bertita E. Compton. 1990. The Smithsonian anthropology collections: planning for long-term use. *Museum Anthropology* 14, no. 3 (August).

Page, Jake. 1983. Return of the Kachinas. *Science '83* 4, no. 2.

Peerman, Dean. 1990. Bare-bones imbroglio: repatriating Indian remains and sacred artifacts. *Christian Century* 107:29 (October 17).

Penney, David W. 1992. Reflections on the Task Force: Museums and First Peoples in Canada. *Museum Anthropology* 16:2 (June).

Pickering, Robert. 1996. Fax transmittal from Denver Museum of Natural History, May 23.

Pipestone National Monument. 2004. An Indian-oriented park: Native Americans and the Monument. Pipestone administrative history. www.npw.gov/pipe. Posted August 21, viewed February 26, 2006.

Pilgrim Hall Museum. 1999. The National Day of Mourning. www.pilgrimhall .org. Posted December 7, 1999, viewed January 24, 2000.

———. 2007. Primary Sources for "The First Thanksgiving at Plymouth." www.pilgrimhall.org. Posted July 14, 1998, viewed February 15, 2007.

Plimoth Plantation. 2007. Mayflower II. www.plimoth.org/visit/what/mayflower2 .asp. Viewed February 15.

Preston, Douglas J. 1989. Skeletons in our museums' closets. *Harper's Magazine* (February).

Price III, H. Marcus. 1991. *Disputing the dead*. Columbia and London: University of Missouri Press.

Pridmore, Jay. 1992. Dickson Mounds: Closing a window on the dead. *Archaeology* 45:4 (July/August).

Prince, Pat. 1992. A Columbus counterpoint. *Twin Cities Star Tribune*, May 20.

Pueblo of Zuni. 1991. Pueblo of Zuni repatriates War God from San Diego Museum of Man. Press release, May 15. Zuni, New Mexico.

Pullar, Gordon L. 1994. The Qikertarmiut and the scientist: fifty years of clashing worldviews. *Reckoning with the dead. The Larsen Bay repatriation and the Smithsonian Institution*, ed. Tamara L. Bray and Thomas W. Killion. Washington, D.C., and London: Smithsonian Institution Press.

Quintal, Margaret and John A. Day. 1982. Introduction. *Oscar Howe. A retrospective exhibition catalogue raisonne*. Tulsa: Thomas Gilcrease Museum Association.

Rave, Jodi. 2004. Indian museum celebrates life, but death is there, too. *Gazette-Times* newspapers, Sept. 27.

Reyhner, Jon and Jeanne Eder. 1989. *A history of Indian education*. Billings, MT: Council for Indian Education.

Riding In, James. 1992. Six Pawnee crania. *American Indian Culture and Research Journal* 16:2.

———. 2000. Repatriation. A Pawnee's perspective. *Repatriation Reader*, ed. Devon A. Mihesuah. Lincoln and London: University of Nebraska Press.

Ridington, Robin. 1997. *Blessing for a long time. The sacred pole of the Omaha tribe.* Lincoln and London: University of Nebraska Press.

Robbins, Jim. 1989. Pilfered remains buried a century late. *The Miami Herald*, May 28.

Roberts, Carla. 1994. Object, subject, practitioner: Native Americans and cultural institutions. *Akwe:kon Journal* 11, nos. 3 & 4 (Fall/Winter). Ithaca, NY: Cornell University.

Rockafellar, Nancy. 2006. The story of Ishi, a chronology. University of California at San Francisco Web site: history.library.uscf.edu/themes_ishi.html.

Rosen, Lawrence. 1980. The excavation of American Indian burial sites: A problem in law and professional responsibility. *American Anthropologist* 82, no. 1 (March).

Roth, Evan. 1992. First Peoples, first steps. *Museum News* (July/August).

Rushing, W. Jackson. 1992. Critical issues in recent Native American art. *Art Journal* 51, no. 3 (Fall).

Sanders, Jacquin. 1998. Despite their rap, mummies are really very chummy. *St. Petersburg Times*, October 23.

Selby, Holly. 1993. Indigenous Americans to receive lists of artifacts. *Baltimore Sun*, November 16, 13A.

Scalplock, Irvine J. 1998. The Syncrude Gallery of Aboriginal Culture. *Muse* 16, no. 2:12–13.

Scheper-Hughes, Nancy. 2001. Ishi's brain, Ishi's ashes. *Anthropology Today* 17, no. 1 (February).

Schneider, Ingrid E. 2001. Collaborative conflict resolution at Devils Tower National Monument. National Recreation and Park Association. Posted at www.highbeam.com/library. July 1.

Science Museum of Minnesota. 1997. *Journey: Museums and community collaboration*. A viewer's guide of conference video. St. Paul, MN.

———. 1995. File copies of position papers, news clippings regarding First Encounters exhibition. St. Paul, MN.

———. 1993. Protest and the Columbus Quincentennial. File report in crisis management category. St. Paul, MN. February 12.

Silva, Tana. 1992. UF Indian exhibit damaged in Minn., *The Gainesville Sun*, June 2.

Simpson, Moira. 1994. Burying the past. *Museums Journal* (July).

———. 2001. Native American museums and cultural centres. *Making representations: Museums in the post-colonial era*. London and New York: Routledge.

Smith, Beverly Foster. 1960. Are Indians real? *Museum Service*. Rochester, NY: Rochester Museum of Arts and Sciences.

Smith, Claire. 2005. Decolonizing the museum: the National Museum of the American Indian in Washington, D.C. *Antiquity* 79, no. 304.

Smith, Paul Chaat and Robert Allen Warrior. 1996. *Like a hurricane*. New York: The New Press.

Society of Colonial Wars in the State of Connecticut. 2007. 1675—King Philips' War. www.colonialwarsct.org/1675/htm.

Southeast Museum Conference. 1995. Mississippi. *Southeast Museum Conference Newsletter* (August).

Spotted Elk, Clara. 1989. Skeletons in the attic. *New York Times*, March 8, Op-Ed page.

Stannard, David E. 1992. *American holocaust*. New York: Oxford University Press.

Stockbridge-Munsee Historical Committee. 1990. Our bibles are coming home at last! *Quin'a Montha'a* 12, no. 1 (May).

Stoll, Michael. 1998. Largest Indian museum opens today—courtesy of world's wealthiest casino. *Christian Science Monitor* (August 11).

Stott, Margaret A. 1988. The Spirit Sings: Artistic traditions of Canada's First Peoples. *Muse* (Autumn).

Strickland, Rennard. 1980. The changing world of Indian painting and Philbrook Art Center. *Native American art at Philbrook*. Tulsa: Philbrook Art Center.

Sturtevant, William C. 1995. Interview by author via telephone to National Museum of Natural History, Smithsonian Institution, May 31.

Swisher, Kara. 1989. Smithsonian to surrender Indian bones. *Washington Post*, September 12.

Tabah, Agnes. 1993. *Native American collections and repatriation*. Washington, D.C.: Technical Information Service, American Association of Museums.

Talmadge, Valerie A. 1982. The violation of sepulture: Is it legal to excavate human burials? *Archaeology* (November/December).

Taos Pueblo. 2006. About Taos Pueblo. www.taospueblo.com/about.php.

Teters, Charlene. 1998. Whose history do we celebrate? *Indian Artist* magazine (Summer).

Thiessen, Thomas D. and Mark J. Lynott. 1989. Nebraska passes reburial law. *Bulletin of the Society for American Archaeology* 7:5 (September).

Thompson, Bob. 2004. Spirit lodge. The Indian museum storage facility feels less like a warehouse and more like home. *Washington Post*, August 2.

Tivy, Mary. 1985. Bones of contention in Ontario museums. *Museum Quarterly* (Winter).

Trescott, Jacqueline. 2004. History's new look. *Washington Post*, September 13.

Trigger, Bruce. 1988. Reply by Bruce Trigger. *Anthropology Today* 4:6 (December).

Turner, Frederick. 1997. No surrender. *Outside Magazine* (August).

Uebelherr, Jan. 1993. Indian faces, voices tell story of museum's "Tribute to Survival." *Milwaukee Sentinel*, September 17.

U'mista Cultural Centre. 1994. Museum brochure. Alert Bay, British Columbia.

United States Commission on Civil Rights. 1981. *Indian tribes: A continuing quest for survival*. Washington, D.C., June.

United States Department of Agriculture (USDA). 1993. *Compilation of state repatriation, reburial and grave protection laws*. Soil Conservation Service, February.

United States Department of Defense. 1996. Frequently asked questions. Naval Historical Center home page: www.history.navy.mil/faqs. Viewed January 18, 2000.

United States Department of the Interior. 2000. Kennewick home site at www.cr.nps.gov/archeology/kennewick. Viewed February 15, 2007.

Vogel, M.L. Vanessa. 1990. The Glenbow controversy and the exhibition of North American art. Reprinted from *European Review of Native American Studies* 14:1; 1990, *Museum Anthropology* 14:4.

Wade, Edwin L. 1981. The ethnic art market and the dilemma of innovative Indian artists. *Magic images. Contemporary Native American art*, ed. Edwin L. Wade and Rennard Strickland. Norman: Oklahoma University Press and the Philbrook Art Center, Tulsa, Okla.

Warner, John Anson. 1986. The individual in Native American art: a sociological view. *The arts of the North American Indian. Native traditions in evolution*, ed. Edwin L. Wade. New York: Hudson Hill Press and Tulsa: Philbrook Art Center.

Weil, Stephen E. 1982. Breaches of trust: Museums, ethics & the law. *ARTnews* (December).

Wilson, Thomas H. 1992. Introduction: Museums and First Peoples in Canada. *Museum Anthropology* 16:2 (June).

Workers World. 1996. Day of mourning: Native protest stops Pilgrim's progress. December 12.

Wright, Ronald. 1992. *Stolen continents: The "new world" through Indian eyes.* Toronto: Pearson Penguin.

Yachay Wasi. 1999. People's voice: protest against Florida International Museum. People's Path www.thepeoplespath.net (home page).

Young, John. 1994. New age assault on Bear Butte decried. *Indian Country Today,* June 29.

Index

A:shiwi A:wan Museum and Heritage Center, 37
AAM. *See* American Association of Museums
Abrams, George H. J., 96, 164
Acoma Pueblo, 118, 146
Adams, Robert McCormick, 98–99
Administration for Native Americans, 160
AFN. *See* Assembly of First Nations
Ahayu:da. See sacred object
AIM. *See* American Indian Movement
Ak-Chin Him Dak Ecomuseum, 138, 157–58, 160–61
Akwe:kon Journal, 158
Akwesasne Notes, 91
Albany State Museum, 40
Albuquerque, 146
Albuquerque Museum, 115
Alcatraz, 8–10, 93
All Indian Pueblo Council, 146
American Academy of Forensic Sciences, 102
American Association of Museums (AAM), 37, 39, 42, 63, 96, 113
American Civil Liberties Union, 98

American Indian Archaeological Institute. *See* Institute for American Indian Studies
American Indian Community House, 67; American Indian Gallery, 57
American Indian Contemporary Arts Gallery, 57
American Indian Movement (AIM), 12, 57, 109, 115, 125, 132–33; birth of, 9; criticism of NMAI, 169; Colorado, 146; Florida branch, 44
American Indian Museums Association (also known as North American Indian Museums Association), 33, 35, 37, 96
American Indian Quarterly, 168–69
American Indian Religious Freedom Act, 31–32, 35, 41, 93, 145
American Indian Society, 57
American Indians Against Desecration, 41
American Indians and National Parks, 140, 144
American Museum of Natural History, 41, 61, 79, 90
Amiotte, Arthur, 166

About the Author

Karen Coody Cooper is the museum training program coordinator at the National Museum of the American Indian, and was formerly training programs manager at the Smithsonian Center for Education and Museum Studies. She holds a Master of Liberal Studies degree, with a museum and anthropology emphasis, from the University of Oklahoma and is an enrolled member of the Cherokee Nation of Oklahoma.